The Terrific Engine

The Terrific Engine
Income Taxation and the Canadian Modernization of the Political Imaginary

DAVID TOUGH

UBC Press • Vancouver • Toronto

Library and Archives Canada Cataloguing in Publication

Tough, David, author
The terrific engine : income taxation and the modernization of the Canadian political imaginary / David Tough.

Includes bibliographical references and index.
Issued in print and electronic formats.
ISBN 978-0-7748-3677-7 (hardcover). – ISBN 978-0-7748-3678-4 (softcover). –
ISBN 978-0-7748-3679-1 (PDF). – ISBN 978-0-7748-3680-7 (EPUB). –
ISBN 978-0-7748-3681-4 (Kindle)

1. Income tax – Political aspects – Canada – History – 20th century. 2. Right and left (Political science) – Canada – History – 20th century. I. Title.

HJ4661.T68 2018   336.240971   C2017-908048-2
                                            C2017-908049-0

UBC Press gratefully acknowledges the financial support for our publishing program of the Government of Canada (through the Canada Book Fund), the Canada Council for the Arts, and the British Columbia Arts Council.

This book has been published with the help of a grant from the Canadian Federation for the Humanities and Social Sciences, through the Awards to Scholarly Publications Program, using funds provided by the Social Sciences and Humanities Research Council of Canada.

A reasonable attempt has been made to secure permission to reproduce all material used. If there are errors or omissions, they are wholly unintentional, and the publisher would be grateful to learn of them.

UBC Press
The University of British Columbia
2029 West Mall
Vancouver, BC V6T 1Z2
www.ubcpress.ca

Contents

Figures

Acknowledgments

This book is the product of what feels like a long journey, over the course of which I have accumulated a number of personal and intellectual debts. The most direct debt is to Dominique Marshall, whose thoughtful guidance of my research echoed the rigour and force of her own scholarship. She was equal parts enthusiastic and skeptical about my ambitions from the start, and I benefited many times from having to muster the evidence and explanation to convince her of something that had occurred to me. That the final product differs so much from what I had originally intended owes a lot to her insistence on my asking the right questions of historical evidence.

James Opp, Norman Hillmer, and A.B. McKillop also made important contributions to the project, as did Jody Mason and Shirley Tillotson, all of whom asked challenging questions and gave me extensive notes for revision at a key stage in my work. John Walsh, Duncan MacDowell, David Dean, and Jennifer Evans also helped to shape the book.

I started talking about studying the effects of income taxation at Trent University in 2005, and I drew on the experience and knowledge of a lot of people there at that time. Jim Struthers was the first person whom I spoke to about studying these effects on the language of political difference. He talked me through the idea and gave me a preliminary reading list, and he advised me strongly to study the period before 1950, when my lack of technical knowledge would be less of a handicap. It is probable that, had Jim not been there to guide me early on, I would have quickly abandoned the idea of studying income taxation, even if it had occurred to me. Other faculty members who assisted me early on included Miriam Smith, Jim Conley, and Dimitry Anastakis.

My colleagues at Carleton University helped me to formulate ideas or work out problems in my work at various stages. David Banoub and I regularly engaged in discussions of our respective projects, their overlaps, and the future of political history in Canada more generally. Specifically, he introduced me to the work of Quentin Skinner, which instantly transformed the direction of my inquiry. Other colleagues who read or heard parts of my work and gave thoughtful critiques include Jess Dunkin, Sara Spike, Natalie Napier, Brian Foster, Jessica Squires, Tom Rorke, Susan Joudrey, Mary-Ann Schantz, and Valerie Minnett.

I was also encouraged by the interest of other scholars in what I was doing. I am thankful to Shirley Tillotson, Elsbeth Heaman, Jean-François Constant, Bryan Palmer, Adam Chapnick, and Tim Cook for reminding me that what I was doing was interesting and important.

In structuring the material, I borrowed key concepts from Shirley Tillotson and Ian McKay. In the case of Tillotson, the borrowing reflects similarity of intellectual project and research expertise and our mutual support for one another's contribution to tax history – hers as a senior scholar, mine as a junior scholar. In the case of McKay, my intellectual debt is not only older but also more complex. I adapt his core concept in a way that he might not support. It's all the more important, then, to acknowledge his work and to note the role that his essay on "The Liberal Order Framework," published in 2000 when my attention was fixed on postcolonial theory and university governance, played in drawing me into the intellectual current of Canadian historical scholarship.

Much of the material in this book was presented at conferences, where I benefited from thoughtful and learned questions and commentaries. Chapter 1 was presented to my colleagues in the Department of History at the Underhill Graduate Colloquium in 2010, and the part of Chapter 3 dealing with "fiscal need" was presented at a conference at McGill University in 2008. Chapter 2 has had a long journey, having been presented at the annual meeting of the Canadian Historical Association at Carleton University in 2009, rejected (with extensive comments from peer reviewers) by *Labour/Le travail* in 2009, and finally published in the *Canadian Historical Review* in 2012. Although the focus of the argument changed significantly through all these stages, I benefited immensely from feedback received along the way.

I owe a particular debt of gratitude to archivists and librarians – in particular those at Library and Archives Canada who remain anonymous to me. Beyond their help, I had assistance from Richard Virr at McGill University's Rare Book Room and Heather Home at Queen's University Archives, as well as from library and information technology staff at Trent University's Thomas J. Bata Library. Christopher Ryan did excellent research work tracking down good-quality images at Library and Archives Canada late in the project and establishing definitively that, sadly, there were no good-quality reproductions of some images that I had wanted to include.

I am grateful to the Social Sciences and Humanities Research Council of Canada for granting me a large amount of taxpayers' money to live on during the research and writing of this book and to Carleton University and the estate of the great intellectual historian S.F. Wise for additional financial support. In addition to the people thanked elsewhere who supported me in securing funding, I am thankful to Jennifer Evans for urging me to apply for the Wise funding at a time when it did me a lot of good. I also did a considerable amount of research and additional writing while I was a postdoctoral fellow at Trent University's School for the Study of Canada, and I am again thankful to SSHRC for that funding.

UBC Press has been wonderful to work with. I'm thankful to Emily Andrew, Darcy Cullen, and Katrina Petrik, who have been my contacts there, for their enthusiasm and attention to my manuscript. I initially approached a competing press and was rewarded with indifference followed by extended, unexplained silence, so UBC Press's professionalism and interest in my work was a much appreciated antidote. I'm grateful to Norman Hillmer for urging me to make the shift and facilitating it and to Lisa Pasolli, whose first book was published by UBC Press while we shared an office at Trent University, for encouraging me to follow her example. I'm also thankful to the three anonymous reviewers for UBC Press who had helpful critiques and identified important sources that I had neglected to reference. I also benefited from the astonishingly learned comments of Jim Struthers on the manuscript that most likely would not have existed without his early guidance.

The greatest debt that I owe is to my family, all of whom have demonstrated remarkable hospitality to my demanding and often inscrutable companion. My sister hosted me on numerous occasions when I was visiting Ottawa to do research after I relocated to Peterborough. My parents not only offered emotional and financial support when it was needed but also provided logistical support on too many occasions to count. More than anyone else, my partner, Jess, has felt the burden of this project and seen my excitement at its promise and my weariness at its challenges in the lines of my face. I hope that they all recognize this book as being worthy of their long and generous investment.

The Terrific Engine

Introduction: A Political History of Possibility

"**N**DP Making Huge Gains as Canada Tilts Leftward," a *National Post* headline pronounced in the spring of 2012. Citing a poll showing that people "think Canada suffers from an income gap, where the rich are getting too rich and the poor are getting too poor," the article said that this concern explained the rising popularity of the New Democratic Party (NDP).[1] The article didn't explain what it meant to tilt leftward or elaborate the connection between income inequality and the electoral fortunes of the NDP. Neither was there an explanation of how electing the NDP would narrow the income gap, though voters' sense that it would was the crux of the article's logic. The editors didn't explain the connections among concerns about income inequality, a leftward tilt, and the fortunes of a political party because they didn't need to. They presumed correctly that readers would know how the terms related to each other. Even though the NDP had never won a federal election, readers shared with the editors and author an *imaginary,* a mental image or map of political reality, that allowed them to imagine political conditions that would increase the possibility of its formation, and they could even imagine what such a government might do – all because they knew what it meant to tilt leftward.

It wasn't mentioned in the article, but progressive income taxation is crucial to the political imaginary that made its claims intelligible. A progressive income tax taxes higher incomes at higher rates, making the rich less rich; the revenue from such a tax can be used to fund social programs and public services, making the poor less poor. The poll respondents who

3

believed that "the rich are getting too rich and the poor are getting too poor" tilted leftward, supporting the NDP as the party most likely to increase taxation on the rich and increase funding for social programs and public services that benefit the poor. Supporters of the ruling Conservative Party leaned rightward, voting in the expectation that the government the party formed would tax and spend only minimally, easing the burden on high income earners who shouldered the greatest weight under the progressive tax and encouraging those with lower incomes to secure income by their own initiatives. Voters support the party that reflects their vision of social relations and of how income taxation should be used to improve those relations. Although we seldom think of it, progressive income taxation is at the heart of how we make sense of politics and how we schematize the complex interrelationships of citizens and the state; it also explains our easy and unremarkable fluency with the political imaginary that maps our political sympathies on a left–right spectrum.

We share this imaginary because we are moderns, heirs to the modernization of politics in the early twentieth century, and we rely on its categories to make sense of our world. The idea that democratic citizenship entails choices among clearly different ways of organizing the economy makes sense to us, even if we never experience party politics quite that way. Parties appeal to our intellect and to our understanding of the shared rights and responsibilities of citizenship, and we use our intelligence and our critical awareness of the world and of the party system to choose among commensurable yet different party programs. Parties that propose a more egalitarian economic arrangement, in which income is pooled through taxation and spent on vast projects to benefit the disadvantaged or the general population, are placed on the left of the spectrum, whereas parties that propose to use taxation only to fund the bare minimum of state projects, thus easing the burden on individual income earners, are placed on the right; those that seek to balance both approaches are placed in the centre. We struggle to understand or even conceive of other political imaginaries in which the differences among parties are about something other than the possible redistributive uses of the treasury and are therefore not amenable to alignment on a left–right spectrum. The core differences among the parties are how income is arranged, and the range of possibilities for different arrangements of public wealth, which we map on a spectrum, from left to right – an arrangement that strikes us as appropriate and clear to the extent that we are moderns.

This modern political imaginary is a language of politics, in a sense, and it arose rhetorically, out of the ways that people talked about and described politics in the early twentieth century. It was the rhetoric through which people expressed the possibilities that income tax offered, rather than the tax itself, that was the engine of political change. Fiscally, income taxation was a powerful instrument of redistribution in the middle of the twentieth century in Canada, funding programs that transformed the overall living standards, and particularly the education and health, of poor and working-class people. It was the fiscal power of taxation, its ability to support generous social programs politically necessary after the First World War, that Stephen Leacock was thinking of when he wrote, in *The Unsolved Riddle of Social Justice,* about "the terrific engine of taxation already fashioned in the war."[2] But its rhetorical effects were even more dramatic. People saw in income taxation the answer to a range of difficulties that haunted politics in the early twentieth century, many of which were themselves rhetorical. The rhetoric through which they articulated their understanding of taxation and the party system set in motion a revolution in political language, overturning an old way of understanding the differences among parties and introducing a new, more modern schema of political differences that underlined the role of the independent intellect in guiding political sympathies. The rhetoric through which people understood and explained income taxation and its overwhelming possibilities to one another was "the terrific engine" of a realignment of Canadian electoral politics along a left–right axis.

This book argues that progressive income taxation and the modern political imaginary were adopted in Canada not just at the same time but also as part of the same process: a vast campaign to modernize politics to make it more meaningful to more people. Income taxation was central to the establishment of left and right as the standard representation of political difference in Canada because of the possibilities that it suggested. The potential of income taxation, its promise of impersonally equalizing incomes and seamlessly transforming an unequal and dysfunctional federation into a mass democracy, had a profound effect on how politics was imagined and discussed. With the introduction of income taxation at the dominion level, it became possible to imagine, and to communicate clearly, the potential for taxation to transform society and therefore to have a much wider range of possible political outcomes of an election. It became normal to distinguish among party platforms that sought to unleash its power and those that sought to contain it. As parties outlined how they would use income taxation, the left–right spectrum, not applied to Canadian political parties before the 1920s, was increasingly adopted to make sense of the new field. *The Terrific Engine* is a history

of those possibilities and of the ways that people found to make sense
of them.

CANADA'S FISCAL REVOLUTION: INCOME TAXATION
AND DEMOCRATIC POLITICS

Income taxation has not enjoyed much attention from historians until
recently. The study of taxation in Canada essentially began and ended with
the work of J. Harvey Perry, a civil servant who published the definitive
two-volume *Taxes, Tariffs, and Subsidies* in the 1950s.[3] Despite its centrality
to questions of national development, state formation, political parties,
and the social welfare state, income taxation has tended to play only a
marginal role even in historical scholarship devoted to these themes. The
implementation of universal income taxation over a few decades in the
early twentieth century, which one scholar has called a "fiscal revolution,"[4]
was touched on in places, most often in journal articles neither written
nor read by historians. The scholarly literature on Canadian politics in the
early twentieth century more broadly, however, is vast. The election of
1911, the First World War, the Great Depression, and the Second World
War, key moments in this political narrative, have been studied extensively.
But these topics fell out of favour along with the rest of political history
in the aftermath of the explosion of social and cultural history emerging
out of the 1960s and have become comparatively dormant since then.
Political history is currently undergoing a revival and a much-needed
methodological reorientation. As part of the revival of political history, a
scholarship on taxation in Canada has developed almost overnight.[5]

The political and social crisis that saw the emergence of the modern
political imaginary was a defining moment for what Donald Wright has
called the "post-1918 generation" of professional scholarly researchers.[6] It
is well represented in their work on Canadian politics. Much of the early
canon of political history in Canada, in fact, grew out of the democratic
struggles of the early twentieth century that are the focus of this book.
Frank Underhill's contributions to the study of Canadian political parties and political culture, informed by his belief that both traditional
parties were "dominated by the business interests of the great Eastern
industrial and financial centres," drew on similar analysis in the *Grain
Growers' Guide* and found their way into articles in the *Canadian Forum*
before being published in academic articles and, eventually, *In Search of
Canadian Liberalism.*[7] Donald Creighton's account of the political and

imaginative challenges in the development of *The Commercial Empire of the St Lawrence* appeared during the Depression, and its arguments about the need for a strong central government were echoed in the historical volume that Creighton contributed to the Royal Commission on Dominion-Provincial Relations.[8] The work of historians such as Creighton and Underhill was criticized after the 1960s for representing only a narrow swath of political reality and implicitly siding with elite conceptions of politics; however, at the time that they were writing, the nature of political parties and the role of the dominion government in creating a national economy were vital questions for popular politics. This book is informed by the understanding that questions of political difference and its effect on democracy were important in the 1930s and remain important. Like those of Creighton and Underhill, this is a history that both interprets the political world and seeks to change it. That it harks back to that older scholarship, in both style and subject matter, is intentional and unapologetic.

The scholarship that is the most direct precursor of this book is the intellectual history of politics that emerged during the long winter of political history in the 1980s and 1990s. Books such as Doug Owram's *The Government Generation* and Barry Ferguson's *Remaking Liberalism* took the focus of political history away from politicians and electoral contests and put it on ideas and the people who produced them.[9] This work underlined the importance of ideas in how politics changed, drawing particular attention to the rapid transformation in ideas of what the liberal state could and should do in the years leading up to 1945. Although it has been valuable in framing key questions of my book, the intellectual history of politics exhibited some characteristics that I have tried to overcome. For one, it displayed a conception of the role of intellectuals in government that tended to idolize liberal intellectuals, presenting their rise to power and influence in the interwar period in whiggish terms. It also presented ideas and intellectuals as necessarily linked, as if workers and farmers had no ideas and ideas were always identifiable concepts imported into government from academia. This book differs from the intellectual history of politics tradition first by examining rhetoric rather than ideas; second, and relatedly, by looking at how various speakers – journalists, politicians, farmers, workers, as well as university-trained intellectuals and authors – reshaped politics through their use of rhetoric; and third by placing these uses of rhetoric in political struggle rather than on an abstract plane. I study how politics changed in the first half of the twentieth century, not just by looking at the formal intellectuals and their ideas, but also by looking at society more broadly and the people's enlightenment that swept through it.

The past decade has witnessed the emergence of a "new political history" that engages with formal politics from a perspective informed interpretively and methodologically by social and cultural history.[10] In response to the proliferation of social history in the 1960s and 1970s, followed by cultural history in the 1980s and 1990s, political history became an intellectual backwater. The isolation of political history had the perverse effect of shielding its methodological limitations from sustained critical reflection, the result of which was an ossification of traditional habits in studying and teaching political history. New political history is a rejection of this isolation and reflects a desire to engage with formal political power in fresh ways. Political history is no longer regarded as a relic or an intellectual backwater, and it is now explicitly promoted as a newly vibrant field of study.[11] Although there were signs of revival beforehand, much of this new interest can be traced back to Ian McKay's essay "The Liberal Order Framework," which proposed seeing Canada as "a liberal project of rule" in which nonliberal practices and aims were either absorbed or suppressed by society and the state.[12] The essay served broadly as a rallying cry for scholars wanting to repoliticize and reinvigorate political history. In addition, though McKay's work was explicitly intended as a "concept of reconnaissance," not as a theory, it has been adopted by scholars as a frame of reference, and it is often cited as the interpretive basis of major research projects.[13] My book is not informed interpretively by "The Liberal Order Framework"; as a study of formal politics informed by social and cultural history's leftism and attention to language, it is a contribution to a wider interpretive culture that can be traced to McKay's influence and example.

As part of this new interest in political history, a new scholarship is emerging that treats taxation as an important social and political fact. The key figure in this new scholarship is Shirley Tillotson, not only prolific in producing her own scholarship but also a leader in spearheading the development of a tax field in Canadian historiography more broadly. Traditional political history, for all of its focus on politicians and governments, paid little attention to taxation. What there is of tax history before the past decade is either intellectual history of politics, as in Owram and Ferguson (in which tax is peripheral), or highly technical and institutional histories of statutes and practices, as in Perry, W. Irwin Gillespie's *Tax, Borrow, and Spend,* or Robert Bryce's *Maturing in Hard Times.*[14] Recent tax scholarship by Tillotson, Elsbeth Heaman, Andrew Smith, and others

has been strongly differentiated from this institutional approach by placing taxation in broader political, social, and cultural contexts, examining
it as a site of social struggle and as a screen for projecting anxieties and
desires.[15] This renewal of interest in taxation is partly a reflection of the
phenomenon of new political history and partly a reflection of a more
interdisciplinary renewal of interest in taxation, as can be seen in what
some scholars call the new fiscal sociology.[16] Like the Canadian historians
studying taxation, these scholars are reviving the field by seeing taxation
as a central fact of political life.[17] *The Terrific Engine* is a part of this emerging national and global scholarship that explores fundamental questions
of democracy and modern politics.

A "Break with the Past": Political Modernism and the Left–Right Spectrum

The use of "left" and "right" as political terms comes from the French
Revolution, the "break with the past" from which scholars conventionally
date the birth of the modern.[18] The terminology, with its abstract clarity
and fierce opposition, inevitably calls to mind the charisma and confidence
of nineteenth-century French enlightenment and citizenship, of the people
and the nation awakening from the sleep of deception to craft a new
people's state that embodied the hope of human progress. Despite its
universal pretensions, however, the left–right spectrum was adopted dif-
ferently at different times in different places. English-speaking countries
were late to take it up, possibly because English parliamentary tradition
already provided another bifurcation – some variation of liberal and
conservative – more appropriate to the narrow ideological range of electoral
contests in Britain, the United States, and the British dominions, where
two parties spoke for overlapping sections of the ruling class.[19] When these
countries did adapt the left–right spectrum to their purposes, it was to
map political cultures that had been shaken by war and depression, by
class conflict and renegotiated (New Deal or Keynesian) liberalism, when
the core themes of the French Revolution – enlightenment and citizenship –
had been translated into English political terminology.

Use of the terminology in politics has prosaic origins. After the *ancien
régime* was violently overturned in 1789, the people's representatives
arranged themselves in the National Assembly, literally left to right,
on the basis of the ferocity of their opposition to traditional authority:
those on the left believed in a strictly egalitarian republic, whereas those

on the right believed that deference to the aristocracy and the church was a public good. The terms "left" and "right" entered English by way of Thomas Carlyle's two-volume *The French Revolution,* which described how, in the heat of debate, "like does begin to assemble itself with like," and, by the seating habits of impassioned speakers, the "rudiments of Parties" began to emerge.[20] Insulting jibes stuck, and the link between physical position and ideological position was quickly fixed in language. Carlyle described "a Right Side (*Côté Droit*), a Left Side (*Côté Gauche*); sitting on M. le President's right hand, or on his left: the *Côté Droit* conservative; the *Côté Gauche* destructive."[21] In this original nineteenth-century usage, the words *left* and *right* were generally nouns: *the* left and *the* right, recognizable groups of people who operated together for shared ends. However, as the terminology spread through Europe, particularly after 1848, when liberals, socialists, communists, and anarchists began proliferating on the continent, threatening the stability of old, aristocratic Europe, the terms became more adjectival, signalling a quality shared by differing things.[22] By the start of the twentieth century, the period in which this book begins, it was possible to refer to not just the left or the right but also to left and right as general directions or inclinations. A profusion of nouns in the years following gave us, according to the *Oxford English Dictionary, leftism* (1920), *right-wingers* (1920), *leftists* (1924), and *rightism* (1934) – truly abstract terms for truly modern political differences.

Modernizing politics necessarily entails what Carlyle called the "Death-Birth of a World!" or, to use a more familiar term from political economy, "creative destruction."[23] The literal violence of the French Revolution is only the most obvious example of a common theme: the establishment of political modernism, like all modernism, is revolutionary in the widest sense, a conscious drive to remake politics, to make it clearer and more efficient by overturning established and ossified political practices. It is a privileging of the new over the old and of the abstract and universal over the familiar and local. It is characterized by what David Harvey has called "a radical break with the past," an awareness of radical novelty.[24] Although, as Harvey says, a true break with the past is not literally possible, the idea of such a break was central to political thought in the period. Political modernism is neither left nor right, but it has been used to express varying political projects. It is concerned with "unblocking energies and releasing flows" by a process of creative destruction.[25] Just as the French Revolution would have been nothing without the "destructive wrath of Sansculottism," the ignorant violence of people without sympathy for the status quo, so too the destructive overthrow of old loyalties, however symbolic, is an inescapable ingredient of political modernism.[26]

The political modernism that established the link between income taxation and the left–right spectrum was also first negative and destructive: its Sansculottism was rhetorical, with farmer and labour newspapers lobbing powerful words at the old difference between Liberal and Conservative, weakening the old affective bonds of party loyalty. This assertion of independence is what McKay calls the "people's enlightenment": a self-conscious sense of growing intellectual and political independence among workers, farmers, and other political groups in the early twentieth century. Building upon a perceived explosion of knowledge and independent inquiry in the eighteenth and nineteenth centuries, speakers saw socialism and other political ideas as a democratic extension of the enlightenment ethos. Immanuel Kant's enlightenment dictum "Dare to Know!" became tied in the twentieth century, McKay argues, to the development of political and intellectual independence among previously unrepresented and marginalized groups.[27] This was linked to a belief that political thought was, or should be, common property, "the possession of all," and should serve social ends.[28] Political activism in the period, McKay argues, was about "unlocking the 'immense power' of knowledge" to create "a genuine people's enlightenment."[29] A wide range of speakers believed that a mass political awakening was both needed and happening in early-twentieth-century Canadian politics and described it in similar terms. Beyond initiating an unprecedentedly blunt conversation about exploitation and taxation before and during the First World War, the destructive phase of the people's enlightenment insisted on the necessity of political and intellectual independence, castigating the old party loyalties as not only ossified and reactionary but also fundamentally false and foolish – and dangerously antisocial.

A period of confusion followed the effective destruction of the Liberal-Conservative imaginary after 1917, during which a new imaginary, premised on the unprecedented possibility of a powerful dominion income tax, began to emerge in new controversies. What replaced the old loyalties of party sentiment was a more abstract relationship between citizens and the state, encapsulated by what Tillotson has called the "citizenship of contribution": a major transformation in the "moral and symbolic meaning of taxation" in the early to mid-twentieth century.[30] In place of the moral obligations of the rich, a new possibility emerged in which everyone contributed in relation to her or his income to fund government expenditures on redistributive social programs and free public services. As a new vista of political citizenship, the working class was being offered, "as an image of their place in a system of collective care," via universal income taxation, a new citizenship "whose responsibility consists in paying part of the price for the services they use."[31] The citizenship of contribution refers to the novelty – the modernity – of the idea of using universal taxation to fund social programs, harnessing the power of taxation as a link among citizens and its overwhelming impact on the rhetoric and imagination of Canadian politics in the 1940s.

The political imaginary that links the left–right spectrum to concerns about income inequality is both historical and modern: it arises out of a particular set of contingencies, but it does so in the explicit hope of effecting a break with the past, a revolutionary shift from an old way of thinking to a new and clearer modern horizon. It is the product of a mass rhetorical project of political modernism, of which McKay's people's enlightenment and Tillotson's citizenship of contribution are both species.[32] At first destructive and wrathful, political modernism's break with the past overthrows the rhetorical basis of the two-party system and, in a process of creative destruction, creates a fertile abyss from which new energies explode. A second, positive stage of political modernism sees these energies coalesce around the novel possibility of income taxation as a powerful instrument of economic equalization and the establishment of a new, more modern, and abstract organization of difference: left and right. McKay's and Tillotson's core concepts together tell the story of how the universal ideals of political modernism – enlightenment and citizenship – became linked in Canadian party politics with the possible uses of income taxation.

"SEEING THINGS THEIR WAY": RHETORIC AND THE MODERN POLITICAL IMAGINARY

The modernization of taxation in Canada in the early twentieth century was a revolution in language in two senses: its outcome, the modern political imaginary, was a radical change in the way that political reality was expressed and represented, and it was a change effected through language or, more precisely, rhetoric. The introduction of a dominion income tax, the income war tax, in 1917, and its broadening into a mass tax in the early 1940s reflected the anxieties, concerns, and possibilities arising out of a previous political or social crisis – and, more importantly, out of a way of understanding a previous political or social crisis. Rhetoric, circulating as images or phrases in speeches, newspapers, cartoons, and books, was crucial to how the immediate events of the period unfolded; words and phrases were consciously chosen for their political effects. To tell the story of the introduction of income taxation in Canada without highlighting its rhetorical implications would be to miss most of what makes the change politically important.

The focus on rhetoric rather than ideas is key to the book's methodological and political ambitions. I focus on the rhetoric through which people made sense of political differences and its connection to changes in the forms of taxation at the dominion level. In part, this connection happened consciously in its own time, as speakers explicitly strove for a new language and a new fiscal regime, but it also happened unconsciously, with speakers adopting language that made sense of their new reality without much active intention. Underlining the *uses* of ideas rather than ideas themselves is implicitly a much more democratic approach to the period's political transformations than the one taken by the intellectual history of politics. That a great number of people who were not professional intellectuals were not only talking about the role of taxation in obscuring and clarifying political differences but also talking about it knowingly reinforces the *political* importance of that methodological stance. The emergence of the modern political imaginary was, in a sense, a democratic story.

My original aim in researching the effect of income taxation on language was simply to trace the change in language, what I assumed would be a largely unremarked increasing use of the terms "left" and "right," and explain its development in relation to changes in fiscal arrangements of the state. My starting assumptions were that the terms used in texts would slowly change and that these changes would be reflected in asides, in parts of writings to which authors had devoted little attention. The sources, however, immediately told another story. In certain situations, speakers were clear and self-conscious about the language that they were using and often commented openly on either a change in terminology or the need for such a change. This discovery changed the nature of the project: rather than simply a history of people using words, it became a history of people using words to talk about words. The development of a new representation of politics through the emergence of the possibility of tax-and-spend politics was not, then, an accident or simply a passive surrender to progress but a kind of mass intellectual project.

The question of how people used language pointed to the study of rhetoric, which Quentin Skinner defines as language used in political struggle.[33]

He argues that "there cannot be a history of unit ideas as such, but only a history of the various uses to which they have been put at different times." The history of the uses of words, Skinner says, is "the only history of ideas to be written."[34] Words and ideas matter, that is, only when they are spoken, and they are spoken only when it is important politically that they be spoken. This approach arises out of philosopher Ludwig Wittgenstein's dictum that "words are also deeds": that is, there should not be too sharp a distinction among saying, thinking, and doing.[35] In Skinner's own field of political philosophy, this becomes an insistence on "seeing things their way,"[36] situating a text in its original context, a call for scholars to "situate the texts we study within such contexts as enable us to make sense of what their authors were doing writing them." Such a method allows students of past political speakers "to grasp their concepts, to follow their distinctions, to appreciate their beliefs and, so far as possible, to see things their way."[37] This approach is critical of much of the discipline of political philosophy, which understands thinkers as elucidating timeless questions rather than engaging in immediate political struggles.[38]

Skinner's insistence that words matter politically and therefore are part of social struggle is the key to how rhetoric is used in this book. The centrality of political modernism in the analytical framing of the book, for example, arose out of the sources. In heralding the possibilities of a federal income tax, the word that people most often used to describe its salutary effects was *modern*. Income tax was modern because it was clear; it was modern because it was destructive; it was modern because it was scientific; it was modern, most often, because it was novel and unprecedented. Critiques of the party system in the early twentieth century invariably characterized it as old, inefficient, or sentimental – that is, as not modern. When people wrote articles or letters calling for a political change, they often spoke of the change as modern, as a necessary improvement, as the realization of a new and better way of understanding things and organizing them. To be true to the sources, to "see things their way," has required engaging with the modernism of taxation.[39]

The left–right spectrum that emerged over the period examined here is characterized as a new "imaginary," a term widely used in political and social theory, though often without much rigour. The imaginary, to the untrained eye, suggests something that has been dreamed up specifically for the occasion, something that allows the author to pull back from the material and reflect on it without subjecting it to a hackneyed and predetermined analytical procedure.[40] But the imaginary, despite its appeal as a blank slate, does mean something. The imaginary is an abstract representation of a field of action, the conditional "world" in which other actions can be intelligibly taken and understood and in which people place themselves. It is a schematic guide to, or simplification of, the repertoire of political and social possibilities available at a given time. For political theorists, the imaginary is a perspective or lens through which abstract phenomena are viewed and given meaning. The imaginary is the fundamental site of social struggle and invention because it is what allows possibilities to be formulated before they coalesce into demands. The French Revolution, for instance, began as a new "egalitarian imaginary" that posited the fundamental equality of people and that, for the first time, allowed a total evaluation of previously unexamined social hierarchies. The core of the revolution, Ernesto Laclau and Chantal Mouffe argue, was this novel perspective, and the vista that it opened up pointed to a new concept of political legitimacy.[41] Beyond being a perspective, though, the imaginary is also a set of possibilities. Political philosopher Charles Taylor defines the imaginary as a "'repertoire' of collective actions at the disposal of a given group of society."[42] He also underlines the visual-spatial aspect of the imaginary, saying that it constitutes "an implicit map of social space."[43] The imaginary is a repertoire of expressions that coalesces into a recognizable and definable spatial representation of a given reality.

My focus on rhetoric and the imaginary undeniably arises out of the linguistic turn in historical scholarship, which interprets the sources of the past in terms of their meaning-making power. But my concern with rhetoric and difference is not simply an outsider's perspective on the past, the result of an overactive methodological imagination enlisting the past against its will in an anachronistic deconstruction. People in the past cared deeply about the rhetoric of political differences, decried its poverty in their time, and pushed, as part of a project of democratic and fiscal reform, for a new delineation of possibilities. This book is a product of modern scholarship and reflects its methodological and theoretical force, but it is also a book about what people in the past had to say about politics and political differences. The language that we use to make sense of politics is in large part their language, and it is as much the product of critical thought and well-honed rhetoric as it is of current scholarship. If they thought that political differences were important for them to think about, then we should as well.

STRUCTURE AND NARRATIVE

The narrative material that follows is organized around four discrete political scenes, in two parts of two chapters each, in which the rhetoric of fiscal politics and political differences is a key concern. Each scene combines a self-conscious interest in the power of rhetoric, a reflection on political differences, and a focus on the politics of taxation as the problem or solution. Spread out over four decades, the scenes demonstrate a long-standing interest in addressing rhetorical questions as fiscal problems and vice versa. They encapsulate the transformation in the political imaginary that characterized the period. The scenes centre first, in Part 1, on the destruction of the two-party system inherited from the nineteenth century and then, in Part 2, on the establishment of a new, more abstract, and more impersonal system of differences characterized by use of the terms "left" and "right." They are, in a sense, two pairs in which a problem is articulated from society and the state responds to it. Although I touch on what happens between these scenes, they do not follow one another directly. Rather, they are pivotal moments in which an awareness of the rhetoric of political differences attached itself to a critique of dominion fiscal politics.

The rhetorical inventions detailed in each chapter are premised on the speakers' deep familiarity with current and recent fiscal politics. Accordingly, each chapter begins with a presentation of the immediate political and economic background as it appeared to the participants. Rather than simply providing contexts for the political struggles, these opening sections offer inventories of the references on which speakers in the period drew. Although these sections are the most directly concerned with political economy, they do not present material bases that determine the rhetorical battles. These sections themselves are rhetorical in that they are concerned with how problems were spoken of and what resources they produced. These sections then build upon speakers' reflections on political differences, on the power of a phrase or slogan, and on the power of a more equitable or powerful tax measure. In each chapter, the core question is the speakers' collective anxiety or excitement over the rhetorical resonances of fiscal questions.

The account begins, in Chapter 1, with the controversy over the tariff, and the Laurier government's intention to lower it as a concession to western farmers, in the 1911 election and the critique of party differences that farmers and other writers produced. At the start of the twentieth century, the tariff, a tax on imported goods, was the chief fiscal instrument of the dominion. Although in a formal sense a tax (or, more correctly, a set of taxes), the tariff was more than simply a fiscal instrument, having been invested with nationalist significance by the Conservative Party in the period immediately following Confederation. This was because the tariff had the practical effect of making imported goods more expensive than goods made in Canada and therefore of protecting domestic industry. It was therefore a tax paid by the consumer, partly to the dominion treasury and partly to Canadian business, in the form of inflated prices. Liberal policy for two decades was in opposition to the tariff, so Liberals and Conservatives presented themselves to voters as having different views on the tariff. To win the election in 1896, however, the Liberals abandoned their opposition to the tariff and, for all intents and purposes, practised the same fiscal strategy as the Conservatives. Nevertheless, both parties continued to campaign on the basis of their tariff differences, in the form of an appeal to party memory and tradition, rather than on their actual positions. Canadian politics from 1896 to 1911 was characterized by force-fully stated differences between parties that governed in essentially the same way. Critiques of the inadequacies of the tariff as a revenue source and as a basis for clear political differences gave rise to calls for a reform of politics through fiscal reform or vice versa. For farmers, the focus was primarily on the tariff itself and secondarily on the party system as an instrument to get rid of the tariff. Farmers and others became increasingly disillusioned with the parties, seeing bitter humour in their rhetorical self-importance and seeing them as important only if useful. Ultimately, the farmers' call was heard in Ottawa, and the Liberals renewed their partisan vigour by campaigning in 1911 on a deal for partial reciprocity with the United States. The defeat of the government by the Conserva-tives' emotional appeal to nationalist sentiment further alienated farmers from the party system.

Alienation from the party system was furthered by the political and fiscal controversies of the First World War, the focus of Chapter 2. The memory of 1911, and of the role of rhetoric in disguising the tariff issue as a question of loyalty rather than of class exploitation, created a fertile field for the appeal of direct taxation as an alternative to the tariff. The domin-ion had stayed away from income taxation, leaving it to the provinces, because the British North America Act allowed the provinces only dir-ect taxation, and the dominion treasury wanted to avoid taxing people's incomes twice. But the First World War made some sort of change neces-sary. With the cost of the war, both in money and in lives, weighing so heavily on the working class, and with military conscription on the table, labour leaders pushed for the "conscription of wealth," in the form of a tax on high incomes, as a necessary corollary. The government reluctantly introduced first a tax on war profits and then a tax on incomes a year later as sops to critics of the tariff and other consumer taxes that fell too heav-ily on the poor and not heavily enough on the rich. As in the lead-up to the 1911 election, the controversy over war finance reflected the increasing irrelevance of the two-party system, which all but expired in the last years of the war. The meaningful divisions were increasingly between the old parties and various groups of political modernists, not between the parties themselves. Strikes ignited all over the country, the most infamous one in Winnipeg, and people ran provincially and federally as farmer and labour candidates. In Alberta and Ontario, they formed the governments, and in Ottawa they held the balance of power.

The income war tax, though it was criticized as weak by Liberal parliamentarians and labour groups outside Parliament, served in the 1920s and 1930s as a suggestion of the possibilities for a new fiscal regime, in which the dominion government would actively use its powers of taxation to direct and shape the economy, a campaign that is the focus of Chapter 3. With a federal income tax permanently in place, though weak enough to be more of an idea than an actual fact for most taxpayers, the modernization kicked off by farmers, workers, and intellectuals shifted into high gear. In the Maritimes, for instance, progressive reformers pushing for public expenditures on public works ran up against the limits of provincial fiscal models, which had to tax a predominantly low-income population, given that so much business leadership had relocated to Toronto and Montreal; they used the Liberal and Conservative Parties interchangeably to advance their progressive ends, employing the two parties' lack of clear differences to strategic advantage. The controversy over fiscal need that emerged out of this realization was a struggle over the role of the federal government in equalizing and correcting for regional economic disparities – which had not been on the agenda previously. In the 1930s, when provinces and municipalities began paying out unprecedented sums for household relief and hung precipitously close to bankruptcy, the critique of the tariff and the possibility of using the federal taxing power to correct for the vagaries of capitalist development began to collide. The growth of third parties, notably the Cooperative Commonwealth Federation (CCF) and various progressive splinter groups of Conservatives, made for a crowded and chaotic electoral field. Combined with the emergence of the possibility of using the federal income tax to effect large-scale income equalization, this led to increasing use of left and right to try to keep track of and agree, often unsuccessfully, on what was occurring. The Royal Commission on Dominion-Provincial Relations, called to address once and for all how the federal government should use its taxing power to stabilize the federation, recommended in its final report that the income tax become solely a federal responsibility. The report also suggested that a single income tax at the federal level would make the political field clearer by allowing the elected government to project a single, clear rate of progressivity, the difference in taxation of high, moderate, and low incomes.

The political realities involved in implementing the commission's idea of a powerful single dominion income tax are the focus of Chapter 4. The commission's recommendations were rejected by some provinces and, in a formal sense, died. Within a few months, however, with the unanswerable justification of the war, Minister of Finance J.L. Ilsley inflated the income war tax to gargantuan proportions, creating a tax base and a budget that exceeded all previous expectations, let alone experience. Over the years that followed, as the dominion further increased income taxation and introduced its first large-scale social program, the Family Allowances Act, the parties increasingly defined themselves in terms of how they would use the treasury to mould Canadian society after the war. The CCF, the Liberals, and the renamed Progressive Conservatives jostled for spots on the left–right spectrum, and, even as all parties insisted on never repeating the catastrophe of the 1930s, commentators proclaimed more confidently than ever that those on the left sought to avoid an economic crisis by using the power of the state to create an egalitarian society while those on the right sought to do so by using tax rates to stimulate growth.

The narrative ends with the establishment of the left–right spectrum as a widely understood representation of difference and universal income taxation as an accepted fact of political life. After the 1940s, the connection between dominion taxation and dominion political differences was seldom noted. The 1945 *White Paper on Employment and Income,* widely acknowledged as marking a new, more central role for the dominion treasury in stimulating growth, also marked the evaporation of the imaginative, modernizing role of income taxation in the period leading up to the Ilsley reforms.[44] Income taxation as a common experience was no match imaginatively for income taxation as an idea: the former produced revenue on an unprecedented scale, but the latter produced rhetoric that in turn produced the modern political imaginary. Once that imaginary was established as a shared norm, it was no longer a "terrific engine" worthy of comment; income taxation stopped producing possibilities and became a largely silent burden.

Over a little more than thirty years, a mass movement to modernize political rhetoric by replacing the tariff with an income tax transformed political possibilities. The old, backward-looking, tariff-based positions of Liberal and Conservative were increasingly loosened, first by a political vanguard and then by political society as a whole. New, modern positions, more fluid and more clearly tied to identifiable fiscal programs, started to dominate, by the end of the Second World War solidifying into a recognizable way of seeing political reality, a political imaginary in which voters chose among parties arrayed on a left–right spectrum according to their propensity to use income taxation to fund social programs and equalize incomes. No single person was involved in this work from beginning to end; it was a shared project across years and regions and, in some cases, deep political divides. It was a mass modernist push to make a more meaningful and democratic politics. To us, its outcome might be obvious, hackneyed, or even frustrating, but to its architects, the taxpayer-funded social state and the left–right spectrum were a radical and important liberation.

PART I

The People's Enlightenment and the Destruction of the Two-Party System

I

A Clear Line? The Great Deception and the Farmers' Critique of the Tariff, 1910–11

The general election of 1911 was a signal illustration of the power of rhetoric in Canadian electoral politics.[1] The election had been called to determine the fate of a trade agreement negotiated between the United States and the Liberal government of Sir Wilfrid Laurier to lower tariffs between the two countries. Highly protectionist tariffs in Canada were linked historically to the Conservative Party, and they were invoked rhetorically by that party as the crux of John A. Macdonald's patriotic National Policy. The Liberals had made peace with the tariff in the 1890s but continued to position themselves rhetorically as the party to vote for in the hope of lowering the tariff, partly by simple virtue of being the only party other than the Conservatives. Starting in 1909, however, organized farmers in the Prairies used their organ the *Grain Growers' Guide* to launch an attack on the tariff as an exploitative tax and on the two-party system that supported it, though one party dishonestly claimed the antitariff vote. Emboldened by the western farmers' organized critique of the tariff, the Liberals championed a move toward partial easing of tariff barriers with the United States and were subjected to an unprecedented barrage of patriotic criticism from the opposition Conservatives and their supporters in the manufacturing and rail industries. In the election on September 21, 1911, the protectionist rhetoric won out, and the Laurier Liberals were defeated.

The outcome of the election, and the role of rhetoric in achieving that outcome, confirmed the dire analyses of the Canadian party system that had begun to circulate in the months leading up to the reciprocity agreement. The *Grain Growers' Guide* in particular saw the election as the ultimate proof of the correctness of its editorial position that the party system was a dysfunctional and dishonest cover for the machinations of a powerful elite (which the *Guide* termed "Special Privileged") that used the state to exploit common people. Its commentary on the election drew bitter attention to the role of nationalist rhetoric in obscuring the issues at stake: "The chief appeal of the Special Privileged and anti-reciprocity forces during the campaign was not to reason but to sentiment. Emotion and not intellect was worked upon by the anti-reciprocity forces ... The appeal to the flag undoubtedly played a very strong part in the decision."[2] The blunt and analytical tone of the editorial, the explicit valuing of reason and intellect over emotion and sentiment, and the critical link between Special Privilege and "appeal to the flag" all reflected the *Guide*'s positioning of itself and its readers as intelligent modernizers up against a dishonest old political machine. For the *Guide* and its readers, the tariff represented everything that was bad and venal about Canadian politics, and the fight against the tariff represented everything that was good and heroic.

Not everyone took the election as seriously as the *Grain Growers' Guide*. Stephen Leacock, chair of political economy at McGill University in Montreal and an energetic orator for conservatism and protection as well as a humourist, devoted the final episodes of *Sunshine Sketches of a Little Town* – a series of vignettes of a fictional Ontario town called Mariposa originally serialized in the *Montreal Daily Star* over February to June 1912 – to an election dominated by talk of trade and patriotism. "I only know it was a huge election and that on it turned issues of the most tremendous importance," the narrator recalls hazily, noting that it had been called to determine

> whether or not Mariposa should become part of the United States, and whether the flag that had waved over the school house at Tecumseh Township for ten centuries should be trampled under the hoof of an alien invader, and whether Britons should be slaves, and whether Canadians should be Britons, and whether the farmer class would prove themselves Canadians, and stupendous questions of that kind.[3]

The passage consists almost entirely of phrases that are heavy with connotation but denote little: the actual question before the electorate is not directly explained, but the emotional nationalism of terms such as "flag," "Briton," "slave," and "alien invader" make clear how the election was represented and understood. What the narrator characterizes as "tremendous questions" are in fact not questions at all but rhetoric through which questions are framed and perhaps even obscured. By parodying the intensity of nationalist feeling that became attached to the election, Leacock was making a statement about the election: its issues, whatever they might have been, were lost on most voters, who understood the election in terms of the overheated rhetoric invoked by the parties. Caught up in the excitement, people mistook the rhetoric for the issues at stake and voted accordingly. "Now that it is all over," the narrator notes coyly, "we can look back at it without heat or passion."[4]

The *Grain Growers' Guide* and Leacock were on different sides of the election, and the tone of their comments was different – the former earnest and analytical, the latter light and mocking – but both showed a keen awareness of the power of rhetoric in defining the terms of the election and shared a sense that the issues were not discussed clearly and honestly. Leacock was a strong supporter of protectionism, and spoke and wrote against the Liberals and reciprocity, but both he and the *Guide,* in total opposition to the tariff and supportive of the Liberals' reciprocity proposal only as a step in the right direction, saw the election as a superficial and even misleading performance. Leacock was strongly invested in the Conservative Party and its traditions, and he enjoyed contributing to its appeals to patriotism, whereas the *Guide* saw the differences between Liberal Party and Conservative Party platforms as mostly meaningless given both parties' deep connections to the country's largest business interests in Montreal and Toronto. However, in the aftermath of the election, both Leacock and the *Guide* saw the rhetoric that the parties used as a distraction from the formal questions that voters were ostensibly being asked to decide. Where they disagreed most fundamentally was in what should be done. For Leacock, the inability to distinguish between issues and affect was charming, an ultimately harmless foible, endemic to humanity, to be mocked in a friendly manner.[5] For the *Guide,* the outcome of the election underlined the necessity of the changes that its writers and readers had been calling for, which amounted to a new, more modern understanding of the party system that substituted clear thinking for muddled patriotism.

The election of 1911 was the first campaign of a political modernism that sought to drain the old party system of its nationalist sentimentality and destroy the old imaginary of parties in clear opposition on the tariff question. Stripping the tariff of its patriotic resonances so that it could be evaluated as a tax went hand in hand with seeing clearly the actual positions of the two parties, both of which were committed to the tariff until the eve of the election. By withdrawing their affective investments in parties and seeing them as instruments of exploitation, the writers and readers of the *Grain Growers' Guide* were enacting a new, consciously modern form of citizenship in which critical intelligence formed the basis of independent political action invested in a party strategically only when its platform aligned with the independent political will of the individual or group. The farmers' agitation against the tariff and its role in framing the issues of the 1911 election provided a perfect laboratory for this new political modernism, but the nationalist rhetoric of the tariff and its ties to industry proved to be too strong. The election was a bitter illustration of the power of rhetoric and tenacity of the two-party system's affective hold, but it also showed the power of the new forces arrayed against that system. Although income taxation was only marginally at stake in the election of 1911, the negative campaign to destroy the imaginary built around the tariff and its patriotic resonances was key to how the fiscal and political revolution of the next decades would unfold.

"Upon This Issue We Engage in Battle": The Parties and the Rhetoric of the Tariff

The tariff was an inescapable fact of Canadian political life at the turn of the twentieth century. A tax on various imported goods, the tariff was not only the dominion's main source of revenue but also the primary hinge on which party differences turned. Although the British North America Act gave the dominion the power to enact any form of taxation, it specifically limited the provinces to direct taxation, which had the effect of confining the dominion to the tariff as almost its sole source of tax revenue. Between the elections of 1896 and 1911, the two parties were committed to maintaining the tariff as an instrument of economic development and protection for industry. Despite this overall agreement, Liberals and Conservatives insistently underlined the importance of the differences between the two parties' tariff policies. Party rhetoric that had originated decades earlier, when the parties were in definite opposition on tariff issues, survived the parties' convergence on this issue and continued to hold the public's imagination. Because of this, the tariff structured how people thought about politics: it determined the outcomes of dominion elections long after the outcomes of these elections stopped determining the tariff.

By 1900, it was impossible to vote against the tariff but also unlikely that beliefs about the tariff would not inform one's voting.

The tariff as a fiscal strategy was born from a crisis in the political economy of the British colonies of North America that started with the end of imperial protection in the 1840s, when the adoption of free trade by Britain forced the colonies to find international markets on their own. Anxiety in the face of this prospect was so acute that merchants in Montreal proposed annexation to the United States. Instead, colonial representatives negotiated a treaty for reciprocity with the United States in 1854. The Americans abrogated the treaty in 1866, and again anxiety and desperation helped to push colonial authorities toward a radical solution: the Confederation of three contiguous British North American colonies – Canada, Nova Scotia, and New Brunswick – into a self-governing dominion. The new dominion government extended invitations to reinstate reciprocity to successive American administrations and was continually rebuffed.

The high tariff policy was originally understood primarily as an irritant to pressure the United States into re-entering into a reciprocity agreement; for the first years following Confederation, high tariffs were invoked as a general retaliatory threat to American protection. However, the dominion also had to support its considerable expenses for infrastructure projects such as railways and canals. The tariff went up and down depending on how negotiations with the Americans were going, and it did well as a source of revenue until the depression of the 1870s, when revenue collapsed. The tariff was always, as J. Harvey Perry said, a "fair-weather friend" that "produces prolifically in good, and abysmally in poor, times."[6] The burdensome and inefficient nature of the tariff became clear in this period and made its performance as a political and fiscal instrument an object of partisan disagreement.

Liberals and Conservatives started investing the tariff and their differing positions on it with increasing partisan sentiment in the depression of the 1870s. Given the depressed conditions, the Liberals were keen not to raise the tariff, even though it was not producing enough revenue to balance the budget. Conservative critics called for an increase that would protect manufacturers. Defending their budgets against proposals for slightly increased rates, the Liberals borrowed the language of free trade, even though their position, like that of the Conservatives, was far from absolute. The result was an increasingly divided partisan dispute over the question of the tariff. "The concrete proposals of the opposing parties differed comparatively little," O.D. Skelton wrote of the 1870s.

"In discussion, however, the advocates of seventeen and a half per cent
and the advocates of twenty per cent frequently took up positions poles
apart."[7] What was actually a difference of degree, that is, was presented
rhetorically as an absolute difference that comprised the meaning of each
pole. Through the next few elections, both parties coined phrases to define
their contrasting positions on the tariff, underlining and amplifying differences to the extent that the parties were seen as absolutely different –
"poles apart," as Skelton said – rather than merely differentiated from one
another by a detail of fiscal policy.

This hardening of partisan positions continued through the decade,
becoming a structuring element of the party system. Although other
issues were involved, "protection and free trade," according to Ben Forster, "were the essential grist for the mill of public discussion in 1878."[8]
The election that year saw John A. Macdonald's Conservatives come
to power with significant help from the Ontario Manufacturers' Association, a pro-tariff lobby group that would rename itself the Canadian
Manufacturers' Association (CMA) in the 1880s. The Conservatives' platform, identified as "the National Policy," resulted in a new tariff in 1879
that was "deeply protective" – not surprisingly since it was coauthored by
the manufacturers.[9] The rhetorical excesses attached to party differences,
their representation as "poles apart," continued through the following
decade. A Conservative pamphlet from 1887, for example, was a single
page on which the two parties' tariff positions were listed side by side
and phrased as opposites (see Figure 1.1). The rhetoric reached a peak
in the election of 1891, the first in which Wilfrid Laurier led the Liberal
Party, when the Liberals ran on a slogan of unrestricted reciprocity and
the Conservatives confidently produced an election poster that, drawing
reliably on years of rhetorical accumulation, said, simply, "The Old Flag,
the Old Policy, the Old Leader." As the tariff became established as a solid
rule of Canadian political life, the partisan rhetoric around it intensified,
and the perception that the party differences were absolute was ever more
deeply ingrained.

The self-identification of the Liberals and Conservatives as "poles
apart" on the tariff question was complicated by a change in policy in
the 1890s that saw the Liberals take a much more pro-tariff stance. Aban-
doning its previous free-trade rhetoric and its 1891 slogan of unrestricted
reciprocity, the party claimed a new position at its convention in Ottawa
in June 1893. Adopted as Liberal Party Resolution #1, the new plank committed the party to a revenue tariff, a moderate tariff intended to raise
revenue for the treasury with minimal effects on the prices and avail-
ability of imported goods. The resolution explicitly affirmed the party's

No. 9.

READ THE RECORD!

The National Policy vs. the Cartwright Tariff.

THE TWO POLICIES CONTRASTED.

UNDER REVENUE TARIFF.	UNDER NATIONAL POLICY.
Period 1875 to 1878.	Period 1880 to 1886.
No Canadian Pacific railway.	Canadian Pacific railway finished.
Only 6,484 miles of railway in Canada.	Nearly 12,000 miles of railway in Canada.
Railway receipts weekly diminishing.	Railway receipts weekly increasing, though rates much lower.
Four per cent. bonds of Canada quoted at 6 *below* par.	Four per cent. bonds quoted at 7 *above* par.
Cartwright could only get £91 for each £100 bond.	Sir Leonard gets a premium of £1 1s 8¼d for each £100 bond.
Cartwright had to pay four and a half million dollars in shaves to the money brokers for his loans.	He secured his last loan at a gain in premiums of $122,000.
Credit of the country down and going down rapidly.	Credit of the country up and rising rapidly.
Net interest on public debt, $1.59 per head in 1878.	Net interest per head (in 1885), $1.59, though fifty-three and a half million dollars has been added to the public debt for public improvements.
Net increase of interest paid per head during period 25 cents more in 1879 than in 1873.	Net interest per head remains the same ($1.59) in 1885 as it was in 1879.
Increase of net interest *every year* of period.	Decrease of net interest every year of period except 1885-6, when to complete the Canadian Pacific railway five years before contract time the whole of the subsidy was paid.
Depression everywhere in Canada.	Confidence and a buoyant spirit throughout Canada.
Business at a standstill.	Business brisk and sales lively.
Real estate lower than ever before known.	Real estate bringing high prices.
Stocks of public companies away down below par and hard to dispose of.	Stocks bringing good prices and above par.
Bank and Dominion note circulation decreasing.	Bank and Dominion note circulation increasing.
Discounts decreasing.	Discounts increasing.
Nine thousand traders fail in five years.	Only six thousand traders fail in six years, with 30 per cent. increase in number of traders.
Their liabilities average $27,000,000 a year.	Their liabilities average only $10,000,000 a year.
Savings bank deposits dwindling month after month.	Savings bank deposits increasing month after month.
Insurances—fire and life—being dropped through the poverty of the people.	Insurances fire and life—greatly increased over every preceding year.
Cities increasing in wealth and population slowly or not at all.	Cities increasing rapidly in wealth and population.
Soup kitchen business lively.	Soup kitchen industry gone into insolvency for want of applicants.
Artisans without work.	Artisans fully employed.
Laborers out of work demanding bread.	Laborers at work on good wages.
Their children starving ; clothing dear and no money to buy it with.	Good prospects for the boys and girls ; clothing cheap and money plentiful.
Everything languishing : Railways, banks, public companies and general business.	Everything active : Railway earnings greatly increased ; bank business developed ; great increase in number incorporated companies, and general business thriving.
The people rise in their might and turn out the Grits in 1878.	1882—People again endorse the National Party.
Exit the party of hypocrisy.	1887—People will do as they did in 1882 and in 1879, only much more so.

FIGURE 1.1   A pamphlet produced by the Conservative Party in 1887 shows the Liberals' revenue tariff on the left and the Conservatives' National Policy on the right. The layout and text suggest that the two parties' positions were completely different. | Library and Archives Canada, AMICUS No. 5307556.

opposition to protection but was widely seen as its acquiescence to the National Policy and the power of industry, particularly through the Canadian Manufacturers' Association, and public opinion in opposition to the party's traditional low-tariff stance.[10] Liberal Party materials, though, strongly underlined the difference between the new position and that of the Conservatives, insisting that, with Resolution #1 in place, "the issue between the two political parties on this question is now clearly defined."[11] Laurier, who had moved Resolution #1 and was widely seen as the moving spirit of the party's embrace of the tariff, noted in his speech at the convention that "from this moment we have a distinct issue with the party in power. Their ideal is protection; our ideal is free trade; their immediate object is protection; ours a tariff for revenue and for revenue only."[12] The implication of the phrase "from this moment" was that the party's shift to a position less different from that of the Conservatives had somehow made their differences clearer. The importance of a clear distinction, indeed an opposition, between the two parties' positions on the tariff was clear. "Upon this issue," Laurier said, "we engage in battle."[13]

Having jettisoned their more sharply differentiated reciprocity position for a more moderate revenue tariff stance, the Liberals won the election of 1896, giving the party its first opportunity to demonstrate its tariff position in action. The Conservative Party, now in opposition, greeted the new budget with apocalyptic warnings about its effect on industry. At the same time, though, the Conservatives appreciated the Liberals' tariff policy as underlining a clear difference between the two parties. Charles Tupper said of the budget that, "from a party point of view, the hon. gentlemen are doing our work; they are showing the people of the country that no reliance can be placed upon the most solemn declaration that they make either in the House or out of it."[14] Both parties had a lot at stake in insisting on the opposition between their respective positions and in downplaying the similarities between Liberal and Conservative tariff policies after the 1890s.

As the Liberal government of Laurier continued its revenue tariff stance through subsequent elections, the parties continued forcefully to underline their opposing positions on the tariff. Speakers would draw attention to the obvious fact of the similarity of the two positions and then quickly insist that they were absolutely different. This was summed up by David Henderson, the Conservative MP for Halton, who stated in the House of Commons in 1902 that "it was said in the early days of the present tariff, that the Liberals had stolen our clothes ... But I do not consider that they have done anything of the kind ... Their tariff is, instead, just the antipode of ours."[15] The remark was reprinted in a Liberal pamphlet that set out to underline the differences between the Liberal and Conservative positions on the tariff and to refute the silent suggestion that the parties' positions were in fact similar and becoming more so. The Liberal authors of the pamphlet allowed themselves some mockery of the Conservative position, calling "adequate protection," the phrase at the centre of a 1902 opposition motion on the tariff, "a very specious" coinage that "might mean anything." Overall, the pamphlet relied on both Liberal and Conservative voices to attest to the truth of their fundamental opposition on the tariff question.[16] The key claim of partisan rhetoric – that "the Liberal policy is directly opposed to the policy of protection" – was one in which both parties were equally invested.[17] "No matter what individuals may say," the pamphlet concluded, "the two parties stand distinctly divided on the tariff: The Liberals for low tariff, the Conservatives for high tariff, and any voter who is interested in tariff matters can therefore have no difficulty in expressing his opinion at the polls."[18] The pamphlet's tone was transparently defensive, implying with some frustration that people had said that the parties were not divided on the tariff issue. Its insistence on the depth of that difference, on its completeness, suggested that there was some doubt that needed to be put to rest. Both parties had a lot at stake in underlining their mutual opposition and in affirming that their differences on the tariff were at the core of each party's electoral appeal.

The insistence that there remained fundamental differences on which voters could decide between the parties was not especially convincing to those outside the parties. Beyond the *Grain Growers' Guide,* whose critique of the tariff and the party system is the focus of the following section, a number of independent commentators observing the Canadian scene between 1893 and 1911 noted the incongruity of political rhetoric and fiscal questions. The most famous of these critiques was André Siegfried's *The Race Question in Canada,* published in 1907. Siegfried, a French social scientist, studied Canadian political life as part of his analysis of the country's handling of the French-English question. He noted with disapproval that Canadian political parties infiltrated every sphere of public life in the federation yet were almost wholly lacking in political content and distinguishing ideology. "Originally formed to subserve a political idea," Siegfried wrote, "these parties are often found quite detached from the principles which gave them birth, and with their own self-preservation as their chief care and aim."[19] Political parties born from the struggles over responsible government had become "mere associations for the securing of power; their doctrines serving merely as weapons, dulled or sharpened,

grasped as occasion arises for use in the fight."[20] Although their struggle
for power dominated Canadian political life, Siegfried concluded, "Liberals and Conservatives differ very little really in their opinions upon crucial
questions, and their views on administration are almost identical."[21]

Siegfried's explanation for this is fascinating and simple: Canadian
politics was about nothing because, if it was about anything, it would be
about race, language, and religion – which would be disastrous for the
future of Confederation. "Let a question involving religion or nationality
be once boldly raised," Siegfried argued, "and all the trivial little questions of patronage and vested interests will disappear below the surface:
the elections will be turned into real political fights, passionate and sin-
cere."[22] Like Leacock, Siegfried believed that meaningful party differences
arose from true bifurcations of opinion. In Canada, however, "far-sighted
and prudent politicians" looking to "preserve the national equilibrium"
did everything that they could "to prevent the formation of homogen-
eous political parties, divided according to creed or race or class."[23] For
Siegfried, the problem with Canadian political life was not that its parties lacked definition and meaningful purpose but that the parties were
too dominant culturally, that one's party "is held in esteem almost like
one's religion, and its praises are sung in dithyrambs that are often a trifle
absurd."[24] The problem, that is, was not that Canadian political party
divisions were baseless but that Canadians invested them with immense
imaginative energy.

A more pointed and less sympathetic view of the party system in Canada
was the one produced by an old friend of Stephen Leacock, Andrew Macphail. He bluntly stated in his 1909 collection *Essays in Politics* that "there
are now in Canada two pseudo-Conservative parties, both standing for
the same privileges and for the interests of the same class."[25] Macphail
underlined the degree to which party labels were based upon the memory of previous stances, not upon the current positions or actions of the
parties: "The electors at large ... have developed an instinct that privilege
and monopoly are the portion of the Conservatives ... [and] that Liberalism has always been the voice of popular discontent and the instrument
by which those evils were to be overcome. They have not learned that
the strife is at an end."[26] For Macphail, the positions of the parties in the
early twentieth century were virtually identical. Whichever of the two
parties was elected to govern, the broad outlines of the economy would
stay much the same. Voters were marking their ballots on the basis of a
difference in image or rhetoric rather than policy. Macphail's proposal
was for the parties to reclaim their old opposition, which amounted to

the Liberals repositioning themselves as the party against the tariff. It was important, abstractly, for the parties to stand for something, or they would become corrupt – "a 'curse' which the country will not endure forever."[27]

It was also important, Macphail insisted, for the parties to disagree on the question of the tariff specifically. The purpose of the legislature was to demonstrate consent to be taxed; if both parties accepted without question that there would be a tax on imports, then effectively there was no democracy. Macphail was keen on the point that it was, beneath its nationalist finery, a tax. It had to be discussed that way, and the political consequences of that discussion had to be faced:

> You may yet convince the consumer that he does not pay the tax ... [or] ... that a tax paid to a manufacturer is as useful to the community as if it were paid into the exchequer – and yet, if his moral sense is outraged; if he becomes convinced that the doing of these things leads to corruption of public life, the degradation of Parliament, ... then he will calmly ignore these excellent arguments, and declare that industrial excitement may be purchased at too high a price, and that prosperity has turned to disaster.[28]

As we will see in the next section, Macphail's sense of the costs of the tariff – "corruption of public life," "degradation of Parliament" – mirrored the position of the *Grain Growers' Guide* from that time, as did his ironic description of tariff rhetoric as "excellent arguments." Macphail was on much the same page as the farmers and as eager to see electoral politics wrestle with an anti-tariff position. "The Manufacturers' Association affirm that they have taken the tariff out of politics," he said, but "the people are very likely to bring it in again when they get the chance."[29]

The protective tariff dominated the party system and the political imaginary in Canada at the start of the twentieth century. From its origin as an irritant to protectionist American governments in the 1860s, tariffs developed in the 1870s into a heavily rhetorical National Policy that kept American goods out of the country and encouraged the growth of local manufacturing. The National Policy of the Conservatives under John A. Macdonald was opposed by the Liberals in opposition using language borrowed from free-trade debates. The differing party positions on the tariff were portrayed by the parties as absolute: as opposites or antipodes. After the Liberals under Wilfrid Laurier lost the 1891 election on a platform of unrestricted reciprocity, they abandoned their harsh anti-tariff rhetoric and adopted a revenue tariff as their rallying cry, and they won the 1896

election on that basis. Although the new position put them closer to that
of the Conservatives on the tariff issue, both parties continued to insist
that they remained absolutely opposed – that the imaginary in which
their opposition structured political debate was still valid and vital. This
insistence was important not just because it made the party system make
sense but also because a growing number of people were noticing that the
parties' positions were increasingly similar.

"Like a Light Shining through the Darkness": The Farmers' Critique of Politics

Western farmers' political awakening began in 1909 with the launch of
the *Grain Growers' Guide,* a weekly newspaper dedicated to cleaning up
politics by getting rid of the tariff. The official organ of three provincial
farmers' associations – the Manitoba Grain Growers, the Saskatchewan
Grain Growers, and the United Farmers of Alberta – the *Guide* played a
central role in organizing farmers by serving as a forum for criticisms of
the tariff and of dominion politics more broadly. The injustice, inefficiency,
and deceptiveness of the tariff were reiterated by the *Guide*'s editors, illus-
trators, contributors, and correspondents, who together produced an
understanding of the tariff as a core corrupting feature of public life. This
understanding was communicated by the farmers' associations to Laurier
during his western tour in the summer of 1910 and to Parliament when
the Canadian Council of Agriculture met in Ottawa in the fall, and it was
the primary inspiration for the government's gamble on reciprocity. As
W.L. Morton has said, the political case promoted by the *Guide* was "the
first act in the agrarian revolt of Western Canada."[30] It was also an important step in the articulation of the relationship between fiscal politics and
political differences and in the modernist campaign to replace the old
party differences with clearer and more honest differences.

The farmers' influence was the conscious product of a process of political modernization and education akin to what Ian McKay has called the
"people's enlightenment."[31] Against the unjust system of "Special Privilege" that cloaked its greed in a rhetorical veil of nationalism, the *Grain
Growers' Guide* cast farmers as the liberators of the nation's democratic
possibilities; they were opening their eyes and seeing honestly what was
before them, and they were acting politically on that knowledge. Whether
that action took place through one or both of the existing parties, or was
embodied in a new party with new principles and a new approach to

politics, the keys were to be knowledgeable and to act on that knowledge to awaken the possibilities inherent in it. In the context of the party system, that meant being honest and intelligent about the relative merits of the Liberals and Conservatives and open to the possibility of acting outside party lines; in the context of the tariff, that meant being honest about what it was and how it worked and which alternatives there were.

The fundamental goal of the *Grain Growers' Guide* with respect to the tariff was to clarify that it was a tax. Where other commentators would call the tariff protection or, with even more nationalist weight, the National Policy, the *Guide* often used the word *tax* in describing the tariff and its effects. In a letter to Laurier in August 1910, for example, a United Farmers of Alberta member complained to the prime minister that "we are now paying taxes on a larger proportion of our imports than fifteen years ago."[32] The *Guide* encouraged its readers to see the tariff burden as a tax, and letters from farmers testifying to the personal burden of the tariff were a regular feature. One correspondent wrote to the *Guide* in August 1910 saying that "I know a person who bought a second-hand gasoline engine from the States and paid $125 duty, tax or tariff, on it. That is a specimen of the burden of taxation for you."[33] Against descriptions of the tariff that underlined its role in creating manufacturing jobs, the *Guide* insistently described it as a tax. By identifying the tariff as a tax, the *Guide* was seeking to dissociate it from considerations that obfuscated what it considered the core issue: exploitation.

Not only was the tariff a tax, but it was also inefficient and unfair. By raising the cost to consumers of imported manufactured goods, the tariff encouraged consumers to buy goods inside Canada's tariff wall; however, this protective effect, the basis of its political and nationalist appeal, meant that very few imported goods were purchased and thus that the duty raised very little revenue. To the extent that the tariff worked to prevent imported goods from finding markets, that is, it failed to raise revenue and vice versa. By combining revenue and protection in a single blunt instrument, the tariff essentially taxed consumers to pay Canadian manufacturers, with an incidental amount accruing to the dominion treasury. For the *Grain Growers' Guide,* then, the tariff was the most egregious form of tax in that it imposed an unfair burden on the taxed without raising significant revenue.

This point was made repeatedly in the paper in various ways. In the words of a November 1910 editorial, the "balance of the revenue, unjustly taken from the people, goes into the treasury of the protected manufacturers."[34] This argument was reiterated in articles, letters, and illustrations throughout 1910 and 1911. An editorial during Laurier's tour in July 1910 explained that

> when a high tariff is placed on a manufactured article it stops to a great extent the importation of these articles, while the Canadian manufacturers of that article add the amount of the tariff to the legitimate charge for such an article. In these cases the farmer or other consumer pays the whole burden of the tariff but the revenue from this tax does not go into the public treasury. It all goes to the treasury of the manufacturers.[35]

Other articles gave the monetary breakdown, estimating the amount that farmers paid in the tariff versus how much went into the dominion treasury, illustrating forcefully how inefficient the tariff was. A letter in December 1910, using census figures from 1906, claimed that

> the enhanced price that the local manufacturers were enabled to charge us for their wares in consequence of this duty, amounted to no less than $2,067,326, which did not go towards the revenue, but into their own pockets. Thus on the plea that we have to impose big customs duties so as [to] procure a revenue, we tax our own people $2,067,326 for the benefit of manufacturers and $323,026 goes to the government. Thus for every dollar that this duty gives to the government, we are made to pay $6.40 to the manufacturers.[36]

Similarly, an editorial in November 1910 argued that

> the farmers of Canada are taxed approximately $2,142,000 per year on agricultural implements alone, to furnish a revenue of just $142,000. Thus, for every dollar of revenue that the government collects on agricultural implements $15 additional goes into the pockets of the manufacturers of implements, and this is supposed to be a tariff for revenue purposes, which our manufacturers tell us is a splendid thing.[37]

That most of the amount that taxpayers had to pay as a result of the tariff went not into the public treasury but into the private treasury of the manufacturers was repeated forcefully in issue after issue. A cartoon titled "How the Farmer Benefits by a Protective Tariff" (Figure 1.2), which ran in the November 1910 issue of the *Grain Growers' Guide*, would have been immediately understood by regular readers. It showed a farmer being squeezed in a vise-like machine labelled "The Protective Tariff Mill" and

Putting on the Screws

How the Farmer Benefits by
a Protective Tariff

FIGURE 1.2 The tariff as exploitation. The operators of the mill, marked "Government" and "Manufacturers," represent the collusion of industry and politics in taking money from the farmer under the guise of protection, money that ends up in the manufacturers' treasury, not the dominion's treasury. The use of a machine to torture and exploit the farmer perhaps is also meant to suggest the exploitative relationship between industry and agriculture – or, more concretely, the industrial regions and the agricultural regions of the country. The image is unsigned but was probably by Dick Hartley. | *Grain Growers' Guide* 2, 38 (1910): 4.

controlled by two identical grimacing figures in three-piece suits, one tagged as "Government," the other as "Manufacturers." The machine was extracting money from the farmer's pockets, and the money was accumulating in a box beneath labelled "Manufacturer's Treasury." The cartoon, like the articles and letters from the same period, was making the point that the tariff was an unjust scheme that amounted to taking money from people under the guise of taxation that mostly ended up in the private treasuries of manufacturers.

The *Grain Growers' Guide*'s critique of the unfairness of the tariff burden was linked to its critique of the misleading and overheated rhetoric that protected the tariff from intelligent criticism and infected the entire political apparatus of the country. The tariff was politically inseparable from its rhetoric, having been established in the public imagination as the key component of the National Policy in the 1870s and since then the basis of the partisan identities of the Liberal and Conservative Parties. That the Liberals, since the 1890s, had abandoned their anti-tariff stance and embraced a nearly identical commitment to the permanence and necessity of tariff protection complicated matters but did not change the fact that the parties still campaigned on tariff differences, thereby contributing to the haze of misrepresentation and confusion that surrounded the issue. The rhetoric that saw the tariff as the necessary basis of loyalty to the British Empire was seen by the farmers' associations and the *Guide* as a cover for exploitation and an insult to the intelligence of Canadians.

That the tariff and nationalist rhetoric were inseparable, and that to argue against the tariff meant to take on that rhetoric, were acknowledged forcefully by the *Grain Growers' Guide.* An editorial in the summer of 1910 said that "advocates of a tariff invariably argue that a tariff spells national unity."[38] Manufacturers and others who benefited directly from the tariff routinely reminded advocates of free trade that it was important to keep in mind the British Empire when devising a trade policy and not be tempted by the easy money that would come from trading with Americans. A cartoon in August 1911 showed an industrialist in a Union Jack vest saying "You must build up the Empire" and waving a flag in front of the farmer to distract him while reaching into his pocket to steal his money, the message being that nationalism was introduced in discussions of trade as a distraction from the real business: exploitation by industry of farmers and other taxpayers. A few months later the editors noted optimistically that "the disloyalty cry is playing out. The farmers of Canada are too sensible to allow themselves to be fooled by such transparent fallacies."[39] The ideas that ignorance and intellectual laziness made people susceptible to the claim that the tariff was a necessary instrument of nationalism and that intelligence was guiding people to a truer understanding ran through the *Guide's* analysis of the rhetoric of the tariff. "To make an intelligent argument either for or against reciprocity based on comparative prices and market requirements entails a considerable expenditure of time and industry in the preparation of facts and figures," an editorial in September 1911 said, "but anyone can say, 'I am not prepared to throw myself into the arms of Uncle Sam and therefore I am opposed to reciprocity.'"[40] That the political rhetoric of the tariff was an insult to the intelligence of educated and politically engaged farmers was a common theme among correspondents as well. As one asked, "Do the parties really think that the Western farmer is fit only for a diet of such bumkum and flap-doodle as their paid press hands out daily or weekly?" The correspondent then commented that, "if so, their estimate of his intelligence is indeed low."[41]

The critique of political rhetoric surrounding the tariff was linked to what, apart from the injustice of the tariff as a form of taxation, was the most well-documented concern of the editors of the *Grain Growers' Guide*: the difference between the two ostensibly opposed parties. The Conservatives were traditionally a high-tariff party and the Liberals a low-tariff party, but under Laurier's leadership the Liberals had accepted the necessity of a tariff, ostensibly for revenue and not protection and therefore apparently milder in effect. To the editors and readers of the *Guide,* however, the difference was unnoticeable. "We cannot see any difference between the two political parties in Canada on this score," an editorial in the fall of 1910 announced flatly. "We cannot see that the names of these two parties stand for anything."[42] During Laurier's western tour, an editorial insisted that "Sir Wilfrid and leader Borden stand on the same platform as regards tariff. There is no hope of ousting one in the hope of securing aid from the other."[43] The hope lay, the editorial claimed, in citizens putting pressure on both parties to insist on change. As a letter a few weeks later asked, "if the Liberal party stands for that infamous doctrine of 'Protection' then how differs it from the Conservative party?"[44] Another correspondent noted the similarities between the parties when they were governing and suggested a new way of differentiating their positions: "It is true that we have two parties or at least two party names, and it is also true that their platforms look different, but it seems to me that the only great difference is that one is in power, while the other is out, so we have the 'ins' and the 'outs.'"[45] The differences between the two parties, the editors and correspondents argued, were not real; the political imaginary that positioned them as opposites was not to be taken seriously.

The political differences between the two parties, the *Grain Growers' Guide* argued, were a distraction from what was really happening: both parties were in league with industry and finance and cared little about democracy or any other principle. "Special Privileged," the *Guide*'s term for the business elite, worked through both parties to advance its material interests, damaging political life in the process. "Both political parties are dominated by these vested interests," one letter argued, "and legislation for years past has been influenced and controlled by the thralldom of this concealed but irresistible force."[46] This meant that the two-party system was a misrepresentation. In reality, the government was in the hands of one power, the Special Privileged, which operated through whichever party was in power. The parties shouted at each other on election day, and attacked one another across the floor of the House of Commons, but ultimately they governed the same way, according to a letter writer in the summer of 1910:

> In public matters there is no genuine opposition at Ottawa in the most important work of any session, even when it gets down (always in its closing days) to voting the public money. Dualism then ... only expresses the number one. It is in the closing days of the session, mark well, it is then, that unity of the two factions – they are no longer parties – begins to manifest itself. It is then that the Liberal and Conservative factions form one camp.[47]

The vagueness of political party labels, and their obscuring of the exploitation at the heart of Canadian political economy, were recurring concerns for the editors of the *Guide,* who lamented that "blind partisanship ... has broken down representative government in Canada and reared upon the ruins the feudalism of privileged wealth."[48]

That the tariff was the bedrock of a corrupt system was a common theme in the *Grain Growers' Guide*'s interpretation of the tariff. An editorial in late 1910 stated flatly that "the tariff is a system under which corruption creeps into our national life; it lowers the moral standard of Canada and undoubtedly does more to injure the common people than any other single law."[49] The editors took great pleasure in citing Laurier, who claimed, before he was prime minister, that "protection, besides being the cause of the worst political corruption, is the deadly foe of all true freedom"; they noted that, "since that time, he has swallowed himself completely."⁵⁰ The corrupting influence of the Special Privileged and their hunger for tariff wealth had destroyed whatever political principles he had held. Another editorial drew all the critiques of the tariff together: "One of the evils of Protectionism is its corrupting influence upon the morals of the people. Protection makes people dishonest; it stimulates selfishness and greed; it is responsible for the corruption of public life and it causes antagonism and strife between countries whose relations should be friendly and harmonious."⁵¹ For the *Guide,* the political dishonesty and economic greed inseparable from the tariff played a central role in damaging the country's democracy. This point was illustrated in a cartoon (see Figure 1.3) in the summer of 1911 that showed the two party leaders, Wilfrid Laurier and Robert Borden, turning the crank on a machine churning up the consuming public to feed the coffers of the rich, as symbolized by financier Max Aitken. The political imaginary and fiscal strategy of the country were equally problematic and mutually reinforcing. To make politics meaningful, the farmers would have to modernize both the fiscal and the political.

Although the primary concern of the editors of the *Grain Growers' Guide* was to expose the tariff as an exploitative and corrupting tax, contributors and especially correspondents devoted considerable attention to fairer, more efficient, and more honest alternatives. This project, the other side of the same coin debunking the rhetoric of the tariff, involved making a case for forms of taxation conventionally seen as unpopular and aggressive and therefore as unrealistic alternatives. Proponents of the tariff defended it on political grounds as a more palatable tax, one that avoided popular discontent because it was subtle and invisible; a direct tax would more clearly and recognizably take money from people and was therefore politically impossible. Even those, particularly in the Liberal Party, who professed to agree that free trade would be ideal, argued that a direct tax would never be accepted generally. Building upon the *Guide*'s critique of the tariff, and readers' sense of themselves as enlightened thinkers, letters and editorials engaged with the possibility of direct taxation as an alternative to the tariff.

The fear of direct taxation was central to the strength of the tariff case and often invoked by people who wanted to dull the appetite for tariff reform or free trade. This was a particularly common tactic of Liberal politicians who differentiated between the protective tariff, which was high enough to dissuade consumers completely from purchasing imports, and a revenue tariff, which was more moderate and only added enough to imports to generate revenue from their consumption; whereas the

Industry leans on the Politician

FIGURE 1.3 The party system as exploitation. "Industry Leans on the Politician" shows Robert Borden and Wilfrid Laurier working the machine that takes money from the public and gives it to rich businessmen, such as Max Aitken. Cement was subject to a 51 percent tariff; the writing on the mixer references this and perhaps the effective merger of the two parties as equally willing servants of the wealthy. The image was probably drawn by Dick Hartley. | *Grain Growers' Guide* 3, 52 (1911): 4.

protective tariff was defended on nationalist grounds, a revenue tariff was defended as an alternative to a direct tax. For example, though he claimed to be a true English free-trade liberal, Laurier argued that the tariff situation in England was different from the one in Canada in that in the former "it was possible to impose direct taxation. In Canada, a new country, it was necessary to continue to secure money for the purposes of the country by customs duties."[52] The *Grain Growers' Guide* answered this argument by insisting that the tariff was in fact a tax and an unfair and inefficient one at that. For example, an editorial pointed out that "Direct Taxation would be a boon of inestimable value to every farmer in Canada" in that "all his tax would then go into the public treasury and none into the pockets of Special Privilege."[53] Both indirect taxation and direct taxation were still taxation, the *Guide* was saying, the difference being that with direct taxation all of the money taxed went to the public treasury, whereas under the tariff a large portion of what consumers paid went into the profits of manufacturers. As with the argument against the tariff, the argument in favour of direct taxation was represented as part of a process of awakening, of seeing reality for the first time, of no longer being misled or deluded.

The political distinction between indirect tax and direct tax was often expressed in visual terms: the former was a misrepresentation, a trick, whereas the latter was honest and therefore democratic. "The present system does not at first glance appear so oppressive as direct taxation," an editorial pointed out, "because the indirect tax is collected in so many ways that the taxed does not realize how heavily they are paying."[54] The visual language – "glance" and "appear" – underlines the idea of indirect taxation as dishonest and misleading, something that keeps people in the dark so that their understanding is incomplete. This visual rhetoric was reflected in the ability of the enlightened farmer to see through the phony distinctions between forms of taxation. Echoing the critique of the tariff, one letter queried the distinction between direct taxation and indirect taxation, pointing out that in both cases taxes are paid; the difference with the former is that all of the money goes to the treasury, so the public pays only what is necessary. "Doesn't [tax revenue] come out of pockets as much now as it would under Free Trade, only more so?" asked David Ross. "Under Free Trade we would save enough in one year on the goods we buy to pay twice over the revenue necessary for the expenses of government."[55] The willingness to bear direct taxation arose from the clear understanding of the exploitative and inefficient nature of the tariff and the conviction that farmers were being overtaxed in relation to their responsibility to the state; this willingness was a key strength in the farmers' political case against the tariff. As one editorial noted, "those protectionists who say that direct taxation is the only alternative to [the] tariff need not fear that the farmers will object to direct taxation because if there was direct taxation in Canada to-day and no tariff every farmer would be money in pocket."[56] The argument that the tariff was exploitative and misleading, the central theme of commentary in the *Grain Growers' Guide,* implied that a direct tax would be a significant improvement both for economic and for political reasons; championing direct taxation, commonly understood as unpopular and confiscatory, took the *Guide's* project of political enlightenment a step further. The case for the elimination of the tariff also had to be a case for the introduction of some alternative instrument for raising revenue – one that would be fairer, more efficient, and easier to make sense of politically, without recourse to mystifying rhetoric that obscured the real issues. The *Guide* and its readers had to offer a positive policy change to buttress the negative policy change: it had to champion direct taxation.

The most commonly proposed form of direct taxation in the *Grain Growers' Guide* during 1910 and 1911 was the single tax on unused land. Popularized by Henry George in his 1881 book *Progress and Poverty,* the single tax was popular with progressives and populists in the United States and Canada.[57] The single tax, in the pages of the *Guide* as in reform thought of the period more generally, reigned as the fairest and most efficient form of taxation. An editorial claimed that "those who have studied the question know that a tax upon land values is the most equitable system of raising revenues." By taxing people who owned land but did not work it, proponents believed, the single tax would "shift the burden from the backs of the farmers and laboring classes and place it upon the exploiters and monopolists where it belongs."[58] As an alternative to the tariff, the single tax was presented as its absolute opposite: where the tariff taxed farmers, workers, and the consuming public for the benefit of the wealthy, the single tax taxed only those who could afford to pay it.

The single tax had appeal beyond its fairness in putting the burden of taxation on those most able to pay it. Proponents argued that it would have the side benefit of encouraging landholders to sell land, thereby making it cheaper to buy. This would make buying a farm easier: "The higher the tax on land values the more anxious the owner will be to get rid of their vacant or half used lots and lands, and the more anxious they are to sell the lower will become the selling price, and easier it will be for a man to get a home or a farm," a letter writer claimed. And that would be good for society because, "the more home owners and independent small farmers there are, the more useful and progressive in all things will be the citizenship which constitutes the state." To have a better citizenry and an improved state, all that was needed was a single tax. "Why should the higher purposes of a civilization be delayed longer," the writer asked rhetorically, "when a slight change in the method of taxation will start it onward and upward on the highway to happiness to all."[59]

The single tax owed much of its appeal to the likelihood that none of its proponents would ever have to pay it. It was therefore the most appealing form of direct taxation because it was directed elsewhere. It was also appealing, however, because it was not an income tax, the threatened outcome of efforts toward tariff reform and free trade in Canada. In fact, in at least one instance, the *Grain Growers' Guide* cited a speaker who suggested that the single tax would save the country from the income tax – assuming that the farmers succeeded in replacing the tariff with direct taxation. Speaking to a Toronto delegation, a farmer spokesperson clarified that "there is [no] danger, from our movement, of the taxation of incomes. More and more we are coming to the opinion that taxation in the main should be levied on unearned increments in land and natural resources."[60] For all of its novelty and its promise of utter social regeneration through shifting the fiscal burden and democratizing land ownership, the single tax was still sold as a bulwark against the spectre of the income tax.

The preference for the single tax over an income tax was marked but not absolute in the farmers' movement. Although the *Grain Growers' Guide* published no articles or editorials endorsing a federal income tax as an alternative to the tariff, some correspondents criticized the idea of a single tax as less fair than an income tax. Income taxation applied the principle of ability to pay and shifted the fiscal burden from the poor to the rich much more consistently and effectively than a single tax on land realistically could. As one critic wrote, "the conclusion, as a farmer, that I have reached, is this: that granting that the taxation of land values to get at the 'unearned increment' is just, then must the principle be extended to include the taxation of all unearned increments of all wealth whatsoever – an income tax does this." The farmer contrasted a rich man who owned land with another rich man – a "capitalist" – who owned financial assets. "How should they be taxed? Henry George would not tax the capitalist at all, as he would allow him 'the full return of his capital.' What a taxless haven of rest for the millionaire lender would this single tax be," he concluded, urging his fellow readers "not to be misled by windy, unstudied statements, but to study" the claims of the single tax "for themselves."[61] Another letter, titled "Some Henry George Nuts," asked rhetorically whether the editors "think a single tax will catch those cunning highwaymen whose methods of evasion and extraction are legion, or a land tax, a wolf hound whose every thought is how not to produce and still secure what others produce."[62] The income tax was put forward by critics of the single tax as a more effective and coherent instrument for accomplishing what, for farmers, was the prime motive for tax reform: shifting the burden of taxation from common people to rich people.

Beyond proclaiming income taxation to be the fairest form of direct taxation, proponents of the former sought to disarm what they thought was an irrational fear that prevented a true understanding of alternatives to the tariff. The key point in this debunking was that farmers, already taxed heavily by the tariff, would pay little to no income tax, simply because their incomes would be too low. The case of England was again important. Opponents of free trade liked to underline the necessity of having other forms of taxation and often cited England as a place where direct taxation was heavy because there was no tariff revenue. Citing various taxes, including the income tax, one correspondent claimed that "these taxes are only paid by the well-to-do people in the Old Country" and wondered "how many of the 5,000,000, or thereby, who live in Scotland, pay income tax."[63] Another pointed out that the income tax, by definition, was "a small tax rising higher as the income gets larger." Again, the appeal for farmers was partly that an income tax would fall on them only if they were fortunate enough to have high incomes. The letter writer asked the editors

how many farmers make an income ... of much more than $800 per year? How many get less? One great advantage of an income tax is that it is necessary for you to prove you have an income of more than $800 before you pay, whereas this duty has to be paid whether you have an income or only an outgo. I wish, sir, I had the figures so I could state what sized income a man in England would have before he would be liable to a tax of $200 per year, the same as we pay in duty.[64]

The income tax, by this reckoning, was less onerous than the tariff. It appeared to be more confiscatory but only because the tariff hid its exploitation behind rhetoric. Although the advocacy of income taxation in the *Grain Growers' Guide* was a minority pursuit, and not the paper's official policy, it resonated with key themes of the farmers' movement: the evils of the tariff and the importance of modern, progressive thought applied to questions of political economy.

As devoted as the paper and its affiliated organizers were to exposing the evils of the party system and the injustice and dishonesty of the tariff, and as interested in promoting direct taxation as a fairer and more honest alternative as they were, their greatest rhetorical flair was reserved for the evaluation and celebration of the role of the movement itself in modernizing politics. Building upon the recognition that the two parties were essentially indistinguishable promoters of identical policies, the *Grain Growers' Guide* repeatedly underlined the role that farmers were playing, and could continue to play, in the renewal of meaningful democratic politics. In the process, contributors and correspondents underlined their increasing disenchantment with party labels and their increasing identification as farmers and intelligent voters rather than party boosters. The *Guide* and its readers were proclaiming a new, modern political identity characterized by a critical distance from party labels and an eagerness to be a political instrument, as an organized interest, perhaps through one of the existing parties or a new third party.

The farmers were uniformly impressed with their efforts at organizing themselves and their example to the rest of the country in terms of exposing the dishonesty of phony politics and embracing the reality of true politics. An early editorial on organization stated that "the farmers should keep out of party politics but should go as far as possible into real politics."[65] The way to do this, the editorial claimed, was to "lay aside party affiliations and work in our own interests."[66] Editorials about farmers and their political promise bore titles such as "Cleansing Political Life."[67] In a letter titled "Let There Be Light," a correspondent argued that "what the country wants is a great man, a statesman of unassailable position and of patriotic character, a St. George who may match our modern dragon, corruption."[68] To most correspondents, though, the "great man" was the farmer himself, whose awakenings "have come as welcome rays of hope out of the darkness."[69] One such farmer wrote that "since I have been reading your paper I realize more clearly the highness of my calling as a farmer. Co-operation seems to me like a light shining through the darkness."[70]

In the most systematic treatment of the importance of the farmers' movement, J.A. Stevenson wrote that, far from simply objecting to the unfair burden of the tariff, farmers "are embarking on an effort to reestablish the proper functions of representative institutions for the people of Canada and to renovate the whole system of national life." Stevenson then explained how the tariff poisoned the whole of society: "The root of the evil lies largely in our economic system. It corrupts our political system, our political system corrupts and degrades the public administration, and the corroding influence extends to the social system and business life till the disease permeates the whole community."[71] The perception of political corruption was widespread in the early twentieth century; what the farmers were doing for the wider public was identifying the root of the evil – the unfair and dishonest fiscal policy of the dominion – and the method of remedying it through education, organization, and cooperation of interest groups in defiance of party labels. The farmers, for Stevenson and others, were the sharp point of modernism in Canadian politics: "Every thinking man realizes the existence of gross evils in the body politic and would fain end them but sees no feasible method and contents himself with waiting until the trail is blazed. This service the farmers' organizations are purposing to perform for the community at large."[72] What precisely the rest of the democratic people would do with the "trail" thus "blazed" was unclear, but the implication was that they would reject party labels and embrace a more modern politics about what was really happening in a material sense that presented clear democratic alternatives.

The farmers' role and political example in refusing party rhetoric was self-conscious and explicit in the months leading up to the 1911 election. The insistence of the *Grain Growers' Guide* on naming and shaming what it gleefully called "miserable peanut party politics" made farmers aware of their self-appointed role in Canadian politics as modernizers and destroyers of party cant.[73] Aware of their starring role in people's enlightenment, farmers, whether as readers of or contributors to the *Guide,* revelled repeatedly in their political modernism and the threat that it posed to the two-party system as the dominant imaginary of dominion politics.[74] As one organizer put it, "let the light shine in the dark places and the muck and dirt which has accumulated in past years will be visible to all and once plainly seen by the people there will be such a house-cleaning that it will make the party politicians tremble with fear."[75] The critique of the tariff, their refusal to play to partisan rhetoric, and their attention to education and organization, the farmers believed, had made them "the most powerful engine for the betterment of social conditions that Canada has ever seen."[76]

"Reciprocity, Neat and Clean": The Election of 1911

The farmers' critique of the tariff and their sense of themselves as a powerful engine for change would have profound effects on Canadian politics in a shorter time than the farmers probably anticipated. Within a year of the founding of the *Grain Growers' Guide,* the paper would inspire an unprecedented gathering and a presentation to Parliament on issues that mattered to farmers, particularly those in the prairie west. Within another year, an election would be fought to a large extent on the basis of the farmers' campaign, and it would clarify the differences between the Liberals and Conservatives on the tariff question. The *Guide's* critique of Canadian politics, of the effects of misleading party differentiation in shielding a bad tax from scrutiny, that is, led directly to a new party differentiation that made the election almost a referendum on the tariff. In practice, the outcome was not as enlightening as the farmers had hoped: the election was dominated by an even more acute spirit of partisanship and an even more inflamed nationalist rhetoric than recent contests had been. But even that result, by driving home the weakness of party differences, contributed to generalizing the *Guide's* modern perspective on parties.

The western farmers demonstrated their growing self-confidence as critics of Canadian fiscal politics during the summer of 1910, when Prime Minister Wilfrid Laurier toured the new provinces by rail. He was greeted at every stop by representatives of farmers' organizations who lectured the Liberal leader on the exploitativeness of the tariff and urged him to lead the party back to a clearer anti-tariff stance. Laurier at first defended the party's position on the tariff as moderate and fair, but he became increasingly impressed with the organized lobbying of the farmers, and his responses became less dismissive as the trip wound down. The farmers' lobbying showed Laurier that a strong feeling against the tariff had been organized into a region-wide movement that could win an election. This awareness inspired the prime minister to ask finance minister W.S. Fielding to approach the US government about the possibility of a reciprocal lowering of tariffs between the two countries. When the talks started in Washington in the fall of 1910, the farmers began organizing to send a delegation to Ottawa late in 1910.

The farmers met at 10 a.m. on December 15 at the Grand Opera House on Albert Street to draw up their platform. There were 500 people present. Although the meeting was dominated by farmers' associations from the Prairies, there were representatives from every province except Prince Edward Island. Some of the speeches were cautious and apologetic. E.C. Drury of the Dominion Grange of Ontario, answering criticisms that the tariff was a necessary source of government revenue, made a speech calling for direct taxation. He said that, "if we are confronted with the proposition that to follow these proposals would be to materially lower the revenue of the country, we must be prepared to make a stand on that question," and he moved to include a clause in the farmers' platform that read thus: "That the farmers of this country are willing to face direct taxation in such form as may be advisable to make up the revenue lost under new tariff relations."[77] It's important to note that his call for direct taxation was for a better tax to replace the tariff, not for a tax that would redistribute income. This is clear in the wording that farmers would "face direct taxation." Drury made it clear that "we are not asking that any system be introduced which would tax the manufacturers for the benefit of the farmers; we are not asking that one single cent be taken from any other class and given to the farmers."[78] As with the *Grain Growers' Guide*'s editorializing on the single tax, his call for direct taxation was both modern and conservative: it was a novel solution to the problem of replacing the revenue from the tariff, and it reflected the farmers' understanding that an income tax would weigh less heavily on most of them than the tariff; at the same time, it reflected an understanding of taxation as neutral – an understanding that minimized the redistributive effects of income taxation and therefore underestimated the likely resistance to it from both parties. Whether this nuancing of the tax question was Drury's own formulation or one agreed on by delegates in discussions beforehand is unknown.

Other speakers were more reflective of the tone of the *Grain Growers' Guide* in celebrating their role in Canadian politics. Roderick McKenzie of the Manitoba Grain Growers' Association said that the farmers' presentation to Parliament "is unique in the history of Canada, and it marks a new era in Canadian history for the farmers to come here in this way to present their views." Their united presentation, Roderick said, "will clearly indicate to everyone that the farmers of Canada are united in their opposition to the present fiscal system, and that there must be a change in the system of collecting revenue and that we should have relief from the burdens that are placed upon us by the tariff."[79] E.A. Partridge, meanwhile, called for direct taxation, specifically the single tax on land. The key, though, was that "we have to educate ourselves along these lines and try to form public opinion so that when the time comes we may form our propositions along the line of equality."[80] Partridge said that he wanted "to put the entering wedge into the thought of these fundamental principles so that we may in the future be able to evolve a better system of taxation."[81]

The farmers' delegation made its way the next morning, December 16, to Parliament Hill to address a joint session of the Senate and House of

Commons. The main speaker, who addressed only the issue of the tariff, was D.W. McCuaig, the president of the Canadian Council of Agriculture. Citing "favourable approaches" on the trade negotiations front, McCuaig called for reciprocal free trade with the United States and for direct taxation to replace the revenue that would be lost. Other speakers continued in the same vein. J.W. Scallion's speech directly addressed the issue of the tariff as an exploitative and inefficient tax, saying that farmers were "willing to meet the requirements of a tax framed to cover the public expenditure of the Dominion, the proceeds from which, less cost of collection, will go wholly into the public treasury." What farmers opposed, Scallion said, was "the further continuance of a tariff which taxes them for the special benefit of private interests." Farmers, he informed parliamentarians, "regard such a tariff as unsound in principle, unjust and oppressive in its operation, and nothing short of a system of legalized robbery."[82] Scallion called for the government to see the tariff question as clearly as farmers did and act in accordance with that vision. "Such a fiscal system is manifestly unjust and should be abolished."[83]

Prime Minister Laurier replied to the farmers in cagey tones, emphasizing that his government was in the midst of negotiations with the US government and that little could be said about the details. He also suggested to the farmers that their views were radical and would have to be moderated in light of contradictory views in other parts of the country.[84] With less in common with the farmers, Conservative Party leader Robert Borden could only remark positively on "the force and earnestness" of the farmers' arguments.[85] A discussion followed in which senators and MPs discussed whether the farmers' speeches would be included in Hansard, the official record of parliamentary debate. They were not.

In the weeks that followed the farmers' presentation to Parliament, political and industrial elites responded to the platform and to the novelty of farmers addressing the political elite directly. On December 29, 1910, Thomas Russell, head of Canada Cycle and Motor and formerly a local branch secretary of the Canadian Manufacturers' Association, addressed the Canadian Club in Toronto on the question of farmers and the tariff. He criticized the farmers' platform as "radical, revolutionary," but he also criticized their tone: "They have made their demands with western vigor," he told the audience, "and I think you will agree ... painted their wrongs with western exaggeration."[86] In his daily editorial in the *Manitoba Free Press*, J.W. Dafoe expressed guarded sympathy for protection but worried that Russell's harshly dismissive tone was alienating. Dafoe had "preached moderation to Western tariff reformers," and now it was the other side that needed correcting.[87] Western farmers, he cautioned, "will resent Mr. Russell's language and will thus be less ready to give due weight to the arguments which he makes in support of the existing order of things." Although noting that the tariff debate was important, Dafoe cautioned that, "if the discussion is not to become so embittered as to be valueless, it will be necessary for the disputants to discard some methods of controversy which have become outworn."[88]

Dafoe's criticism of Russell did not extend to George Foster, who commented critically on the farmers' platform a few days later. Foster was adamant and clear in his support for protection, for which Dafoe thanked him on behalf of the farmers, noting that "his unqualified declaration is a reminder, if one were needed, that the Conservative party is traditionally and by conviction Protectionist." Russell's harsh words were a problem, Dafoe was saying, but clear and believable differences of policy were to be appreciated, even if – or especially if – they were policies with which one disagreed. He underlined the value of partisan clarity of the kind that Foster was exhibiting in contrast to the general tone of deference to the strength of anti-protection feeling in the west:

> Western farmers, who by the smooth talk of vote-hunting politicians, assisted by an opportunistic press, are induced to believe that by some magical hocus-pocus the Conservative has been transformed into a zealous believer in lower tariffs and free trade, will have an unpleasant awakening if Mr. Foster is given the power and the opportunity to replace the present tariff with one more to his liking.[89]

A very different Conservative position was outlined momentarily when Arthur Meighen, a rising star in the opposition party and a westerner, gave his response to the farmers. Meighen called for a reduction of tariffs on agricultural implements. The *Manitoba Free Press* criticized the speech, ironically noting that the "voice of the west calling for tariff reductions was again heard in the Commons to-day," but the call "came from the ranks of the party that originated and holds still sacred the doctrine of protection."[90] The paper argued that Meighen was contributing to confusion, for clearly the policy would not be carried out by his party if it was elected. In contrast to Foster, Meighen was not being honest about his party position. In fact, the *Free Press* pointed out, what Meighen was calling for "has been the avowed policy of the Liberals some years past"; the young Conservative MP was merely "drawing a red herring across the trail of Tory high protection."[91]

These initial volleys over the tariff were a prelude to the furor over the reciprocity deal, which began when Fielding returned from the United States in late January. He appeared in the House of Commons on January 26, 1911, and outlined the basis of a deal that would lower tariffs mostly on agricultural products and keep manufacturing protected, and he expressed his vain hope that "the matter would be regarded as outside party politics."[92] That was not to be the case. Instead, the next few months would see voters "inundated with a flood of rhetoric that was a mixture of patriotic bombast, nationalistic fear-mongering, jingoistic support for the Empire, and pure anti-Americanism."[93] A particularly extreme example occurred just after the election was called, when President William Howard Taft noted that Canada found itself at "a parting of the ways."[94] Opponents of reciprocity seized the phrase as evidence that, to the Americans, the reciprocity agreement represented Canada's breaking away from the British Empire.

The anxious rhetoric of protectionists who saw every expression of sympathy for reciprocity as radical and extreme was regretted not only by partisan Liberals, who had a lot to lose by framing the issue in this way, but also by liberals more generally, who wanted a political culture in which ideas could be discussed plainly and civilly. Echoing Siegfried and Macphail, these writers warned that overheated partisan rhetoric was ultimately bad for democracy and would alienate voters who wanted to support parties that wanted real change. Writing on the eve of the election, with partisan rhetoric already heating up, Dafoe warned that, "if business men and financiers consistently and successfully prevented the satisfaction of the needs of the Western farmers, the traditional parties would disappear and be reformed on class and sectional lines."[95] Although he was a Liberal, Dafoe was defending the party system as a whole by contrasting it to another possible system in which parties with very different ideological bases vied for power. He saw the intensity of the farmers' critique of the tariff and party system up close, and, though he was only partly sympathetic to it, he understood its implications as a possible break with the past, an imaginary framed around a struggle between two parties equally sympathetic to capitalism.

For the farmers themselves, meanwhile, though the *Grain Growers' Guide* criticized the patriotic rhetoric on which opponents of reciprocity relied, for the most part they welcomed the opportunity for an election in which the tariff would be contested, not only by rival parties but also by clearly differentiated fiscal positions. Finally, the election offered the chance for a real test of public opinion on the tariff. "Reciprocity, neat and clean, will be the issue before the public between the parties," an editorial on the eve of the election announced. "Not in a generation has an election been fought in Canada on a farmer's issue, or on any issue as clear and distinct as this."[96] On the question of whether the country was at a parting of the ways, and whether the party system could survive the election, the *Guide* was less nervous and more brash than Dafoe in its confidence in the democratic intelligence of the people. A cartoon published during the election and titled "A Parting of the Ways" in cheeky reference to President Taft's controversial phrase showed the farmer at a crossroads with democracy in one direction and plutocracy in the other. Plutocracy was marked by the *Guide*'s familiar rich man in a suit, in this instance holding a spiked club, with dark clouds of exploitation in the background. Democracy, past the scarecrows of blue ruin and annexation, led to a rising sun. For the *Guide,* the image encapsulated the real issue in the election, the choice between submitting to the continued exploitation of the tariff under the weight of Special Privilege or walking down the path of reciprocity toward freedom. That the political parties were now arranged clearly on the question of the tariff was good, and an important sign of changing times, but the difference that mattered in the 1911 election and beyond was the choice between plutocracy and democracy.

"BETWEEN TWEEDLEDUM AND TWEEDLEDEE": THE MODERN RHETORIC OF THE PARTY SYSTEM

Although the Liberals did well in the Prairies, they lost badly in Ontario and were defeated in the election of 1911. The reciprocity agreement was cancelled, and the new Conservative government reiterated its unwavering support for a strongly protectionist tariff. The *Grain Growers' Guide,* like Liberal partisans and supporters of tariff reductions, was extremely disappointed in the result and bitter about how the election had been fought. In the aftermath of the election, the *Guide*'s critique of the party system sharpened and became more common. A deep cynicism about the two-party system, and about dominion politics more broadly, was the lasting legacy of the partisan rhetoric of the 1911 election.

The reciprocity agreement itself was not terribly radical in relation to the history of the tariff and the nationalist rhetoric that surrounded it. It lowered rates primarily on food, and this was meant to appeal to farmers, who produced more food than could be eaten in Canada or realistically exported to Great Britain and who hated the tariff in any case; it kept tariffs on manufactured goods high, the crux of the National Policy and the only issue that realistically mattered in industrial Ontario, where reciprocity was most fiercely denounced. What was defeated, many commentators insisted, was not the agreement itself but a caricature of it, cloaked in a rhetoric of disloyalty and national danger. Voters were invited to cast their votes on the dangerous possibility that the agreement would lead to further agreements that would erode manufacturing tariffs, sap the country's industrial capacity, and ultimately make the dominion another vassal state of the United States. If elections were to be meaningful exercises in informed participation in determining the actual policies of the government – if they were going to be democratic – then a new and clearer rhetoric was urgently needed.

Letters to the *Grain Growers' Guide* after the 1911 election reflected the deep bitterness over the clear issue of the tariff having been overshadowed by partisan rhetoric. "Despite all the flag-waving and the call to loyalty," one reader wrote in a letter titled "The Future Outlook," "the real issue lay between a high and low tariff." The reader pointed out bitterly that "both political parties are dominated by these vested interests" and that "legislation for years past has been influenced and controlled by the thralldom of this concealed but irresistible force."[97] Edward Porritt, whose 1910 book *The Revolt in Canada against the New Feudalism* had been advertised in the *Guide* all through the campaign, opined after the election that "it was the New Feudalism that raised the annexationist cry, and infused into the campaign the rancor against the United States by which it was characterized."[98] Overall, however, the *Guide* did not dwell on the election results – except to make the case unequivocally for a new party, neither Liberal nor Conservative, to push for progressive reform in Ottawa.

The perception was most commonly articulated by the *Grain Growers' Guide,* but it was also echoed by many writers not tied to the farmers' cause or linked to one of the parties. Commenting glumly on the role of rhetoric in the outcome of the election, O.D. Skelton wrote that "the party of 'moderate' protection is out and the party of 'adequate' protection is in." A serious examination of the issues, Skelton thought, would lead one to the conclusion that there was precious little "difference in tariff policy between Tweedledum and Tweedledee."[99] Skelton, actively sympathetic to the Liberals in the election, pointed out that "the proposed agreement followed exactly the lines long accepted by both political parties as eminently desirable, if only they could be obtained."[100] Because the

Liberals were advocating a good agreement and the Conservatives were opposing it, he noted bitterly that, "both on broad considerations of the mutual advantages of free intercourse between neighboring peoples not unevenly matched in those fields, and on detailed study of market conditions in the two countries, the advocates of reciprocity had the better argument."[101] With all the frustration of an expert political economist, Skelton claimed "beyond doubt that it was the political rather than the economic aspect of the case that carried most weight."[102] The idea that the agreement was an economic one and should have been examined on its merits rather than on political terms was a common position for Liberals. William Lyon Mackenzie King, who lost his seat in 1911 and did not return to Canadian politics for almost a decade, complained that "the whole question was taken out of the realm of economics, and fears and passions were aroused, which today men are ashamed of."[103] In a letter to a colleague, King wrote that the Conservatives won by not talking about the issues: "Annexation, not reciprocity, was the issue on which the government was defeated."[104]

The parties that Skelton dubbed the "Tweedledum and Tweedledee" of tariff policy had precious little to differentiate them. They were effectively machines for winning elections and, having won them, for using office to improve their position to fight the next election. No great principle divided the two parties, though they were rhetorically differentiated, particularly during the 1911 election, by their stance on the tariff. For the *Grain Growers' Guide,* the election illustrated the tendency to become excited about words rather than policies and to inflate tiny, poorly understood, and vaguely articulated differences into absolute oppositions. A better definition of the parties, some basis on which to make clear their purpose for existing and contesting elections, was wanting. New forms of politics were emerging that would force this clarity on both Liberals and Conservatives. The farmers and their *Guide* were leading the way, and intellectuals were following them. However bitter their perspective on the parties, this disenchantment was based upon the firm modernist belief that, as Macphail said, "words do occasionally convey a meaning to intelligent persons, which cannot be entirely taken away by further arrangement of words."[105] Skelton's study of socialism, which gave Skelton his first monograph – titled *Socialism* – in 1911, was premised on the insistence that it ought not to be seen as just a scary or seductive shadow or spectre, that it was "a word with a definite and ascertainable meaning."[106] That the same could not be said for Liberal or Conservative in Canada went without saying.

There were high hopes for the election of 1911 arising out of the farmers' self-conscious efforts to transform dominion politics, the Liberals' embrace of a policy of lower tariffs, and the possibility of clear differences between Liberal and Conservative on the tariff question. Those hopes, however, were more than disappointed: the outcome of the election, and the rhetoric widely seen as having been responsible for that outcome, suggested that the party system was beyond repair and that simply to reaffirm the old nineteenth-century partisan oppositions would not be enough. The election underlined, for critics of the tariff and party differences attached to it, the need for a new solution, a break with the past that would overcome and overturn rather than clarify the differences of the nineteenth century. This new awareness, this loss of investment in the two-party system, was entirely negative at this point: what had seemed to be meaningful was no longer meaningful, and what had made sense of the political landscape no longer did so.

***

The protective tariff was the issue on which political differences were forged in the 1870s and held fast into the early twentieth century. These differences, according to the *Grain Growers' Guide,* were expressed in the phony poses and windy phrases of party apologists and masked a corrupt and oligarchic system of exploitation of the consumer. The fiscal system and the party system were inextricably linked. Reforming the political system and reforming the taxation system were inseparable. Because the party system was corrupted by tariff wealth and its own dishonesty, the leadership to create meaningful political differences would have to come from outside the two parties. This happened in 1911, but the rhetoric of party and nation was too powerful, and the decision was made on an emotional basis to keep the tariff. For farmers and others eager to see a real contest between different fiscal strategies discussed clearly and intelligently, the 1911 election was a bitter disappointment. For those who had begun to see the two-party system from a detached perspective, the performances of the parties – especially the Conservative Party – in 1911 led to an even deeper and more permanent alienation from the old political imaginary in which two parties defined themselves by their positions on the tariff.

The failure of the hopes of 1911 made the ground fertile for linking tax reform with political modernism, both in the form of new political parties and in the clarity of political differences, in the aftermath of the Borden victory. Over the next few years, political priorities would shift dramatically. First, the long boom associated with the entry of the western region into the national economy came to a sudden and nerve-racking stop. Then the war in Europe dominated and distorted every aspect of public life. Throughout all of these changes, the memory of 1911, both its promise and its disappointment, served as a pivotal moment, an inspirational text for modernist desires and ambitions. The desire for direct taxation as the basis of more meaningful political differences was expressed through the war and moved to the centre of dominion political culture.

The 1911 election was hailed as an event, unique in Canadian politics, in which both parties offered a break with the past, a direct challenge to the established orthodoxies of Canadian political economy and public life. It marked the more direct influence of new political groups on the political process, and as such it was the beginning of the end of the period in which the parties were the totality of political life and the start of a period in which self-conscious social groups increasingly organized themselves independently of parties. It marked the culmination of a desire for "a clear line," a more meaningful, more intelligible, and more effective system of party differences – as well as the bitter disappointment of having those desires thwarted.[107]

2

The Brink of the Abyss: The "Conscription of Wealth" and the Party System, 1917–19

Fire engulfed the Centre Block of Parliament in the evening of February 3, 1916, devouring the Senate chamber and the House of Commons before it tore up and through the Victoria Tower, destroying the building built fifty years earlier, on the eve of Confederation, by the following morning. Only the Library of Parliament survived the blaze (see Figure 2.1). The First World War had begun a year and a half before, but the fire, which forced the business of the Senate and House of Commons to relocate a few blocks south to the Victoria Memorial Museum on Metcalfe Street, was the political elite's first experience of direct danger and indignity. Anxious rumours of a German saboteur armed with explosive chemicals were investigated, but the fire turned out to have been started by cigar embers.[1] For the next five years, until a new Centre Block was completed in 1921, the king's representatives were relegated to a temporary home. While the war raged in Europe and industrial unrest threatened revolution and civil war at home, parliamentarians made do with cramped quarters and complained about the heat. The five years that Parliament spent in its temporary home would be the greatest test of its political relevance in a "world on fire."[2]

Parliament in the last years of the war was increasingly pushed to the sidelines even of domestic politics by a bitter struggle between the state and its people. Writing toward the end of that ignominious period, as the greatest of the many strikes of 1919, the one in Winnipeg, dissolved in a storm of Royal Canadian Mounted Police hoofbeats, Stephen Leacock lamented the polarization between defenders of the old order and

FIGURE 2.1   The aftermath of the Parliament buildings fire, summer 1916. The Library of Parliament was the only part of the Centre Block left standing six months after a fire destroyed the meeting rooms of the House of Commons and Senate. The photograph shows crews at work, but rebuilding would be slowed by the war, and a new building would not open until 1921. | Government of Canada, Public Works, 1916/Library and Archives Canada PA-130624.

proponents of the new order at the end of the war. "To some minds the demand for law and order overwhelms all other thoughts," he complained. "To others the fierce desire for social justice obliterates all fear of a general catastrophe. They push nearer and nearer to the brink of the abyss. The warning cry of 'back' is challenged by the eager shouts of 'forward!'"[3] To a writer like Leacock, a sardonic but affectionate critic of the Canadian political tradition, the attack on the liberal order struck a harsh blow. In a telling phrase, he wrote that "parliamentary discussion is powerless. It limps in the wake of popular movements."[4] Part of the anxiety and horror with which Leacock viewed the political struggles at the end of the First World War was a sense that the charisma of parliamentary debate was being undermined; if the representative state was not to become redundant, then it had to get on board, or try to, with "popular movements," "limp[ing] in the wake" of a polity less and less impressed with the old differences between Liberals and Conservatives.

An excellent illustration of Leacock's point that Parliament was the follower, not the leader, was the debate on the income war tax in the summer of 1917. The debate was remarkable for both its intensity and its self-consciousness as Liberal members, many of them veterans of Wilfrid Laurier's cabinet, vied to say the most outrageous and shocking things while criticizing the bill. George Graham, once the minister of railways and canals, expressed the hope that the minister of finance would "increase somewhat the amount of taxes on these men. I do not want to use the word 'somewhat,' but I would say to increase radically the taxes on the large incomes."[5] Charles Murphy, who had been the secretary of state for external affairs, hoped that Thomas White would amend the bill to "provide for a more equitable distribution of this Income Tax, and [to] see that those in receipt of large incomes shall pay a much larger percentage than they are going to pay under the present measure."[6] And Michael Clark, the Liberal member for Red Deer, claimed that "I know millionaires who have expressed their very highest satisfaction with this income tax, and I do not think that is a good compliment to the tax. I would lower the satisfaction of these gentlemen if I were in the position of the minister; I would give them less satisfaction and more taxation."[7] Frederick Forsyth Pardee, the chief Liberal whip under Laurier, called the tax "a flea-bite; a mere cheese-paring." Lamenting that the tax "does not take from men enough to make it hurt," Pardee said that "the rich man and the rich corporation who are protected by the men who are fighting our battles at the front should give to such an extent that it will hurt."[8] Other members spoke with equal ferocity and directness about the limitations of the tax as a burden on the wealthy and the importance of increasing the rate of taxation for high incomes. In the end, members ruthless in their criticism of the bill's weakness voted in favour of the bill.

The Liberals' self-consciously radical rhetoric in the debate on the income war tax tells us a lot about that particular moment in political life. For one thing, the rhetoric wasn't their own; it came from the labour movement in particular. Its purpose in the parliamentary debate was simultaneously modern and conservative. It was intended to maintain the centrality of the party system and Parliament itself in political life and by extension the fiscal system of the tariff that, as we saw in the previous chapter, was so tightly entwined with the party system. But it was intended to maintain that system under the unprecedented conditions of the war, which drove profits and prices up and made the tariff even more exploitative and unpopular. Labour unions joined farmers as aggressive critics of the government's fiscal politics and as confident champions of people's enlightenment. As the government's musings on introducing conscription for overseas service became louder, a corresponding call for the "conscription of wealth," generally interpreted as a steeply graduated tax on high incomes, gained traction. As labour criticisms became threats to the industrial basis of the war, Liberals and Conservatives slowly and uncomfortably agreed on the need to forge a ruling coalition of parties – a move that gave credence to modernist claims that the opposition between Liberals and Conservatives was a subterfuge. Neither the government nor the opposition really wanted to introduce income taxation, but they needed to – not for fiscal reasons but for political (i.e., rhetorical) reasons.

The introduction of income taxation reflected the further ascendancy of political modernism during the First World War and the increased desperation of maintaining the old political imaginary under new conditions. The parliamentary debate, and the self-consciously radical rhetoric of certain parliamentarians, reflected the heightened political tensions of wartime politics, and even more so the unprecedented centrality of new political actors, notably the labour movement, which had done so much in the lead-up to the debate on the income war tax to make "conscription of wealth" a powerful and ubiquitous phrase. The centrality of labour reflected a further progression of popular disenchantment with the Liberal and Conservative Parties as key sites of political and rhetorical identification and a deepening of the tendency of the farmers of 1911 to see the parties as meaningless and phony pseudo-enemies. More than this, though, the centrality of labour in determining the rhetorical stakes of the income war tax reflected the rising force of a new and self-consciously modern opposition between both parliamentary parties – the Liberals and the Conservatives – on one side and popular movements, whether farmer or labour or otherwise, on the other. The parliamentary debate that marked the introduction of income taxation at the federal level perfectly illustrated the break with the past of people's enlightenment that sought not to reform the old parties and their nationalist images but to burn parliamentary politics, and its tradition of gentlemanly rhetorical combat, to the ground.

"The Burden of Government": The People and the Costs of the War

The enormous and unequal costs of the war in terms of displacement, debt, and death gave rise to a rapidly polarizing political culture and what was arguably the most controversial parliamentary session in the history of the dominion. The Military Service Act, which conscripted men for military service overseas for the first time in Canada's history, and which was debated at the same time as the income war tax, was at the centre of this political controversy. To pass conscription, Robert Borden's government took unprecedented measures: it negotiated a coalition with pro-conscription Liberals, called the Union government; it enfranchised women who were either in the armed forces or had relatives serving in them; and it disenfranchised recent immigrants. The income war tax, similarly, was the first dominion income tax and, along with the business war profits tax of 1916, represented the overturning of a long tradition of resistance to direct taxation by the federal government. It was a break with the past that, like the Union government and the enfranchisement of women, was a political gesture by the government to enlist support for conscription, and it had little to do with paying for the war in a literal sense.

The income war tax was introduced by Thomas White, a minister of finance who had entered politics at the top, following the 1911 election. One of eighteen prominent Liberal-identified businessmen who threw their support behind the Conservative Party's anti-reciprocity campaign, White was enthusiastically welcomed in Borden's cabinet as a symbol of nonpartisan elite rule.[9] A hard-core fiscal traditionalist, White encountered serious problems shortly after becoming finance minister. The long economic boom identified with Laurier and the delayed success of the National Policy in the 1890s came to an end in 1913, with the result that Canada's credit dried up and its revenue from trade tariffs fell just as railways and other major public projects turned to the dominion government for desperately needed financial support. White spent most of the year before the war anxiously assessing the extent of the damage to the country's financial reputation while endeavouring to appear unconcerned.[10] The crisis illustrated the core problem with the prewar fiscal model, as R.T. Naylor has demonstrated. Government operations were financed with loans paid with revenue from tariffs; in a depression, when trade slowed down, revenues fell, and credit dried up precisely when the state needed it most.[11] Traditional resistance to the imposition of direct taxation by the federal government (in part because the provinces – and hence their creatures, the municipalities – could levy only direct taxes) had forced the dominion to rely on tariff revenues, leaving the Borden government with no alternative but to wait for trade conditions to improve so that revenues could revive.[12] When the war began in the summer of 1914, in fact, White's chief concern was that interruptions in trade would cut even further into dominion revenues.[13] Although White was advised in

Parliament and by correspondents that an income tax would be both possible and perhaps necessary, he refused to adopt what he called a "minor" measure and repeatedly emphasized the government's intention to rely on the tariff for revenue.[14] The government maintained a studied conservatism on tax questions, resisting calls for the introduction of income taxation right up to its introduction of the income war tax.

The conservatism that had prevented the governing Conservatives from introducing an income tax in response to the war had not prevented the introduction of other taxes. War taxes had in fact been introduced, particularly in Ontario, but they were indirect and regressive taxes on consumer goods, and they weighed more heavily on lower incomes than higher incomes. The new war taxes simply built upon the previous method of collecting tax revenue, with all of the inefficiency and exploitation decried by the *Grain Growers' Guide* in 1911. The war economy made the regressive system of finance more regressive in other ways. War loans, a central financing instrument that provided income in the form of interest payments to banks and wealthy individuals, and that ultimately had to be paid in revenue raised through the tariff and other sales taxes, were essentially income transfers from the poor to the rich.[15] That wealthy Canadians were actively encouraged to profit from the war by investing in war bonds muddied the distinction between the antisocial war profiteer and the patriotic investor that the government was keen on emphasizing and underlined the deep inequity of the government's traditional approach to war finance.

Critics of the government's traditional resistance to direct taxation made their stand on the grounds of fairness and modernity. O.D. Skelton, the Queen's University political economist frustrated by the tariff debate in 1911, was impressed in 1915 that "for the first time in our fiscal history the Minister of Finance found it advisable this year to devote a part of his Budget speech to a serious discussion of the income tax." The fact that White "urged strong objections against its adoption" was disappointing but not surprising.[16] A less genial criticism came from the labour movement, the war's premier purveyors of people's enlightenment. Much as it had for farmers, the unfair tax load shouldered by workers became for the *Industrial Banner* key evidence of the profound injustice of Canadian fiscal policy, which, an editorial in November 1916 claimed, placed "the whole burden of maintaining humanity on the shoulders of the industrial classes."[17] Characterizing the tariff as "an insidious system of taxation, which enters the home by stealth, with no invoice or voucher, and which costs $60.00 to collect $100.00," the editorial, titled "The Burden of Government," urged readers to "overthrow this tyranny and make this country truly the 'land of the free and home of the brave.'"[18] The *Banner's* anti-tariff stance, like that of the *Grain Growers' Guide* in 1911, arose from a materialist opposition to unfair and burdensome taxation, but it was linked explicitly to highly rhetorical appeals to democratic revolution.

Adding to the burden of the tariff and the new war taxes was the rising cost of living, which had taken hold before the war but accelerated sharply when the economy picked up in 1915. Like the tax burden, the rising cost of living was a recurring theme of articles in the *Industrial Banner*. Also like the tax burden, high prices were cast in explicitly political terms as a problem of democracy. An editorial in September 1916 on "The High Cost of Living" described rising prices as a "direct and unconcealed tribute levied upon the people by unscrupulous combines and speculators" and called on "authorities at Ottawa to wake up and do something to regulate the heartless exploitation of the consuming public." Underlining the point that the issue was a political one, the editorial urged the government to "get its ear to the ground and find out what the electorate, the people, are talking about."[19] Another editorial noted that "unscrupulous speculators, taking advantage of existing conditions, have developed a systematic scheme of exploitation of the general public by unduly and altogether unnecessarily inflating the price of commodities that it is necessary for people to buy in order to exist."[20] The question of high consumer prices dovetailed well with the question of whether gaining profit was moral in light of the material suffering of families and of the sacrifice of lives on the battlefield. An editorial in March 1917 asserted that, "undoubtedly, the amassing of wealth has become an insanity that dooms millions to degradation, hardship and want," and it stated that political attempts to deal with the cost of living "are clearly useless so long as it is legal and respectable for the big interests to monopolize and control the natural sources of wealth and the avenues of trade and commerce." The problem, the *Banner* said, is that retailers "are able to intimidate parliaments and legislatures and force them to do their will and all for the sake of dividends and profits so immense as to be undreamed of a dozen years ago."[21]

Within a year of the start of the war, in fact, munitions production had revitalized the Canadian economy, and employment and trade conditions improved.[22] By reviving industrial production and increasing the cost of living, the war boom strengthened and revitalized organized labour. The economic crisis of 1913–15 had reversed many of the gains that the labour movement had made during the Laurier boom. Massive unemployment gutted unions, and labour struggled to maintain basic rights with a severely weakened bargaining position and became conciliatory. The advent of war and munitions contracts, Myer Siemiatycki argues, "revived sagging trade union fortunes by turning the flooded labour market of 1914 into a dire manpower shortage by 1916."[23] Organized labour was a rising power, particularly in Ontario and Quebec, where workers threatened strikes that would have seriously undermined imperial war production.[24] The introduction of national registration, which implicitly subjected industrial labour to the same power of compulsion as military service, created more resentment among workers, and the introduction of conscription, in the form of the Military Service Act, further inflamed class resentment of a government that compelled military service while it invited the rich to contribute voluntarily to finance the war – for a profit.

Organized labour clearly relished its new power, but it was a rhetorically delicate matter for unions eager to enjoy the opportunity to influence unsympathetic governments to express themselves on the question of the war while their power derived from their ability to stop production. (It was precisely this tension between supporting the war and opposing the economy of the war that conscription of wealth was so deftly to elide.) The important thing was to position government and industry as reactionary and labour as people's enlightenment. In practical terms, this meant characterizing rising tension between workers and industry as both a great disgrace for which the government was responsible and a welcome sign of the maturation of political intelligence among working people. Accordingly, when a strike began in Hamilton, the *Industrial Banner* was quick to blame the "bungling of the Dominion Government and its refusal to safeguard the interests of the workers in munitions and war supply factories in Canada by the insertion of fair wage clauses in all contracts."[25] At the same time, the *Banner* clearly relished its sense that,

> throughout the length and breadth of the Dominion of Canada, public sentiment has become thoroughly aroused at the inexcusable inaction of the federal Government in failing to legislate to relieve the consuming public from the heartless exploitation of trusts and combines which have organized to take advantage of war conditions to unduly advance the price of foodstuffs and commodities, upon which the said consumers are absolutely forced to depend for life and sustenance.[26]

The conditions that created the necessity for revolt were appalling and unconscionable; the acute awareness of those conditions was inspiring and could only be good news in the long run: the editorial was titled "The Spirit of Revolt Is Everywhere Apparent."

Calls for the conscription of wealth, as articulated by labour in 1916 and 1917, drew on moral opposition to the further enrichment of wealthy Canadians, especially as viewed against the conscription of other Canadians. It drew on sharpened moral indignation at the social inequalities that had characterized prewar Canadian society but were deepened by the war. The rising cost of living combined with a number of new regressive sales taxes on top of the old regressive tax, the tariff, to produce an unsupportable burden for the families of soldiers, workers, and farmers who tried to survive on low incomes. Business profits, meanwhile, were unprecedented, and investment in the war, either directly in government bonds or indirectly through private companies filling war contracts, was lucrative for people with extra income. The war was making the rich richer and squeezing the poor harder than ever. Labour was determined to fight back, and conscription of wealth was its rhetorical bludgeon. The introduction of the income war tax in the summer of 1917, which constituted a reversal of the government's previous position, was a response to labour's criticisms, not the expression of a changed attitude by White regarding the value of income taxation. It was a political solution to a political problem, and it was greeted as such by critics of the government.

"The Awakening": The Conscription of Wealth and People's Enlightenment

The rhetoric of the conscription of wealth developed out of the exploitative political economy of the war and served as a sharp indictment of the Conservative government's management of the war. It rested on a concept of fairness that implied an equivalence between conscription and taxation. The conscription of wealth rhetoric was in fact both complex and vague, often conflating a number of distinct arguments. Sometimes wealth was paired with labour in that both were resources comparable to natural resources and professional expertise and should be made available, in all fairness, to the state to prosecute the war efficiently, usually via some specific mechanism such as income taxation. At other times, the conscription of wealth was presented as a kind of punishment for the rich – as illustrated by Frederick Forsyth Pardee's insistence that taxation should "hurt" – who benefited from the war through war bonds or actual profiteering and who should be made less rich. Whether arising out of a technocratic idea of service to the state or a bitter class resentment of the inequities of wartime economic conditions, or both, the conscription of wealth rhetoric found expression in the statements of a wide range of speakers in the year leading up to the income war tax debates.

At the centre of the class critique of conscription and war finance was the insistence that conscription, in defiance of its official universality, meant conscription of the working class. This point was illustrated forcefully in the *Industrial Banner* in an article citing a study by the Canadian Manufacturers' Association, which pointed out that an overwhelming majority of those already enlisted were workers: "Out of 268,111 enlistments up to February 15, 1916, 170,369 are to be credited to 'manual labor,' and 48,777 to 'clerks.'" "In other words," the editorial concluded, "mechanics, labourers and clerks have furnished more than eighty per cent, or four fifths, of all Canadian enlistments."[27] The numbers were not intended to suggest that professionals and managers, who made up the other 48,995, were less patriotic or brave; rather, they were meant to remind readers that there were far more poor people than rich people, especially among those young enough to be conscripted. Conscription was therefore primarily conscription of the nonrich.[28] Another story in the *Banner* on September 15, 1916, stated forcefully that "the principle of conscription is one thing – the practice is quite another. In principle, it is an instrument of national defence; in practice, it is made an instrument of working-class subjugation."[29] The headline "The Government Has Promised There Shall Be No Conscription" was paired on October 20 with the subtitle "Insistent Demand for Conscription of Wealth." The articles reported that members of the Trades and Labour Congress (TLC) Executive were meeting with Borden and quoted Simpson as saying that, "if a man is computed to be worth $100,000 a good portion of that wealth should be conscripted if it is found necessary to force conscription on men."[30] Conscription of wealth could therefore be an argument against conscription (on the basis that men were already doing enough for the war by enlisting), but it drew on a class understanding of war service, valorizing the contributions that workers made to the war short of being forced to fight.

The calls for the conscription of wealth became more insistent as the government moved to introduce conscription. These calls rested on a critique, forcefully articulated in the *Industrial Banner*, of the political economy of the war. This critique focused on both the rising consumer prices and the new, regressive war taxes, both of which were evidence of the collusion of government and industry in placing the burden of the war squarely on the shoulders of the working class while the rich got richer from the war. A cover story on May 25, 1917, under the headline "Will the Government Allow Wealth to Go Free Now Labor Is to Be Conscripted? – Or Will It Conscript Money and Use the Whole Resources of the Country to Win the War?" asked, "now that the government has announced that it proposes to conscript blood and muscle in the service of the State," whether "the profiteers and coupon clippers, the new crop of millionaires that is being created in Canada as a result of enormous profits, nor earned, but buccaneered out of the Empire in its hour of need, are to be exempted."[31] Later, after the government announced its willingness to introduce the income war tax, the *Banner* again linked exploitative political economy and military service, explaining that people's indignant awareness of the injustice of the conscription of men without the conscription of wealth had moved the government. "The policy of the Government, which aims to conscript the manhood of the nation while graft and exploitation runs riot in the land," it noted, "has called forth a storm of indignation such as no former administration has been called upon to face – a storm before which even the indifference of said government has been forced to give way."[32] The brutality of war, the *Banner* insisted, weighed more heavily on the poor than on the rich and made profit itself immoral, necessitating a fairer and more modern form of taxation that would weigh more heavily on the rich than on the poor and use the country's wealth for a common purpose.

The idea of the conscription of wealth was so effective and powerful, as Ian McKay has noted, because it attached a critique of wealth to the patriotic culture of war.[33] Indeed, by representing the conscription of wealth and the conscription of manpower as two halves of an inseparable whole, labour intellectuals were able to portray free enterprise as unpatriotic and the government that nurtured its continued success as negligent in its execution of the war effort. The originality of this rhetorical gesture was illustrated in a June 22, 1917, editorial in the *Industrial Banner*, which aimed to reframe the range of possible positions on conscription: "Individuals may honestly and conscientiously differ on the question of conscription," for "some honestly advocate it and some honestly oppose it, but neither Borden nor Laurier are to be placed in that class."[34] The *Banner* insisted that it was inconsistent and dishonest to support the conscription of men and not the conscription of wealth. An even more forceful equating appeared on the front page of the *Banner* on July 6: a registration form for the conscription of men beside one for the conscription of wealth (Figure 2.2). The image encapsulated

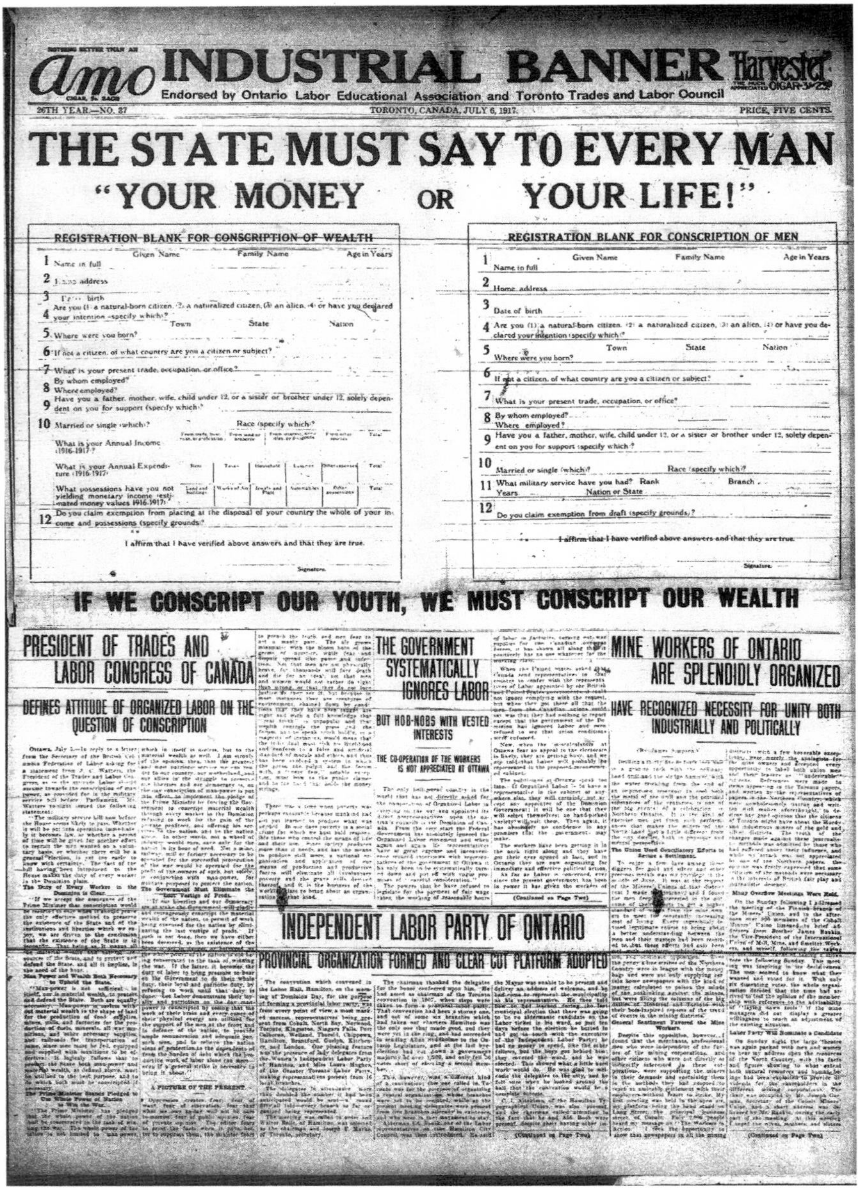

INDUSTRIAL BANNER

Endorsed by Ontario Labor Educational Association and Toronto Trades and Labor Council

26TH YEAR—NO. 27 | TORONTO, CANADA, JULY 6, 1917. | PRICE, FIVE CENTS.

THE STATE MUST SAY TO EVERY MAN "YOUR MONEY OR YOUR LIFE!"

REGISTRATION BLANK FOR CONSCRIPTION OF WEALTH

1 Name in full — Given Name — Family Name — Age in Years
2 Home address
3 Date of birth
4 Are you (1) a natural-born citizen, (2) a naturalized citizen, (3) an alien, (4) or have you declared your intention (specify which)? — Town — State — Nation
5 Where were you born?
6 If not a citizen, of what country are you a citizen or subject?
7 What is your present trade, occupation, or office?
8 By whom employed? Where employed?
9 Have you a father, mother, wife, child under 12, or a sister or brother under 12, solely dependent on you for support (specify which)?
10 Married or single (which)? Race (specify which)?
What is your Annual Income (1916-1917)?
What is your Annual Expenditure (1916-1917)?
What possessions have you not yielding monetary income (estimated money values 1916-1917)?
12 Do you claim exemption from placing at the disposal of your country the whole of your income and possessions (specify grounds)?

I affirm that I have verified above answers and that they are true.

Signature.

REGISTRATION BLANK FOR CONSCRIPTION OF MEN

1 Name in full — Given Name — Family Name — Age in Years
2 Home address
3 Date of birth
4 Are you (1) a natural-born citizen, (2) a naturalized citizen, (3) an alien, (4) or have you declared your intention (specify which)?
5 Where were you born? — Town — State — Nation
6 If not a citizen, of what country are you a citizen or subject?
7 What is your present trade, occupation, or office?
8 By whom employed? Where employed?
9 Have you a father, mother, wife, child under 12, or a sister or brother under 12, solely dependent on you for support (specify which)?
10 Married or single (which)? Race (specify which)?
11 What military service have you had? Rank — Branch — Years — Nation or State
12 Do you claim exemption from draft (specify grounds)?

I affirm that I have verified above answers and that they are true.

Signature.

IF WE CONSCRIPT OUR YOUTH, WE MUST CONSCRIPT OUR WEALTH

PRESIDENT OF TRADES AND LABOR CONGRESS OF CANADA

DEFINES ATTITUDE OF ORGANIZED LABOR ON THE QUESTION OF CONSCRIPTION

THE GOVERNMENT SYSTEMATICALLY IGNORES LABOR

BUT HOB-NOBS WITH VESTED INTERESTS

THE CO-OPERATION OF THE WORKERS IS NOT APPRECIATED AT OTTAWA

MINE WORKERS OF ONTARIO ARE SPLENDIDLY ORGANIZED

HAVE RECOGNIZED NECESSITY FOR UNITY BOTH INDUSTRIALLY AND POLITICALLY

INDEPENDENT LABOR PARTY OF ONTARIO

PROVINCIAL ORGANIZATION FORMED AND CLEAR CUT PLATFORM ADOPTED

FIGURE 2.2 An equivalence: conscription and the conscription of wealth. This cover of the *Industrial Banner* showed paired registration cards for the conscription of men and the conscription of wealth – the former real, the latter invented. The image illustrated the point that the editors of the *Banner* had been making in textual form for more than six months. | *Industrial Banner,* July 6, 1917, 1.

the rhetorical claim that the *Banner* had been making for more than six months: that men and wealth should be conscripted equally and that to conscript the one it was fair and necessary to conscript the other.

The position that the conscription of soldiers demanded the conscription of wealth was a powerful one taken up by many commentators otherwise unsympathetic to either labour or direct taxation. Stephen Leacock, a noted Conservative, took the argument up in his pamphlet *National Organization for War*, part of which Charles Murphy cited in the debate on the income war tax. In typically immoderate style, Leacock bemoaned the wastefulness, in the context of war, of selfish activity and insisted that all resources should be made available to the war effort:

> If a war were conducted with the full strength of the nation, it would mean that every part of the fighting power, the labour, and the resources of the country were being used towards a single end. Each man would either be fighting or engaged in providing materials of war, food, clothes and transport for those that were fighting, with such extra food and such few clothes as were needed for themselves while engaged in the task.[35]

For Leacock, the efficient use of resources for the war should be the singular priority of political economy. "This is the fashion in which the energies of a nation would be directed," he noted with evident approval, "if some omniscient despot directed them and controlled the life and activity of every man."[36] The implication that individual freedom and property rights, in a wartime context, are antisocial came to the surface when Leacock addressed taxes specifically. He estimated that consumers were paying 10 percent of their income in war taxes, noting that this "means that nine-tenths of the man's work is directed to his own use and only one-tenth for the war."[37] He depicted war finance as unscrupulously capitalistic and profit seeking. Taxation was devised with "one eye on the supposed benefits to industry," and the "so-called patriotic loan is so issued that the hungriest money-lender in New York is glad to clamber for a share of it."[38]

A more moderate call for the conscription of wealth in the form of income taxation came from Newton Rowell, the Ontario Liberal leader who would run as a Unionist candidate in the 1917 dominion election and play a central role in Borden's second government. In a speech on July 26, 1917, later reprinted in a pamphlet entitled *Conscription of Wealth*, Rowell said that

> men at the front feel and feel keenly that while they are giving their all for Canada and for liberty, men at home are making huge profits out of

the war. In justice to the men at the front as well as to the cause for which they are fighting, we must require wealth to bear its share of the burden. Men who are profiting by the war must make a full contribution to the cost of the war, and in addition, a radical, progressive income tax measure is urgently required.[39]

Here Rowell linked a sense of justice and fairness in war sacrifice and connected the large profits arising from the war to the need for an income tax – which he described as "radical" (like his federal colleague Graham in the parliamentary debates cited above) and "progressive"; although "progressive" is a technical term in taxation, referring to the taxation of higher levels of income at higher rates, "radical" has no equivalent technical meaning. In another speech, on August 2, 1917, reprinted in the same pamphlet, Rowell brought up the issue again, this time specifically commenting on the income war tax, in its second reading at the time, criticizing its weakness by noting that "a progressive income tax is a step in the right direction, but we need a war measure not a peace measure like the present Bill."[40] Rowell again emphasized equality of sacrifice but framed it in explicitly economic terms, saying that "the whole capital of the working man is in his life and his capacity for work" and arguing that, "if he is placing that at the service of his country, the contribution of a man of large income, who only gives the surplus over reasonable living expenses, is but dust in the balance compared with the contribution of the man who offers his life."[41] His insistence on what he called a "radical" income tax, and his rejection of the income war tax as a peace measure, reflected both a deep sense of injustice with the wartime economic conditions and a modernist interest in a break with the past.

The phrase "conscription of wealth" articulated a critique of the inequalities generated by the Borden government's handling of the war effort. It built upon an existing critique of the tariff as the dominion's central financing instrument but sharpened that critique in the context of war finance, which exacerbated the regressivity of the tariff and of the threat of the conscription of men for military service. As the debate over conscription intensified, the link between income taxation and conscription encapsulated in the phrase "conscription of wealth" was widely reproduced and articulated in various ways by Liberals and Conservatives as well as labour voices. The idea that taxation had to be higher and fall more heavily on those with higher incomes for the burden of war service to be fairly apportioned held appeal across a wide range of political views. But beyond its status as an appeal to equal sacrifice, the phrase was appealing for its political effects. For Liberal and Conservative parliamentarians, as for the editors and readers of the *Industrial Banner,* the conscription of wealth was a useful rhetorical instrument in clearing a path to a new way of doing politics and a new way of understanding political differences.

Rather than simply an expression of class fear or political opportunism, or a critique of the political economy of war sacrifice, the rhetoric of the debate on the income war tax can be seen as a reflection of the widely shared but contested project of political modernism. Conscription of wealth wove together competing strands of critique and was voiced by speakers from differing and opposed political positions. Although Borden and White's undeveloped project of progressive reforms, and the emergence of the coalition Union government after the election of 1917, were the political fruits of the elite project of political modernism, the emergence of independent labour parties and a wave of strikes after the war (including the one in Winnipeg in the spring of 1919) reflected a labour project of modernism. As with the conscription of wealth rhetoric with which it overlaps, however, the modernist project reflected some similarities between elite and labour politics. In particular, both saw the war, and the general modern era in which it was unfolding, as forces awakening people to new possibilities and, in particular, to a clearer awareness of the world.

That the time had come for independent political action by labour was a near-constant theme in the *Industrial Banner* over the year up to the summer of 1917. Although the efforts of the TLC Executive to influence Borden and other members of the political elite were applauded and endorsed by the editors, the paper exhibited a pronounced distaste for the old political parties. What it called the "strike at the ballot box" was partly an expression of ultimate frustration with labour's marginalization by the ruling Conservatives in particular and partly an expression of the full flowering of the working class's own political emancipation and intellectual independence – or people's enlightenment.[42]

The link between mass political enlightenment and a break with the Liberal and Conservative Parties was a recurring theme in the *Industrial Banner*. An editorial on July 16, 1916, made this point clearly, arguing that the creation of a party for workers was the logical expression of labour's political education:

> The ballot must supplement political organization on the industrial field, and the lessons that labour has learned of late in the school of hard experience should itself be the incentive to spur it into action to organize a great political party of its own in order to capture and control the law making power of the state, in order to lay the foundations for a real and enduring democracy in which the people should rule and justice finally triumph.[43]

The same editorial ridiculed workers who still defined themselves as Liberal or Conservative, arguing that "the man who carries a union card today and can insult his intelligence in order to follow round in the rear of an old party bandwagon should be caged in some zoo as a curiosity for sensible people to gaze upon."[44] This insistence on independent political action as the essence of political modernism, and on old elite-led parties as relics of political ignorance, recurred in the *Banner,* most clearly in an editorial on the importance of independent political action that explicitly drew on the modernist imagery of mandatory progress:

> There is not an intelligent observer to-day but realizes that great changes, industrially and politically, are in the making; that things will not go on as they have done as in the past; in the old worn-out run that resulted in worldwide exploitation and disaster. None know this better than the professional politicians, who fully realize that the old parties are losing their hold on the people, that the old pleas have lost their efficacy, and that ancient traditions must be quickly relegated to the scrap heap.[45]

An eloquent and forceful expression of the idea of a break with the past, the passage celebrated the growing independence and awareness of workers as an expression of a modern consciousness and even acknowledged the forces in the old elite-dominated political parties that pushed for a rejection of partisanship.

The threat of conscription also inspired threats of extraparliamentary forms of independent political action: general strikes. As Myer Siemiatycki has argued, the idea of a general strike against the Canadian economy began in the munitions factories of Toronto and Hamilton in 1916.[46] With the rise of the conscription issue, locals of the Trades and Labour Congress began passing resolutions for a general strike in the event of conscription and pushing their national executive to adopt a similar stance on a dominion-wide basis.[47] Although these efforts were unsuccessful, TLC President James Watters reflected this link in his comments to the *New York Times* on July 4, 1917. Asked how labour organizations would respond to the Military Service Act, he said that they would

> demonstrate their loyalty and patriotism on the day man-power is conscripted by seeing that the work of their brains and every ounce of their physical energy is utilized for the support of the men at the front and in defense of the nation, to provide ample remuneration and adequate pensions for the men in khaki and a full measure of protection to the dependents of such men, and to relieve the nation from the burden of debt,

which the productive work of labour alone can meet – even if a general strike is necessary to bring it about.[48]

Here Watters used the rhetoric of the conscription of wealth to make the general strike – the ultimate expression of the power of workers independent of the state – a patriotic gesture. Whether or not this move would have resonated far, whether or not it would have found a sympathetic audience, it undoubtedly would have registered with the dominion cabinet and might have influenced the introduction of the income war tax.

The demand for the conscription of wealth, which developed from labour's criticism of the political economy of the war and was articulated most forcefully by the *Industrial Banner*, was taken up by speakers from across the political spectrum by the summer of 1917. Its insistence that the dominion government use its coercive power not just to force men to fight but also to curb the inequality that the war produced resonated with widely held beliefs about profit and sacrifice during the war. Calls for the conscription of wealth were not uniform: for some, the argument was a technocratic insistence that all resources should be used to fight the enemy, whereas for others it was a moral question of making the rich suffer as much as the soldiers at the front were suffering. That the conscription of wealth was part of a radical and modern break with the past was most forcefully articulated by the *Industrial Banner*, which placed the rising power and independence of organized labour and the need for a clearer understanding of politics in the context of people's enlightenment. An editorial on December 15, 1916, entitled "The Awakening," linked independence of thought with a break with the past that would inaugurate a new politics. "There never was a time in the history of the Province," it read, "when people were thinking so seriously on real problems as they are at the present moment."[49] Serious thought on real questions, for the *Banner*, was partly about a critical understanding of the tariff and the promise of the conscription of wealth. But it was inseparable from a move toward political independence and away from the old, tired allegiances of the party system and its mouthpieces in Parliament.

"A Blast of Taxation": National Government, the Conscription of Wealth, and Parliament

The conscription of wealth rhetoric had been widely disseminated by the time the income war tax was introduced in the summer of 1917. Parliamentarians using intemperate language calling for "more taxation" and "less satisfaction" were therefore at the end of a long rhetorical arc. Similar rhetoric in response to the weakness of a self-styled war tax on income would have been anticipated, given that the conscription of wealth and the political threats from labour were crucial inspirations for the introduction of the tax. The opposition's keenness to use radical language, like the government's introduction of the income war tax, was an attempt to appeal to the critique of war finance happening outside Parliament and, in the process, to pass conscription. But it was more than a mere reflection. As Richard Krever has argued, the debates on the income war tax reveal legislators from two parties seeking to work out a pro-conscription coalition, which would become, later in 1917, the Union government.[50] As John English observes, the Union government grew out of an elite criticism of partisanship radicalized by the war, creating what he calls an "ideology of service" that argued for Liberal and Conservative identities to be folded into one governing elite that would defend the state against threats from without and within.[51] The conscription of wealth rhetoric, then, was tied to elite attempts to undermine Liberal and Conservative differences by working out a coalition government that would embody and defend the shared values of the whole political class. The obverse of people's enlightenment, English's ideology of service also relied on the power of income taxation, and its critique of inequality, to initiate a break with the past of a different kind.

The intricacies of the Liberal and Conservative alliance that would become the basis of the Union government were signalled in the debates on income taxation, as Krever says, which "showed the price the Conservatives would have to pay to entice Liberals into the ranks of a union party."[52] Opposition members indicated repeatedly and forcefully that they supported conscription but would support the government only if it introduced an income tax. These Liberals also indicated their inclination to join a coalition for the purpose of winning the war. Pardee, for example, the day before White presented the income war tax, said that "the affairs of this country to-day demand a National Government, if it can be formed on a proper basis for the proper administration of those affairs."[53] The shift in the political culture that English sees happening in 1917, a shift away from partisanship and toward a shared elite ideology of service about governing the economy and winning the war, was expressed through the conscription of wealth rhetoric.

However, as useful as this rhetoric was to the working out of Liberal and Conservative differences, it was a potentially dangerous import. Using extreme language to create an unprecedented arrangement to defend the status quo is an awkward exercise and can easily go awry. It was important for the Liberals to express the discontent that the government's reliance on the tariff was causing, but it was risky to make Parliament simply a reflection of popular and radical ideas; it had to be done with finesse. In the debate on the income war tax, however, Thomas White did not respond to the onslaught of criticisms unleashed by the Liberals, a reflection of the convention that, in budget debates, "members of the Opposition conduct almost the entire debate."[54] The government's silence presents us with a provocation without effect and prevents us from assessing how much of a threat to the functioning of Parliament it was thought to be.

Other expressions made in Parliament in the summer of 1917 illustrate clearly the anxieties associated with intemperate speech related to the government's handling of the war. On June 22, George Graham rose to say that he supported the introduction of an income tax but that what he really meant was the imposition of a tax on high incomes:

I would not have an income tax for the man with the ordinary income because he has difficulty enough now in living, but there are in Canada a great number of men who receive a great deal more money than they earn, and a portion at least of their excess income ought to go hand in hand with the labour and the soldiery of Canada for the prosecution of this war.[55]

He followed up with a resolution that he presented for the consideration of MPs:

That in the opinion of this House it is desirable that steps should be taken forthwith by the Government to provide that accumulated wealth should contribute immediately and effectively to the cost of the war, and that all agricultural, industrial, transportation and natural resources of Canada should be organized forthwith so as to ensure the greatest possible assistance to the Empire in the war and to reduce the cost of living to the Canadian people.[56]

Graham made a point of drawing attention to the fact that unlike "some people [who] have spoken of conscription of wealth, ... I have not used that term."[57]

Despite Graham's evident circumspection and explicit distancing of his resolution from the conscription of wealth, Thomas White rose a few weeks later, on July 10, to clarify the risks of inflammatory speech. In a formal "Statement of the Finance Minister," White said that

it has been officially drawn to the attention of the Government that the use of the expression "conscription of wealth" in the debates in Parliament and by public and other bodies outside Parliament and by the press in its news reports has caused a certain uneasiness among those whose savings constitute a vital factor in the business and industrial life of the Dominion and are so essential to the credit and prosperity upon which our efforts in the continued prosecution of the war must largely depend.

A number of things were at work in this statement. First, White was reminding MPs and the public of the importance for the dominion of private credit, the basis of federal finance and, crucially, the war effort. An "uneasiness" among holders of capital was a potentially serious problem. White therefore asserted that "there need exist no apprehension on the part of the public that any action of a detrimental character will at any time be taken with respect to the savings of the Canadian public," clarifying that the government might introduce "income taxation upon those whose incomes are such as to make it just and equitable that they should contribute a share of the war expenditure of the Dominion."[58] Second, White was distinguishing between taxing accumulated wealth (or savings), which was not under consideration, and taxing income, which was. Third, he was issuing a condemnation and a caution to parliamentarians to avoid frightening holders of capital with intemperate and imprecise speeches.

Understandably concerned that his comments had been misconstrued, Graham immediately rose to defend his parliamentary record:

I did not use the term "conscription of wealth." The resolution which I introduced was in these words: "That in the opinion of this House it is desirable that steps should be taken forthwith by the Government to provide that accumulated wealth should contribute immediately and effectively to the cost of the war."

The observations that I made were, I think, perfectly in harmony with the wording of this resolution and with the remarks just made by the Minister of Finance.[59]

White made no reply, but the prime minister stood and said, clearly enough for the parliamentary reporter to hear and record, "hear, hear."[60] Thus ended a particularly self-conscious display of cross-partisan concern about the risks of parliamentary rhetoric.

The anxious insistence that parliamentarians be circumspect in their criticism of the government's conduct of the war spoke to the concerns of the political elite, both Liberal and Conservative, about the risks that rhetoric along the lines of conscription of wealth might pose to political and economic support for the war. This anxiety was evidence of a widening polarization between a political elite committed to continuing and even increasing Canada's involvement in the war and an array of opposition groups increasingly intransigent in opposing it – a polarization that historians have underlined repeatedly. Debates on the income war tax reflected this polarization, both in the sense that Liberal members were unrestrained in their criticism of it and in the sense that the tax itself was introduced to dull opposition to conscription, the most divisive element of the government's war policy. But the conscription of wealth was also a key instrument in working out an unprecedented alliance of Liberals and Conservatives seeking to introduce conscription. This was possible not only because a new political culture had emerged among the elite that was disdainful of partisanship but also because the desire for a more active – indeed radical – instrument of taxation was widespread.

The debate was full of energetic and humorous remarks, all intended to underline the weakness of the tax and the members' interest in having it strengthened. It consisted entirely of Liberals criticizing the Conservative government, but it also featured some surprising examples of interparty agreement. Murphy quoted at length from a pamphlet by noted Conservative Leacock entitled *National Organization for War,* which complained that "our present taxes are, for war time, ridiculously low, as far as people of comfortable, or even of decent, means are concerned" and suggested that "every cent of the money that can be gathered up by national thrift should be absorbed by national taxes and national loans." (A part of the pamphlet that he did not cite read thus: "We need a blast of taxation – real taxation, income tax and all, that should strike us like a wave of German gas."[61]) The copy of the pamphlet that Murphy read from was published by the National Service Board of Canada, a wartime agency headed by Conservative MP R.B. Bennett, and was therefore, Murphy noted, government literature.

The conscription of wealth, the rhetoric that motivated this response, though it arose from the polarization of political positions on the war, also served as a bridge between political positions; unlike other increasingly absolute oppositions, it admitted a spectrum of differences. It could be an expression of a range of desires, from those of labour thinkers in the *Industrial Banner* for a more equal industrial order to those of pamphleteers of the Conservative and Liberal Parties for a more efficient war effort. The extraordinary appeal of radical critiques of war finance was in part an effect of the unprecedented violence and upheaval of the First World War and in part simply a deepening and widening of earlier critiques of the tariff as regressive and unfair. The conscription of wealth resonated, that is, not only because of the unique circumstances of the war but also because of a shared desire for a radical break with the past, a political modernism that ran across more obvious political differences.

The income war tax itself, in fact, was welcomed, even by MPs critical of its weakness, as a necessary instrument in modernizing politics. In this case, rather than severing old political affiliations, modernity was cast as a clarifier, eliminating confusion and allowing taxpayers and citizens to make informed and intelligent political choices. Clarity and intelligibility were the necessary conditions for a healthy political culture and for justice in government. The links among income taxation, modernity, and clarity were not new in the war context, but the introduction of the income war tax – justified by the special exigencies of the war and inspired by the unique conditions of class conflict produced by the war – served as an invitation to make the connections explicit.

This appeal to modernity, and to the potential for income taxation to bring directness, legibility, and clarity to Canadian politics, can be seen most clearly in the contributions of F.B. Carvell, another Liberal MP who later became a member of the Union government, to the debate on the income war tax. When the bill got to the Senate, senators broke with convention (under which the upper house passed all money bills passed by the lower house without revisions) and amended it, allowing investigations into tax evasion to be held in camera, out of view of the public. White expressed concern about the move but was primarily concerned about avoiding a confrontation over the issue. Carvell rose on September 15, 1917, to denounce the Senate amendments and linked income taxation to modernity and clarity. Such taxation, he said, "produces a condition of affairs by which, after the war is over, we can discuss questions of trade, commerce, and tariff much more intelligently than we have been able to discuss them." His interest in more intelligent discussions of the tariff might have been an oblique reference to the Liberals' defeat in 1911 and the role of nationalist rhetoric in framing questions of taxation. Carvell also noted that "the financial condition of Canada has so changed during the last three years [since the war started] as to revolutionize our whole method of taxation." He continued that "we have to get down to direct taxation, and to adopt a system so efficient, straight and above board that every man will know whether or not his neighbour is paying his fair share of taxation."[62] Here Carvell linked modernity and direct taxation in the need for political clarity, for visibility and transparency. His enthusiasm for income taxation, and his linking it to modernity, echoed a comment that Michael Clark made on August 17: "The war ... has been a great fiscal schoolmaster, as well as a great schoolmaster along other lines." Clark also congratulated White that "he has learned from the course of the war the necessity of putting on some direct taxation."[63] Like the necessity for the *Industrial Banner* of independent political action, the necessity of direct taxation was represented by these Liberal MPs as the lesson of the war, the awakening that the war forced on a sleep-walking polity.

Throughout the summer and fall of 1917, Liberal MPs continually took rhetorical shots at the Conservatives' management of the war, and at the injustice of their method of financing it, in ways that clearly echoed critiques of the war by the *Industrial Banner*. In August, Louis-Joseph Gauthier pointed out that "the honourable gentlemen are continually talking about sacrifices, about contributions, about living a life of privation," and he asked a number of questions: "Who are those who are making sacrifices? Who are those who are giving contributions? Who are those who are living a life of self-denial? It is the common people."[64] Later, in September, Frank Oliver, who had been the minister of the interior in Laurier's cabinet, took the radical rhetoric of the conscription of wealth even further, linking the government and its industry allies to the enemy. "The Kaiser in our country is our Government," Oliver said, "an oligarchy self-selected." He continued that "it is supported, as it was created, by an aristocracy of wealth, an aristocracy which includes the munitions profiteers, the men who corner the food of the people, the manufacturing monopolists, the railroad exploiters, and the boa-constrictors of high finance."[65] His rhetoric was vivid and harshly condemnatory. His speech sounded less like the usual parliamentary banter and more like an editorial in the *Banner*.

That so much of parliamentary discussion in 1917 sounded like the statements of organized labour tells us a lot about how much the House of Commons was becoming a forum for radical critiques of politics – that parliamentary discussion, in Leacock's vivid phrase, limped in the wake of public discussion. The debate was partly about establishing the necessary conditions for pro-conscription Liberals to join a Union government; however, the conditions were not those of the Liberal Party or the Conservative Party or even the two of them combined. They were the conditions of labour itself. This was a fact of which the *Industrial Banner* itself was proudly and even gleefully aware. An editorial on October 5, 1917, surmised that "the insistent and growing demand that is being voiced from every province in the Dominion that action shall be taken, immediately, for the conscription of wealth" was "giving the ballot-stealing administration at Ottawa not a little concern," noting with satisfaction that "amongst its 'now' most insistent advocates are to be found thousands of those who formerly were vehemently opposed to" the conscription of wealth. This state of affairs, the paper pointed out, was the work of organized labour itself, which had "boldly insisted that wealth and special privileges should help bear the war burdens of the state."[66] Although the editorial mentioned neither the income war tax nor the parliamentary debate about it directly, they were the perfect illustration of the *Banner*'s point: the fiscal and rhetorical fruits, respectively, of organized labour's wartime awakening.

"The Spirit of Revolt": Creative Destruction, People's Enlightenment, and "the Era of the Great Parties"

The war, at its grimmest in 1917 with no discernible end in sight, ended with an armistice in 1918 and a peace treaty the following year. The passions of the earlier period cooled, and the desperate need for bodies to send to the front evaporated, but deeply felt resentments continued to bubble up as soldiers returned to bleak prospects. Passions stirred by the debates over conscription and taxation left a bitter taste and made a quick return to the prewar politics of engaged partisanship impossible, even for those who might have desired it. The break with the past envisioned by farmers in 1911 had come about, not entirely or solely through people's enlightenment but through collaboration between increased engagement and awareness of common people and the horrifying cost of waging a war and the response to those factors by a government and an opposition eager to make Parliament relevant to its radical critics. The result had been an income tax that targeted the wealthy and a political imaginary that had been all but destroyed.

The political modernism that overturned the dominion's party politics and fiscal conventions in 1917 bore more fruit as the war ground to a halt, with new differences taking the place of old differences. The Union government, the alliance of Conservatives and pro-conscription Liberals arising in part from the conscription of wealth debates, held power in Ottawa until 1921, three years after the basis for its existence had ended. Also in dominion politics, the Progressive Party, arising from the farmers' movement against the tariff and re-energized by the conscription issue, was founded in 1920 and became an important player in dominion politics (usually supporting the Liberals) after 1921; farmer candidates were particularly successful in the west, where Progressive or United Farmer governments were formed in Alberta and Manitoba. In Ontario, the "strike at the ballot box" predicted by the *Industrial Banner* came in 1919, when United Farmer and Independent Labour members formed the provincial government. Although the

Liberal and Conservative Parties returned to their original names by the mid-1920s, and Ontario soon reverted to a two-party system, the two-party basis of dominion political culture was forever altered. Liberals, Conservatives, farmers, and labour together had brought an end to the old nineteenth-century divisions. As Liberal journalist J.W. Dafoe later wrote, the war "brought to a definite close what might be called the era of the Great Parties."[67] The political modernism that took hold after the war – "the efforts at the realignment of parties, the attempt to newly appraise political views, and to redefine political relationships" – all of this was "testimony to the dissolving, penetrating power of the impulses of 1917."[68]

In their place, of course, new divisions deepened. High prices and the return of prewar depression combined with the return of soldiers and the intransigence of employers and the state in the face of the demands of labour to create a violent storm of industrial upheaval. Strikes and other political actions erupted across the country; the most famous of the strikes was in Winnipeg in the spring of 1919, but every province in every region saw a major increase in union activity in the period.[69] The Union government responded fiercely to the workers' revolt, labelling its leaders "Bolsheviks" (the new catch-all term imported from the Russian Revolution for political dissidents) and deporting anyone whom they could identify as a foreign influence.[70] As the country "raced towards the abyss," in Leacock's phrase cited above, one bright spot for critics who wanted the liberal state to be the site of meaningful political debates, rather than the boot heel of capitalist repression, was the income war tax, which O.D. Skelton affirmed "has now become an important and doubtless permanent feature of our fiscal system."[71]

Although the tax was still a minuscule part of the overall tax system, estimated to have brought in 1 percent of the revenue used for the war, it loomed large in the aspirations that people had for it and in the possibilities that it suggested.[72] The ideas that the income tax would be permanent and that the rates and base of the income war tax would slowly evolve to where it represented the major source of revenue, and therefore the major source of political division over social spending, were implicit in some of the critiques of the tax on its introduction in 1917. These critiques became more explicit in the years that followed. For instance, F.B. Carvell, a Liberal critic of the weakness of the income war tax who joined the Union government, told the House of Commons in early 1919 that

I am a firm believer in the Income Tax; in fact I am one of those who believe that the scope of this tax should be very largely extended. I believe the scope of the tax should be extended upward and downward so that it might take in practically every man and woman who earns an income in this country ... I know of nothing that will conduce to better government, and the more honest administration of public affairs, than the fact that common people realize they are paying a tax straight into the coffers of the Government.[73]

Echoing his 1917 cautions about the importance of taxation being open and honest, and therefore the inappropriateness of in camera appeals, Carvell was repeating a common equation between income taxation and knowledge that would lead to good government.

A similar sentiment in favour of a direct tax was voiced by prairie editor C.W. Peterson in 1919 in *Wake Up, Canada!* With one thought on the tariff and another on the new taxes, he said that "a direct tax involves positive knowledge on the part of each taxpayer of the exact amount of his contribution ... An indirect tax shrouds the whole transaction in mystery. No one knows what he pays ... The system is, consequently, unsound and unscientific and should be avoided as far as possible."[74] Peterson offered that "the income, being the fairest basis of taxation, should assuredly be made the corner-stone of our taxation rather than merely incidental to the scheme."[75] Beyond correcting for and eventually replacing a worse tax, the income war tax suggested another possibility that the tariff had negated: using taxes to redress economic inequalities. Peterson predicted that a dominion income tax would allow the fiscal function of the state to "graduate from the narrow field of exacting more or less nominal tribute upon the earnings of the citizen for defraying the cost of public services, into the much wider and more important sphere of becoming an effective instrument in promoting a more even distribution of wealth amongst all the citizens of a nation."[76] An income tax was a good instrument, Peterson said, and could be used by a progressive government to protect free enterprise from the destructive extremes of inequality – a boon to socialists – by calmly and rationally adjusting the levels of taxation: "If the Government of Canada does its job intelligently, the scheme of taxation will be so adjusted, that net earnings on private capital will never be what they were in the past, and thus the levelling process will presently remove the more glaring inequalities that now furnish the favourite text of socialist propaganda."[77] Leacock, coming from a similar perspective of enlightened (and therefore, in the context of the late First World War, anguished) conservatism, wrote that "the period of five years of war has shown [the problem of inequality] to us in a clearer light than fifty years of peace."[78]

The clear light through which the war had shown inequality to those at the top and the bottom was, to a large extent, the discontent with taxation as embodied in the phrase "conscription of wealth" and the sheer weight of the cost of the war distributed through the ungainly and unfair system of the tariff. Presaging what would become a common rhetorical theme in the next war, Leacock commented that, in a war, "national finance seems turned into a delirium. Billions are voted where once a few poor millions were thought extravagant."[79] Skelton made much the same point but more concretely and learnedly, noting that the dominion in the postwar period "must raise in a single year a sum greater than the total expenditure of the Dominion ... during the whole generation from 1867 to 1900."[80] From the postwar perspective, however, with cities erupting in class war, it was clear to Leacock that "the financial burden of the war ... will prove to be a lesson in the finance of peace. The new burden has come to stay." Reiterating the concern that unfettered capitalism, with its extremes of wealth and poverty, was unfair and therefore unstable in the modern world, Leacock underlined the importance of easing inequalities to modern liberal statecraft: "No modern state can hope to survive unless it meets the kind of social claims on the part of the unemployed, the destitute and the children," and this task necessitates that it "continues to use the terrific engine of taxation already fashioned in the last war." Taxes on incomes, which can be intelligently adjusted to redress changes in the pattern of inequality, would become central to the liberal state "to an extent never dreamed of before."[81]

Looking ahead from the political wreckage of the end of the First World War, Leacock, Skelton, Peterson, and Pardee all predicted increased centrality and importance for income taxation. It was important because, unlike the tariff, it was clear and easily understood, and it allowed for intelligent awareness and informed democratic debate. Beyond its legibility, it was efficient and progressive, meaning that in theory it was capable of influencing the distribution of income and the financing of public spending projects; the war, the debates on the conscription of wealth, and the workers' revolt all having driven home the relevance of inequality to political stability, the capabilities of income taxation, it was predicted, would become increasingly important in shaping dominion politics.

The opposition that Leacock worriedly noted was growing every day between those who clung to law and order and those who strove for social justice – both facing the abyss, as he saw it, one crying "forward" while the other cried "back" – was real, but it masked important similarities. All politics were modernizing at the end of the First World War. The Union government, which aimed to unite the only two parties that vied for power, thus undermining the old, established political imaginary of ostensibly polar differences, reflected what Dafoe called the end of "the era of the Great Parties" as decisively as did the Winnipeg General Strike, which sought to replace parliamentary opposition with class opposition. Victoria Museum, where parliamentarians debated the income war tax and unravelled the party system by cross-party cooperation (Figure 2.3), shared more than an era with the public gatherings held in Victoria Park during the strike (Figure 2.4): they shared an ethos of overturning the old, of breaking with the past. The introduction of income taxation at the dominion level was a product

FIGURE 2.3   The end of the great parties I: The Union government in Parliament's temporary home. The House of Commons in 1918, shortly after the formation of a Union government that brought together Conservatives and pro-conscription Liberals, meeting in the main hall of the Victoria Museum, its temporary home after the 1916 fire. The fact that members all sat at the same level and on chairs that moved might have contributed to a less formal way of operating and interacting. | Library and Archives Canada, Arthur Beauchesne Fonds, PA-139684.

FIGURE 2.4   The end of the great parties 2: The People's Parliament, Victoria Park, Winnipeg, 1919. Winnipeg was the site of the most iconic of a series of strikes between 1917 and 1921 that shook the elite's confidence in liberal capitalism. In the spring of 1919, a general strike shut down the city for four weeks. During the strike, people often assembled in formal or informal assemblies called parliaments. These assemblies were intended as a more egalitarian and democratic version of representative democracy than that reflected by the parties in the House of Commons, and they pointed toward a new, more modern order in which the people were central. | Archives of Manitoba, L.B. Foote Fonds, Foote 1679. Winnipeg General Strike – Crowds at Victoria Park, 1919, N2745.

of both forms of political modernism and of the destructive impulse to overthrow the old party system and its rigid, unconvincing imaginary once and for all.

***

The break with the past in dominion fiscal practice that political modernists had long been seeking came in 1916 and 1917, when the House of Commons voted for the first time to use direct taxation. The move was unorthodox, reversing a tradition in which direct taxation was left to the provinces while the dominion relied on the tariff, and the immense borrowing power that it supported, to fund the federal government. It was not the cost of the war directly that triggered the shift to the new form of taxation but the spectre of a popular revolt against how the burden of the war was apportioned, and the need to forge a parliamentary coalition to enforce conscription, that led the government reluctantly and half-heartedly to introduce an income tax. With the threat of massive labour revolt on its hands, the dominion responded with as little as it thought possible. Although the weakness of the tax on income elicited a vociferous opposition attack, the fact that such a tax existed at all suggested the possibility of new and more modern politics. The memory of the dominion election of 1911, when the obscurities of the tariff were wrapped in nationalist rhetoric sold to voters as the issue at hand, played a part in the government critics' satisfaction with the introduction of the new taxes. The income war tax was weak, still tiny next to the tariff at the end of the war, but the possibilities that it held for clarifying politics and even, at a bit of an imaginary stretch, for blunting the struggle between socialism and capitalism by equalizing incomes made it undeniably exciting.

The conscription of wealth rhetoric that marked the introduction of the first dominion income tax had been instrumental in working out the intricacies of an unprecedented coalition between Liberals and Conservatives while illustrating the growing gap between both parliamentary parties and increasingly active and informed political groups outside the two-party system. However mild it might have seemed at the time in the context of the labour revolt and the background of the war, however meek it would seem as the enormous burden of expectation was loaded onto it through the interwar fiscal crises, the income war tax was radical and important at the time as a break with the past, the first concrete act in the destruction of the political and fiscal system of the tariff and an invitation to think of what political imaginary came next. Debates about the role of income taxation in the distribution of wealth were crucial to undermining the two-party system by the end of the First World War, leaving in its place a kind of void rapidly filling with fantasies of what income taxation could do if it were made more powerful.

PART 2

The Citizenship of Contribution and the Construction of the Modern Political Imaginary

3
The Curve of Progressivity: "Fiscal Need" and the Constitution, 1921–39

Norman McLeod Rogers rose in the House of Commons in early 1939 to deliver one of his many blasts of wit at the opposition's expense. The clever Liberal minister of labour was a favourite of his party and the community of intellectuals engaged in government work to which he belonged, but he was a source of continual annoyance to Conservatives.[1] Speaking as part of the debate on the Speech from the Throne, Rogers kidded R.J. Manion, the leader of the opposition, about his success in reabsorbing H.H. Stevens, a renegade Conservative who had fled the party in 1934 to found the Reconstruction Party, into the front ranks of the Conservative Party. "We," Rogers noted, meaning either the government or Parliament or the country as a whole, "have yet to learn what the terms of the reconciliation have been" – whether, that is, "the Reconstruction [P]arty is to be conserved or the Conservative Party reconstructed." And then, in an extravagant display of wit, Rogers noted that Stevens, in returning to the front row, had "moved, at least in the physical sense, from the extreme left to the extreme right of the Conservative Party benches." What did his reappearance mean, Rogers asked, for the principles of either the Conservative Party or the Reconstruction Party, which voters had been asked in 1935 to see as competing parties?[2] Although Rogers was politically better connected and better educated than most Canadians, he was not alone in wondering how to make sense of bewildering changes in the party system and in using the left–right spectrum as his instrument of attempted clarification.

The two decades between the end of the First World War and the start of the Second World War were marked by catastrophic depressions in various regions of the country, by great innovations in party politics, and by a prolonged constitutional crisis over the fiscal powers of the dominion state. Although this constitutional complex is popularly identified with the 1930s, it developed first in the Maritimes in the 1920s, shifting to the west when economic conditions worsened there in the decade that followed. At the peak of the Depression in 1934, 30 percent of the workforce was unemployed, and an unsustainable 2 million people were dependent on public relief.[3] In the course of trying to understand and resolve the prolonged crisis, politicians and intellectuals struggled with new ways of conceptualizing political difference. New possibilities suggested by the introduction of a dominion income tax in 1917 created political cleavages no longer containable in the old nineteenth-century differences of Liberal and Conservative. A more distanced relation to the old political imaginary, one that read the opposition between Liberal and Conservative platforms somewhat ironically, became more common. New third parties, some with clear ties to the people's enlightenment of farmers and workers, others with more abstract and modern positions, proliferated, complicating the political scene. The changes in the party system and the insistent demands for constitutional modernization underscored the need for a new political imaginary but also made finding agreement on one more difficult. The Royal Commission on Dominion-Provincial Relations, or Rowell-Sirois Commission, created in 1937 to try to resolve the constitutional crisis caused by the Depression, tried to make sense of a political scene in the midst of unprecedented innovation and change.[4]

When the commission reported its findings in late 1939, it called for the federal government to have sole control over the taxation of income. Why? Because, the report claimed, "the personal income tax is the most highly developed modern instrument of taxation" – the most equitable, the most efficient, the most transparent, the most precise tool for raising revenue – and, because it is drawn from "surplus income" and is internally self-adjusting, the tax least likely to be burdensome to taxpayers and the economy as a whole. The problem was that "the income tax (made up as it is in many provinces of a Dominion tax plus a provincial tax) has failed to fill a role in Canada commensurate with its abilities."[5] As a remedy, the report suggested, "the income tax should be used in accordance with modern practice, as an equalizer and chief instrument of adjustment in the whole tax system." To be an effective instrument, income taxation had to be spared from the federal division of jurisdiction and made into a unitary power. "The rate and the appropriate curve of progressivity necessary to reform and control the tax structure," the report claimed, "can only be achieved if this equalizing instrument of taxation is under one authority. That authority can only be the Dominion."[6]

In underlining the potential power of income tax as an equalizer, however, the report emphasized that equity was a political concept – and that income taxation could accurately reflect the politics of taxation through its curve of progressivity. A mathematical image of the relative burdens of taxation under a progressive income tax, in which higher incomes are taxed at a higher rate and lower incomes at a lower rate, the curve is a graph with a horizontal *x* axis representing income, a vertical *y* axis representing the rate of taxation, and a curved line extending from the lower left to the upper right: at the lower left, the income (*x*) is low, as is the tax rate (*y*); at the top right, the income (*x*) is high, as is the tax rate (*y*) (see Figure 3.1). The flatter the line, the less progressive it is; the more the line is curved upward, the more progressive it is. Income taxation, through the curve of its progressivity, could be made to reflect a range of competing ideals of equity between regions and citizens. Equity was understood, that is, not as a fixed ideal but as a contested terrain. Income tax simply provided a more legible illustration of those differences, provided that it was both unitary and powerful. Writing at a time when new political parties and new languages to represent political differences were complicating the political field, the commissioners seemed to suggest that a powerful dominion income tax would not only solve the fiscal problems of Confederation but also allow for a clearer and more modern representation of political differences.

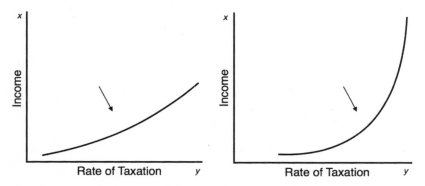

FIGURE 3.1   The curve of progressivity, illustrating the rate of progressivity between income and taxation. It was referenced repeatedly in discussions of taxation in the report of the Royal Commission on Dominion-Provincial Relations (the Rowell-Sirois Report). The image on the left shows a mildly progressive income taxation in which taxes rise moderately as incomes rise; the image on the right shows a more pronounced progressivity, symbolized by a deeper curve in which taxes rise more drastically as incomes rise.

The commission's highly rhetorical understanding of dominion income taxation as "an equalizer" can be fully understood only in the context of the crisis of Confederation that gave rise to it and of a wider political and rhetorical context in which the grounds of political disagreement were changing as new forms of authority emerged on the political stage. Arising from the political upheavals of the previous two decades, the commission was a staged encounter between the rhetoric of regional protest movements and the fiscal powers of the dominion state, with university-educated intellectuals serving as increasingly powerful mediators. Intellectual historians of politics have told the story of the rise to power of the "mandarins" or "government generation" of civil servants in the 1930s in ways that underscore the autonomy of intellectuals who generated ideas to fix the constitutional and fiscal problems that affected people.[7] Here the emphasis is reversed: rhetoric arising from political struggle provides the entry point for intellectuals such as Norman McLeod Rogers to bring critical policy reforms to the elite. Political modernism, the rejection of party politics and the advocacy of an unprecedented role for the dominion treasury in shaping the distribution of income, came from the margins to the centre and brought its rhetoric to the dominion cabinet and the Rowell-Sirois Commission. The dominion power of taxation, the inspiration for much of the political unrest in the regions and provinces in the late 1920s and early 1930s, was cast as the solution to the problem of Confederation, and a new political imaginary rooted in what Shirley Tillotson calls a "citizenship of contribution" emerged from a powerful dominion income tax capable of being adjusted to the appropriate curve of progressivity.[8]

"An Outworn Instrument"? The Constitution versus the "Equalizing Instrument of Taxation"

Political debate in Canada in the 1930s was dominated by the question of the Constitution. The catastrophic collapse of the economy left unprecedented millions of workers unemployed and swelled the ranks of those living on municipal relief, straining meagre provincial budgets. The Great Depression exposed the weakness of the Canadian fiscal framework and inspired calls for a new framework in which the dominion, which had greater fiscal capacity, would fund social programs at the provincial level. The great question of the decade was whether the existing constitutional framework, the division of powers set out in the British North America

Act in 1867 and interpreted by the Judicial Committee of the Privy Council since then, was a barrier to modernizing the fiscal framework – whether a new role for the federal treasury as an equalizer was merely a further evolution of its traditional role in Confederation or a revolution requiring a new, modern Constitution custom-built for redistributive tax policies.

Those who saw the Constitution as a barrier to a new fiscal framework were, like the farmers and labour unions of the 1910s, political modernists who appealed to a progressive view of history to justify eliminating institutional barriers. The catastrophic economic conditions of the 1930s strengthened popular support for egalitarian solutions to the problem of unemployment and poverty. But even advocates of social welfare and labour reform were focused primarily on improving the conditions of possibility of reform in the 1930s. The weakness of the state as a redistributive agent before the 1930s, Matt James has argued, meant that the left "had to dwell on considerations that were essentially preliminary to the economic advocacy that was the top priority for working-class organizations during the Depression."[9] Although their ultimate goal was to create legislation, "proponents of welfare state solutions had to grapple with a range of obstacles" to the development of a powerful taxing and spending authority, and clearing these obstacles became the key concern of political actors in the period.[10] Political modernism of the kind that would eliminate obstacles to reform was a necessary step in improving the conditions of possibility for the development of any kind of politics based upon income redistribution. The campaign involved many actors – provincial and regional protest movements, intellectuals working in the government – whose interests overlapped. The campaign culminated, via a long and contested route, in the Rowell-Sirois proposal for a more precise and powerful federal income tax.

The fiscal powers of the dominion and provinces of Canada were laid out in the British North America (BNA) Act, legislation passed by the British Parliament in 1867 that became Canada's Constitution. The BNA Act permitted the dominion to levy any tax but restricted the provinces to direct taxation; in practice, though, the dominion had relied overwhelmingly on the tariff as a source of revenue and had left direct taxation to the provinces until 1916, when it introduced the excess profits tax, followed by the income war tax the following year. The centrality of the tariff to the dominion's finances combined with the nationalist meanings invested in its rate structure, especially in the 1870s when the National Policy became the core Conservative Party position, made the tariff a key point of division between Liberal and Conservative electoral appeals, as discussed in

Chapter 1. In keeping with its division of the taxing powers, the BNA Act also gave a specific list of powers to the provinces while granting all other powers in addition to those listed in the act to the dominion.

This original conception of the respective taxing and spending roles of the dominion and provinces was altered significantly over the first half-century of Confederation by the Judicial Committee of the Privy Council (JCPC), the British court that served as Canada's highest court of appeal. Although the BNA Act gave the dominion the power to levy any tax, as well as a comprehensive scope of possible action, in a series of decisions the JCPC limited the powers of the dominion but left its taxing power absolute. The JCPC defined the power of direct taxation allocated to the provinces under the BNA Act narrowly and extended considerably the provinces' responsibilities. This arrangement left the dominion government with lots of potential revenue but little to do with it and the provinces (and municipalities operating under their auspices) with lots of responsibilities and comparatively little revenue. The situation was addressed semi-satisfactorily before 1914 because the dominion government relied primarily on the indirect tax of the tariff, and left direct taxation to the provinces, and because provincial governments were not overly ambitious. The dominion government's expansion into direct taxation in 1916–17 with the business profits tax and the income war tax, and the emergence shortly thereafter of demands for more generous social welfare programs at the provincial level, created what many political commentators called a constitutional "deadlock."

The controversy over the JCPC's interpretation of the BNA Act was at its most acute in 1937 when the court ruled on R.B. Bennett's 1934–35 New Deal reforms, a ruling that many saw as a verdict on social reform of any kind. Elected shortly after the Depression started, Bennett had been in trouble almost from the moment that he took power in 1930, as the Depression unfolded and expanded, putting pressure on the entire economy but especially on provincial and municipal governments as relief rolls expanded. Under pressure to abandon laissez-faire liberalism, Bennett's Conservative Party started to tear itself apart, H.H. Stevens breaking off to form the Reconstruction Party and W.D. Herridge threatening to do the same, which he would in 1939. Bennett belatedly agreed to introduce a package of reforms, modelled on Roosevelt's New Deal, that would see the federal government take a more active role, in some cases openly infringing provincial jurisdiction. In public, Bennett claimed that recent court decisions on broadcasting and transportation had signalled a "widening sense of the power of the central authority"; in private, he admitted that there were "grave constitutional difficulties" with federal legislation that sought to interfere in the economy.[11] Bennett lost the election in 1935, thanks partly to competition from the Reconstruction Party, and King sent the New Deal legislation to the JCPC for reference on its constitutionality.

The JCPC ruled in 1937 that much of the New Deal legislation was unconstitutional. Those who held hope in calmly and rationally changing the economic basis of the country without troubling the constitutional status quo were bitterly disappointed in the ruling. This was especially true of the League for Social Reconstruction, a group of university-employed intellectuals founded in 1932 to promote socialist ideas. The league served as an informal "brain trust" for the socialist Cooperative Commonwealth Federation and assumed control of the *Canadian Forum* in May 1936.[12] As recently as 1935, the league had written hopefully in *Social Planning for Canada* that "the BNA Act is a mere political framework, not inextricably tied up with a particular economic system," downplaying almost to nothing the political and constitutional barriers to Parliament's introducing socialism to Canada.[13] The league's constitutional expert, F.R. Scott, called the decision "another example of the way in which the [JCPC] has compelled the adoption in Canada of an interpretation of the constitution unfavourable to a strong central government."[14] The *Forum* opined that the ruling amounted to "a reactionary and stupid ... amendment to the Constitution" and complained that "everything is unconstitutional that does not fit into the social and economic preconceptions of a few senior judges."[15] Now the BNA Act was judged to be "an outworn instrument."[16]

The JCPC's interpretation of the BNA Act was a particular bone of contention for political economists, historians, and other intellectuals in the 1930s, and it has remained so ever since. It became an explicit political problem, however, only because of the sudden increased demand for government action in the 1920s and 1930s. The primary inspiration for the establishment of the Royal Commission on Dominion-Provincial Relations was discontent among the provinces, particularly the Maritime provinces, with the political economy of Confederation as the old tariff-fuelled National Policy was awkwardly and half-heartedly modernized during and after the Great War. The adoption of an income tax by the dominion did little to change the actual economics involved in federalism, but it did a lot to change what was seen as possible. It exacerbated some of the practical problems of Confederation, but it also indicated a way forward for some of them – particularly in the Maritimes, where the idea of a new role for the dominion treasury originated.

For many political commentators, the British North America Act in
the 1930s needed to be modernized to admit the political possibilities
that had moved onto the political landscape since the introduction of the
income war tax in 1917.[17] The desire to do something about the failure
of capitalism pushed more and more people to the realization that the
first step was to eliminate the barrier to action, the JCPC's limitations
on the development of taxing and spending policies. The belief that the
dominion power of taxation needed to be strengthened substantially to
correct for the inconsistencies of capitalist development across Canada
was common by the end of the 1930s. The Constitution, which had been
interpreted in such a way as to deny the possibility of using either provincial or dominion power to redistribute income, became the target of
a modernist campaign, one that aimed to remove the barriers to a new
relationship between the provinces and their citizens using the power of
taxation. Although the west had led the push against the tariff and called
for a direct tax to replace it in 1910, in the aftermath of the Great War it
was the eastern part of the country that pushed for a more active role for
the federal treasury, a demand that eventually focused on an expansion
of the federal direct taxation introduced in 1917.

"An Invidious Doctrine": "Fiscal Need" and the Dominion Taxing Power

The crisis of the 1930s that pitted the new taxing power of the dominion
government against the constitutional division of powers actually began
in the 1920s. As in the 1910s, when the movement that ultimately led to
the introduction of the income war tax in 1917 began in the Prairies in the
mobilization against the protective tariff, the agitation for a new role for
the dominion income tax as an "equalizer" after the war was at first marginal, originating in the Maritimes and making its way, by way of modernist
rhetoric, to the centre. The structural tension that saw the dominion with
the potential capacity, though not the political will, to raise an unprecedented amount of tax revenue and the provinces with growing demands
for social programs – particularly mothers' allowances – was first expressed
in regional terms as a demand for redress of a specific set of local problems.
When the same problems that plagued the provincial governments in
the Maritimes spread to other provinces in the 1930s, the dominion was
forced to respond more enthusiastically and act accordingly. But the crisis
in the Maritimes helped to frame that ultimate response by originating a

rhetorical frame through which the Rowell-Sirois process would view the dominion taxing power. The Maritimes' regional protest called forth a new, modern concept of federalism that would see Ottawa use its extensive and potentially lucrative taxing power to transfer funds on an automatic basis to provinces with limited taxing capacity to fund their social programs – a scandalous concept knotted, like conscription of wealth, into a controversial slogan: "fiscal need."

The Maritime Rights movement began in the early 1920s when the governments of Nova Scotia, New Brunswick, and Prince Edward Island pressed Ottawa for better terms and for a modern, reformed fiscal federalism. The movement was an expression of profound discontent with and alienation from Confederation in the region caused by changes in the Canadian economy.[18] The turn to hydroelectricity in Ontario and Quebec as the fuel of the manufacturing economy meant a diminished market for coal, the region's premier export to central Canada. At the same time, the dominion government removed the subsidy on the intercolonial rail line, making shipping coal and manufactured goods west prohibitively expensive. These factors made the recession of the early 1920s the Maritimes' "Great Depression," a more catastrophic economic meltdown than the 1930s would be in the region. Rather than simply a cry of regional despair or another crafty attempt to wrestle better terms from central Canada, though, the movement that arose in the three Maritime provinces in the 1920s was an expression of a newly energized political power.

The Maritime Rights movement is best understood, in fact, as a movement of political modernism, a hinge between people's enlightenment in the immediate postwar period and a new, modern politics focused on the role of the dominion taxing power in generating greater equality among regions. Indeed, as E.R. Forbes has made clear in his classic study of the Maritime Rights movement, the regional campaign for a more active and egalitarian federalism was an outgrowth itself of movements for progressive reform. A coalition of professionals, businessmen, organized labour, and intellectuals began calling for more active state involvement in various spheres of civic and provincial life. As Forbes notes, "all these progressive proposals placed strong pressure upon provincial governments to inaugurate or expand programmes for which revenue was not available."[19] The demands for reform, that is, exposed the weak fiscal capacity of the Maritime provinces; this weakness in turn "led progressive elements ... into a ... campaign for Maritime unity, one object of which was to wrest from the federal government a 'fair' share of Dominion revenues."[20] For full citizenship to be available to everyone in the Maritimes, reformers argued, the Maritime provinces needed a guarantee of increased tax revenue – which would have to come from outside the region. To create even the possibility of government spending on social programs, that is, required a new role for the dominion treasury.

Provincial governments began demanding emergency funds from the dominion government. The introduction of the income war tax was key to transforming the regular demand for a subsidy into a more modern demand for an automatic transfer of tax revenue from the dominion to the provinces. It was the discrepancy between rising dominion revenues from new taxes that had been brought in during the First World War and rising provincial expenditures that caused dysfunction and resentment. But the focus on income taxation wasn't the only modern theme.

Like the farmer and labour movements in the period before the introduction of the income war tax, the Maritime Rights movement was characterized by a new, modern understanding of the party system; although electorates in the Maritimes elected members of the old parties to Parliament in the 1920s, they did so in a modern way, using the parties as instruments of popular grievances, investing little in their partisan differences.[21] Rather than supporting parties based upon the attribution of meaningful differences to the Liberal and Conservative Parties, that is, Maritime Rights used elections to express the movement's dissatisfaction by strategically denying support to parties that ignored their concerns. The first phase of this campaign was in 1921, when support for the Union government collapsed. "The striking change in voting patterns," Forbes says, "was an indication of the Maritimers' attempt to secure their 'rights' through a change in government."[22] Defeating Union candidates meant electing Liberal candidates, who swore during the election "to advocate and stand by Maritime rights first, last, and all the time." Led by a prime minister fixated on the more obvious threat posed by the Progressive Party in the west, however, these candidates disappointed their supporters once in office.[23] The next time around, in 1925, Maritime Rights targeted the Liberals, delivering "a crushing verdict of the Maritime Provinces in criticism of the non-recognition of [the King] government of the Maritime Provinces' rights."[24] Although political observers were "accustomed to discover political storms in the West," the Maritime Rights campaign had wiped out two parties in the region in a decade.[25]

The Maritime Rights storm had at last succeeded in attracting the attention of a much weakened King, who, concerned about the survival of his government, acted quickly to give the appearance of being concerned about the issues. He set up the Royal Commission on Maritime

Claims in April 1926, under the leadership of Andrew Rae Duncan, to examine the case. By the time it reported in September, Governor General Viscount Byng's rejection of King's request to dissolve Parliament had triggered a scandal (the King-Byng crisis) that culminated in an election that restored King to surer ground. The Duncan Commission recommended an immediate emergency transfer of funds, which Ottawa did, dulling the immediate threat of lost seats. But the more fundamental and controversial question, whether Ottawa should provide ongoing support to the Maritimes to meet their fiscal needs, was left to a later investigation. After a series of delays, Ottawa agreed, following a conference with representatives of the Maritimes in August 1934, to appoint a new royal commission to carry out the reassessment of subsidies proposed by the Royal Commission on Maritime Claims in 1926.[26] In the end, that is, that later investigation had to wait eight more years and likely would not have happened at all if the government of Nova Scotia had not called a commission of its own.

The province's Royal Commission of Economic Enquiry, chaired by J.H. Jones, was called in 1933 and reported in 1934. Although it is often relegated to the status of a footnote, the Jones Commission "foreshadowed" the Rowell-Sirois Commission in important ways, as Stephen Henderson has argued: it gathered "the latest in constitutional and liberal thinking in Canada," and, in considering the constitutional and fiscal crisis of the period, it "reached many of the same conclusions as Rowell-Sirois."[27] It relied extensively on the contributions of two noted political economists: Harold Adams Innis and Norman McLeod Rogers. Innis was the founder of the staples theory of Canadian history and, despite his contribution to the Jones Commission, a vocal critic of intellectuals' involvement in politics. Rogers had served as an assistant to King in the 1920s and was comfortable both in academia and in partisan politics. His brief on fiscal Confederation and Nova Scotia's place in it was the centrepiece of the Jones Commission in terms of its reputation and influence. As the star of the reform-minded intellectuals, Rogers was invited to present a shorter version of his brief in the pages of *Canadian Forum*, which he did in a series of articles in the fall of 1934.

In explaining the challenges of public finance in Nova Scotia, Rogers echoed the *Grain Growers' Guide* in underlining the fact that the tariff needed to be understood as both "a tax and a subsidy."[28] The National Policy, by creating a single national economy, had had the effect of concentrating wealth and industrial development in one part of the country. This seriously undermined the ability of most provinces to raise money through

direct taxation, as the BNA Act dictated, because of the low incomes of
the residents of those provinces. "Differences in taxable capacity of the
provinces may have existed in some measure at the time of Confederation," Rogers acknowledged, but "it is undeniable that such differences
have been greatly accentuated as a result of fiscal policies in operation since
the adoption of the National Policy in 1879. Largely as a result of these
policies the industrial life of the Dominion has been concentrated more
and more in the central provinces of Ontario and Quebec."[29] The tariff
made Ontario and Quebec wealthy, but more importantly it made the
other provinces less so. The development of a strong manufacturing economy in central Canada "has been accompanied in considerable degree by
a corresponding decline in the wealth and income of the other provinces
in the Dominion." Rogers argued that "tariff incidence" had to be key to
considering the overall fairness of dominion-provincial fiscal relations.[30]

The income war tax, though it was not intended to have any effect on
dominion-provincial relations, was a lucky break for those who wanted
to find a way out of the fiscal malaise of the Canadian Constitution in
the 1920s. The income tax, Rogers argued, "enables the Dominion to
act as a redistributing agency through which some portion of the profits
accruing through the protective tariff can be utilized either for direct
subsidies to the provinces which have suffered most through the effects of
the tariff or for the maintenance of common standards of social services
throughout the entire Dominion."[31] Were the dominion to use its taxing
power to be a "redistributing agency," taxing across the country to fund
social programs in low-income provinces, Rogers argued, it would be an
effective offset of the regional effects of the tariff, which had undermined
industrial development outside Ontario and Quebec. "Unless these services are assumed by the Dominion with its unrestricted taxing powers,"
Rogers said, "the provinces with low taxable capacity will be compelled
to maintain standards of governmental service inferior to those supplied
in the provinces which have been the chief beneficiaries of the fiscal policies of the Dominion during the past sixty years." The "assumption by
the Dominion" of the costs of social programs in less wealthy provinces,
Rogers insisted, was "the only satisfactory means of alleviating the continuing effects of the unequal incidence of the tariff upon the financial
position of the provinces."[32] On the strength of his brief, the commission
recommended that the shelved portions of the ten-year-old commission
on Maritime Rights be re-examined.

Provincial governments across the country, not just in the Maritimes,
were facing bankruptcy, while the dominion government held all the

taxing power, when a second royal commission was established in 1935 to clarify the applicability of fiscal need in federal-provincial relations. The man chosen to chair the commission was Thomas White, the retired former minister of finance who had grudgingly introduced the income war tax in 1917. White and his commission spent most of the year looking into the issue, receiving submissions from the provinces, and disagreeing. In his majority report, he acknowledged that the Maritimes had serious fiscal problems: high rates of taxation that yielded very little revenue (because incomes were low) and a lack of basic administrative infrastructure largely caused by low tax revenue.[33] White agreed "that the Maritime Provinces are, unlike the other Provinces, not able to adequately finance expenditures for public welfare, in particular Old Age Pensions, Mothers' Allowances and Child Protection," and he observed that "New Brunswick has no Old Age or Mothers' Pensions system. Prince Edward Island has provided Old Age Pensions on a limited scale but has no Mothers' Pensions system."[34] Taxes in the Maritimes were heavy compared with those in Ontario and Quebec yet raised little revenue. The old economic hardships of the early 1920s and the current economic hardships of the early 1930s made a bad situation even worse.[35] White recommended that Ottawa send a further subsidy, arguing that this kind of emergency response was how the relationship had worked historically and should continue to work.

The recommendation of an additional subsidy was tied to an explicit rejection of the more controversial aspect of the Maritime Rights case: the insistence on fiscal need as a legitimate basis for a modernized fiscal federalism. In recommending a new subsidy, that is, White explicitly rejected the idea that fiscal need could be the basis of an ongoing and automatic transfer of funds from the dominion to the Maritimes. He argued that establishing a formal mechanism in which the dominion would fund provincial expenditures would be irresponsible and even unconstitutional, for it would give Parliament direct responsibility for provinces' finances. At the same time, it would allow provinces to spend beyond their means, in the knowledge that their "needs" would be met by the dominion. Parliament would be responsible for financing a legislative program approved under the authority of a provincial legislature. The province's legislative program would be dictated by the dominion's finances, or the dominion's finances would be affected by the province's legislative program. Either way, the basic principles of responsible government and parliamentary supremacy would be jeopardized. "Responsibility must go hand in hand with authority," White concluded. "Power to spend must entail responsibility for expenditures."³⁶ The concept of need, he argued, was too vague to be workable politically, constitutionally, and administratively, and it would, if made a practice of political economy, perilously undermine parliamentary federalism and responsible government.

White's rejection of fiscal need echoed the dominion's brief to the commission, heaping scorn on the region's "alleged fiscal need," insisting vehemently that it was without legal or constitutional basis, and asserting that "the Dominion has been fully alive throughout to the danger of an invidious doctrine of this kind" from the time of Confederation.³⁷ A permanent fiscal relationship based upon the provinces' needs, the brief noted, "would obviously be an incentive to extravagant spending on the part of recipient governments."³⁸ Nor did the argument that modern industrial society required a more active role for government impress the dominion's lawyers, who noted that "the Maritime Provinces make repeated reference to the expansion of functions of government," but they pointed out that "it is a matter of common knowledge and in fact is evident from their submissions that opinions differ considerably from time to time and among different communities as to the necessity for such expansions and as to their direction and extent."³⁹ As well as denying the validity of the doctrine of fiscal need, the brief argued against the immediate subsidy.

The centrality of the income war tax to the controversy over fiscal federalism was made clear by commissioner John A. Mathieson, who disagreed forcefully with White's dismissal of fiscal need and whose dissenting opinion was included in the commission's report. "The fields of taxation surrendered by the provinces to the Dominion have proved prolific sources of revenue, far in excess of what the 'fathers of Confederation' could have anticipated or even dreamed," Mathieson noted.⁴⁰ Similar statements appeared throughout the 1920s and 1930s, drawing attention to the increasing inappropriateness of the original division of federal powers. But more powerful than the actual revenues accruing to Ottawa based upon its power of taxation was the *potential* revenue. And here, especially, the income war tax was important: a weak tax, it was really more an idea of what might be, of the role that the dominion could play, if its latent powers were made significantly more manifest, than a material fact. The idea of the income war tax inspired equal parts of concern and excitement and was an inspiration to more than just the advocates of Maritime Rights. The pressures on the Maritimes to provide municipal services comparable to those in other provinces were fuelling demands for the dominion government to leave direct taxation once again to the provinces, but the pressure from western provinces to lower or abolish

the protective tariff, Ottawa's key source of indirect taxation, was pushing in the opposite direction. Some sort of tax agreement between the
provinces and the dominion was clearly necessary, but the Duncan and
White Commissions, which had examined the case in the Maritimes, had
shied away from recommending comprehensive and systematic changes
to the constitutional and fiscal arrangements between the governments.
The dominion-provincial conference of 1927 had ended with a call for a
commission of inquiry to look at the problem nationally, a call repeated
regularly by individual provinces and at any gathering of provinces over
the eight years that followed.

The Maritime Rights controversy over fiscal need introduced the novel
idea that the dominion should use the income war tax to redistribute taxing capacity from province to province. By the time Rogers and Mathieson were articulating this idea, the Depression was in full force across the
country, and the belief that the BNA Act – as interpreted by the JCPC –
was a political problem was widespread. The rejected idea of fiscal need
was part of the intellectual context that the commissioners absorbed in
addressing the solution to the Depression. Nova Scotia Premier Angus L.
Macdonald, addressing the commission in 1937, suggested that "Ottawa
could serve as the distributing agent for the wealth of other provinces,"
distributing taxable capacity "on a more equitable basis."[41] Although the
Maritimes were seen throughout the period as a reactionary backwater,
the region in fact made the most direct contribution to what would be
the key recommendation of the Rowell-Sirois Report: the federal government's monopoly of income taxation.

The idea of using dominion revenue to fund social spending arose out
of catastrophic economic conditions in the Maritimes in the 1920s, was
the basis of innovations in party politics in the region, and was clarified
and legitimized by the intellectual work of Norman McLeod Rogers, who
served first as an expert political economist to the government of Nova Scotia and then as a dominion cabinet minister. By the 1930s, the catastrophic
collapse of capitalism and of faith in the old political order had spread to
the west, prompting the dominion to call the Rowell-Sirois Commission.[42]

"A Clear and Definite Minimum Program": Parties and the Rhetoric of Political Difference in the 1930s

The Great Depression undermined the relevance of traditional party politics, which had been concerned with the question of which party, Liberals

or Conservatives, should be trusted to direct the development of a capitalist economy. "There is a great body of public opinion that is disgusted with the two older parties," H.H. Stevens said in 1935 on the occasion of his leaving the Conservative Party to found the Reconstruction Party.[43] Although he overstated the contempt with which Canadians regarded the major parties (which continued to hold power federally through the 1930s), the belief that "the distinctions between Tories and Grits are nothing more than those between the ins and outs" was becoming much more common in the 1930s.[44] The self-consciously modern perspective of the *Grain Growers' Guide,* that the parties were interchangeable instruments of the country's business interests, was formalized in the Progressive Party, which emerged from the conscription crisis in the west and held the balance of power in the House of Commons through the 1920s. The Progressive Party was not just a third party competing for power against the other two parties; it embodied the modernist rejection of party and of "the mock warfare of government and opposition."[45] The detachment with which organized farmers and labour had viewed the partisan appeals of Liberalism and Conservatism in 1911 and 1917, and which the Progressive Party represented, became increasingly widespread in the 1920s and 1930s. New parties with more distinct and less liberal programs emerged, some of them as breakaway factions of the Conservative Party, and some from social movements outside parliamentary politics, but all of them were more attuned than the old parties to the crisis of capitalism.

With a wide expansion of political possibilities, and a rapid proliferation of third parties, political differences were undergoing a chaotic modernization. New parties emerged between 1919 and 1939, but the main period of innovation was 1934–35, when the Social Credit Party, the Cooperative Commonwealth Federation (CCF), and the Reconstruction Party all emerged. Liberals and Conservatives had to redefine themselves within a new political landscape in which their old appeals meant little. The National Policy of tariff- and railway-fuelled development was breaking down as a basis of shared assumptions, and political differences were increasingly tied to competing visions of what the state should do to correct for the economic crisis – visions in which income taxation, not the tariff, played the central role. The language of left/right differences was increasingly referred to as a way to clarify differences, though in practice it could do little to order a mixed field.

The Liberal and Conservative Parties were in awkward positions as politics began to radicalize around questions of fiscal power and public responsibility for welfare in the context of the Depression. The Liberals under King did their best to avoid appearing to take a position and attacked the Conservatives for either exposing or obfuscating their true nature as an ideological, right-wing party. Under Bennett, the Conservatives actively sought to elude banishment to the right extreme by launching the New Deal, a set of dominion social reforms that, not surprisingly, was declared unconstitutional by the JCPC. In opposition again, the Conservatives under Robert Manion went in the other direction, painting the Liberals and every other party as communists. The *Canadian Forum* editorialized that the electorate was to be "provided with one simple, false election issue by the Conservative Party. The Canadian people, it appears, must choose between Mr. Manion and Communism. There are no half-way houses." The editorial described Conservatism as "a residue of reactionary left-overs" that would "absorb its truculent left wing with modest concessions of social legislation."[46] It is notable that a party of "reactionary left-overs" could have a "left wing": that the language of "left" and "right" applied even within the Conservative Party meant that the terms had been completely unmoored from their original context. Also, that its "left wing" would demand any social legislation indicated that the label might have been a simplification.

The prospect of presenting a clear choice to the electorate between socialism and capitalism was a great dream to socialist intellectuals in the 1930s, one that inspired a lot of writing aimed at teasing out the differences and similarities among the various parties that had popped up and claimed the mantle of political modernism in the period. The true dream for social democrats, of course, was that King would frame the election as being a contest between the CCF and Liberals rather than between the Liberals and Conservatives. "If the Liberal party proved unwise enough to accept the gauntlet of socialism thrown down by the C.C.F. and thereby made capitalism versus socialism the election issue," Graham Spry noted giddily, then "the election would have a supreme educational value and the results would have an enduring significance" – adding that such a contest would be forever deferred by "Mr. King's facility for erecting the unimportant into the significant."[47] Many authors, though, blamed the divided field of alternatives to the old parties for splitting up the modernist vote. A 1936 editorial noted sourly that "a million voters broke away from the old parties and marked their ballots for candidates opposed in various ways to the present system" and asked "can these million voters be organized in a single political movement that will present a greater challenge to the old parties than the competing groups presented?"[48] An answer was provided in the following issue by David

Lewis, the CCF's organization man, who pronounced that "a fusion of the C.C.F., Communists, Social Crediters, Reconstructionists, [and] Left Liberals ... would, under present Canadian conditions, create confusion, compromise the socialist objective and the C.C.F. as a party, and might even, by way of reaction, call forth a strengthening of the right forces."[49] The fusion of left groups, and the electoral threat that they would pose as a unified bloc, raised the obvious threat of a unified bloc of Conservatives and Liberals, which would be all the stronger at the polls. (It is interesting to note that the same concerns arose on the right in the early 1940s.)

How to define the new parties, and how to determine whether they were ultimately on side with or at odds with the CCF and socialism, were common and recurring sources of debate in the *Canadian Forum*. An editorial in August 1939 defined "Progressive candidates" as "all those opposed to the two old parties" and argued that such parties "should not stand in each other's way."[50] The assertion that opposition to the old parties itself was progressive suggests that the word *progressive* still carried its old definition as "nonpartisan" or at least not subject to the party machines. The editorial clarified that any noncompetition proposals would depend on "a clear and definite minimum program which the various progressive parties can accept and for the sake of which they agree to bury their differences until those measures are achieved."[51] What that "minimum program" would be the editorial did not say.

A number of letters appeared in response to the editorial on noncompetition among progressive parties. One letter writer said that "I agree that the C.C.F. leaders are correct in refusing anything like a 'popular front' with" other new parties, "for with the present confusion of policies in this country it is necessary to have one party which will insistently keep the issue of socialism before the electorate. But it is also necessary to avoid splitting the progressive vote whenever possible if more than a handful of leftists are to be elected."[52] It is unclear in this letter whether the words *progressive, leftist,* and *socialist* are being used as synonyms or whether one or more of them is considered a subset of the other. Whether Social Credit or the Reconstruction Party, a faction of the Conservative Party under Stevens that contested the 1935 election, were progressive, they certainly were not socialist. Spry noted in a 1935 article that the platforms of the Reconstruction Party and CCF were "very similar in language though fundamentally different in policy."[53] In this instance, the language of the left–right spectrum did little to clarify an inescapably messy political reality.

A number of authors underlined the point that fiscal policy, correctly interpreted, served as a better line of division than party platforms, which tended to be vague and self-inflating. How a government taxes and spends, and how it affects the division of wealth and income, seemed like good ways to define political programs if they could be made legible to the public. Frank Underhill, in his critical review of Bennett's New Deal proposals, claimed that "the acid test of a capitalist government's sincerity in desiring to distribute more evenly the benefits of the capitalist system is its taxation policy." Somewhat pleased with the generalities of the proposed changes, he was suspicious of the lack of specifics, saying that "the fiscal system of the Bennett government so far has been devoted to passing the burden of taxation from the rich to those of smaller incomes."[54] A few years later Eugene Forsey, a CCF adviser and perennial candidate, concluded his regular review of the national economy in the summer of 1939 by saying that "it is ... clear that the Dominion government need not be anything like as hard up as it is, or anything like as niggardly in social service expenditures." Turning up the partisan dials, Forsey continued that "clearest of all is the fact that no Liberal or Conservative government is going to apply any of these measures. An intelligent electorate should be able to draw the moral."[55] The clear line, for CCF intellectuals, was between those who wanted to use the power of the state to fund social programs and those who did not. J.L. Ilsley, neither a socialist nor a social scientist, offered the thought in 1940 that politics had changed dramatically in a few years:

> I am not very old, but in my lifetime I have noticed a great change in public opinion in Canada as to what creates cleavages ... The divisions that arise in the Dominion of Canada to-day are economic divisions, not racial and religious divisions; they are due to trouble between various classes of society, between various occupations and various industries, and such trouble is economic.[56]

The party system might not have been a clear reflection of such cleavages; however, for a partisan Liberal and minister of the crown to draw attention to them in public, they must have been fairly obvious.

The party system in the 1930s was in turmoil. A growing disenchantment with the old parties and their appeals couldn't overcome a lack of coherence in the development of new, modern parties with competing and incommensurable programs. It is a historian's cliché to say that such a situation, viewed in retrospect, was too much in flux to allow much generalizing. However, an editorial in the *Canadian Forum* said the same thing – "the situation is very fluid" – adding that "historians a generation hence will demonstrate in the society of our day there was going on an inevitable evolution towards some goal of which by that time they have become conscious."[57] What it is possible to generalize about is that, on the left during that time, at least, the frustration with the intricacies of the ever-changing party system was matched by an equivalent sense of possibility, a feeling that the time had come, or was coming soon, for a new kind of citizenship. "Is it not time," Dorothy G. Steeves asked, "that we visualized the possibility of a Dominion-wide social insurance scheme on a contributory basis, where feasible, but extending equal benefits to those who were not privileged to pay their share?" Steeves was commenting on the Rowell-Sirois Report, but her remarks show something more expansive. "Now is the time to prepare our social machinery," she insisted, claiming that "social security in the future will be the real unifying factor of Canada and the basis of a new Canadian culture."[58]

"As if Speaking of an Undivided Power": The Rhetoric of Dominion Taxation

The recommendation of the Royal Commission on Dominion-Provincial Relations that the collapsing fiscal patchwork of the 1930s be replaced by a single, modern, unitary, and powerful income tax at the federal level was the product of a complex of crises that dominated Canadian politics between the two world wars: a crisis in the party system originating in the Liberals' abandonment of reciprocity in the 1890s and brought to a head in the elections of 1911 and 1917, which had metastasized by the 1930s into a chaotic and convoluted field of parties; a crisis of capitalism originating in the Maritimes in the 1920s and spreading to other regions by the 1930s, which called for a new relationship between the federal and provincial governments; and a constitutional crisis arising from the inapplicability of the British North America Act to that new relationship. Certainly, there were other factors involved: intellectuals drawn into dominion service from university departments of political economy played key roles in pushing for and shaping the commission. Norman McLeod Rogers, fresh from his success as the author of the Jones Commission brief on Nova Scotia's place in Confederation, was elected to the House of Commons as a Liberal in 1935 and appointed minister of labour. Rogers became the dominion's principal recipient of correspondence from municipalities and other organizations complaining about the administration of relief and calling for a commission to examine its financing – much of it citing his own analysis back to him. But the Rowell-Sirois Commission's recommendations reflected a wide social consensus on the desirability of a new, modern fiscal framework. Intellectuals were merely the instruments of that consensus.

The commission's recommendations, however without precedent they might have appeared, were wrapped in the authority of historical interpretation. Donald Creighton, who wrote the historical study of Confederation, cites the views of A.T. Galt and John A. Macdonald as arguments against the JCPC's interpretation of the BNA Act. Galt's reference to "the power of taxation" – "as if speaking of an undivided power," in Creighton's evocative and telling phrase – having been "confined to the General Legislature" was proof that the dominion was intended to have, at least in principle, all of the taxing power in the country. What is more, the BNA Act "gave the Dominion unlimited powers of taxation" because the "magnitude of the burdens, actual and prospective, which were being transferred to the Dominion, called for commensurate fiscal resources and powers."[59] The exhilaration of dominion power was a common trait among those connected to the commission. Alex Skelton's copy of the *British North America Act and Amendments 1867–1927* has a lone enthusiastic pencil mark next to section 92, 10, c, which reads thus: "Such Works as, although wholly situate within the Province, are before or after their Execution declared by the Parliament of Canada to be for the general Advantage of Canada or for the Advantage of Two or more of the Provinces."[60] Clearly, the prospect of increasing Ottawa's power was exciting as both the belated fulfillment of a derailed history and for its own sake.

The imaginative power of the dominion that Creighton, Skelton, and others demonstrated is linked in the report to the imaginary power of income taxation itself, producing an electrifying unification of power. Throughout the report, the dominion tax is referred to as an "equalizing instrument," an echo of Leacock's description of it as a terrific engine, or as a mechanism. These descriptions suggest that income taxation is powerful, modern, and a precise tool for achieving some purpose. Like the contributions of scholars and experts to the government, and of statistics to the analysis of economic policy, it is also increasingly identified as scientific. Above all, it is effective but works only if it is one instrument whose action is legible and coherent.

Certainly, there were other motives, on both what would have been increasingly called the right and what would have been increasingly called the left, for centralizing income taxation. Business groups had repeatedly been asking Rogers for a reprieve from the "irksome multiplicity of returns and tax forms" by having what one group insistently called "ONE INCOME TAX," preferably at the provincial level but if necessary at the dominion level. Socialists, inspired by Fabian example, also believed that there should be a single income tax. Although the League for Social Reconstruction, the intellectual wing of the CCF, was not enthusiastic about taxes, noting that "in a fully socialized economy ... taxes will disappear," it still spoke of income taxation in *Social Planning for Canada* as if it was only a dominion measure.[61] These requests from groups at different places along the political spectrum arose out of different desires and concerns. The fact that they all wanted a single income tax at the federal level helps to explain why the Rowell-Sirois Commission reached the conclusions that it did and perhaps suggests that there was something beyond party and position that motivated their demands.

The appeal of income taxation was that it was modern and scientific and could help to rationalize not only the tax system but also the system of political differences. It was powerful and necessary and, if centralized in the dominion, could be the instrument that would fix the conceptual problems dogging Canadian politics. This was undoubtedly a major inspiration for the report's core recommendations. The report pointed out that, "as consumption taxes make up nearly 60 per cent of total government revenues (which in turn, it will be remembered, equal some 30 per cent of the national income), and as various forms of business tax make up another 30 per cent," regressivity was the dominant characteristic of the fiscal structure. This meant that, in the words of the report, "only 10 per cent of total government revenues are in forms to which any scientific principles of progressivity can be applied in order to redress the regressivity inherent in the heavy Canadian consumption taxes."[62] This passage is interesting for a number of reasons. The Rowell-Sirois Report accepted regressive consumption taxes (including the protective tariff) as a central feature of the Canadian tax system. But income tax is associated directly with modernity and science: only income tax can offer "scientific principles of progressivity." Progressivity is understood as a corrective, something that one adds to existing tax systems to offset or "redress" the perverse effects of existing taxes. More than that, though, the passage laments that so little of the dominion's taxing power is capable of being used with precision for political ends of any kind.

In fact, however, the report declared, because of the combination of dominion and provincial income taxes, progressivity in Canada, far from being scientific, "has been carried to a fantastic extreme." The poor are overtaxed by consumption taxes, the rich are overtaxed by income taxes, while the middle class is undertaxed. "It is primarily by adjustment of the income tax curve of progressivity," the report argued, "that this trough in the curve of progressivity in the tax system as a whole can be removed, and the extreme impositions at each end of the curve modified."[63]

The report was not suggesting that there was an ideal rate of progressivity; rather, it was claiming that it was possible to administer the income tax, to use its power of progressivity, to elicit political effects. In that sense, the rate of progressivity might be scientific but not absolute. It can clearly reflect different political beliefs and different and competing conceptualizations of what social justice between classes might look like – what the commission called "social philosophy" or political differences. As its report said, "equity as between income classes is basically a matter of social philosophy, and it must be left to the political crystallization of the prevalent philosophy to determine, for example, whether taxation should be progressive, and if so, at what rate."[64] The progressivity of an income tax will reflect the political outlook of the government in power. Income taxation is, or ought to be, a clear measure of the political position of the party in power.

The dominion-provincial division of powers, however, made it difficult for any social philosophy to be reflected in what the report called scientific principles of progressivity. In direct response to its suggestion about the prevalent social philosophy determining progressivity, the commission claimed that "it is important to note the obstacles to the use of the income tax as an instrument of either social philosophy or efficient social practice which are presented by the existing division of tax powers and the joint occupation of the field by the Dominion, provincial, and even municipal governments." Although income taxation should reflect, through its application of scientific principles of progressivity, the dominant conception of social justice, in fact "the joint occupation of the field makes it mechanically impossible to develop an income tax which will, in itself, apply to different income groups in what is currently considered an equitable manner, and which can be adjusted to the desired degree of progressivity of the tax system as a whole."[65] This was one of the arguments for assigning income taxation exclusively to the dominion: only with a single taxing authority could income taxation be politically legible and lend clarity and order to a crowded field of political options.

The report did not directly address the question of differences among parties and the desirability of bringing clarity to a chaotic field of electoral options. The authors might have had those concerns less immediately on their minds than contributors to the *Canadian Forum* and other partisan intellectuals, for whom drawing clear lines among parties and separating friend from foe were higher priorities. But the fact that the report made a point of bemoaning the effect of divided jurisdiction on the legibility of the governing party's social philosophy suggests that the question of the relationship between parties and taxation was in the air in the 1930s. The desire for clarity, for a mechanism that could accurately reflect the governing philosophy through its curve of progressivity, was one of the arguments that it presented for a single taxing power, the dominion income tax. Read alongside the agonized hair splitting of left-wing intellectuals who tried to use the left–right spectrum to make sense of a confused party system, this preoccupation reads like a fragment of a shared mood, a common enthusiasm for a new and clearer political imaginary, freed by the operation of the "equalizing instrument of taxation" from the dissimulating sentimentality of the past and the anxious confusion of the present.

***

The belief that the dominion power of taxation needed to be strengthened substantially to correct for the inconsistencies of capitalist development across Canada was common by the end of the 1930s. The Constitution, interpreted by the Judicial Committee of the Privy Council in a way that effectively denied the possibility of using either provincial or dominion power to redistribute income, became the target of a modernist campaign, one that aimed to clear the ground for a new relationship between the provinces and their citizens using the power of taxation. Whereas the west had led the push against the tariff and called for a direct tax to replace it in 1910, in the aftermath of the Great War it was the east that pushed for a more active role for the federal treasury, a demand that eventually focused on an expansion of the federal direct taxation introduced in 1917. The idea of using dominion revenue to fund social spending arose from catastrophic economic conditions in the Maritimes in the 1920s, was the basis of innovations in party politics in the region, and was clarified and legitimized by the intellectual work of Norman McLeod Rogers, who served first as an expert political economist to the government of Nova Scotia and later as a dominion cabinet minister. By the 1930s, the catastrophic collapse of the economic order spread to the west, prompting the dominion to launch an investigation of its fiscal relations with the provinces.

The Rowell-Sirois Commission proposed a centralization of the power of income taxation in Canada under the authority of the federal

government. Income taxation was cast as the solution to the fiscal problems of Confederation, as the "equalizing instrument of taxation" – just
as it had been cast as "the terrific engine" in the period immediately
following the war. The commission offered a strengthened dominion
income tax as the solution to the constitutional stalemate over the federal
division of taxing and spending power. With its proposed new power,
the dominion treasury could undo some of the damage that the tariff
had done to provincial equality by financing more equitable government
services across the country. On a practical level, then, the recommendations were the outcome of the long, messy battle over economics and
the Constitution originally expressed as fiscal need. Using the federal
power of taxation to fund provincial spending on relief and other social
programs pointed the way to a practical resolution of the immediate
problem of paying for the support of indigents within the framework of
the BNA Act and established the script that would dominate postwar
social politics.

On a more imaginative level, the Rowell-Sirois recommendations
also seem to reflect a widespread urge to find a new, more modern language of political differences. Building upon the movements against the
tariff and for a steeply graduated dominion income tax, the movement
of Maritime reformers for a radical solution to the fiscal inequalities
among provinces extended the modernist project of renewing politics
by displacing the tariff and nationalism from the centre of the Canadian
political imaginary and substituting income inequality and a progressive income tax. The concept of fiscal need, though officially dismissed
as a principle of public finance, connected to the earlier critiques of
dominion finance and – as the economic catastrophe of the Maritimes
in the 1920s became nation-wide in the 1930s – forcefully underscored
the need for a new political imaginary. The brittleness of the old fiscal
system, tethered to nineteenth-century principles of public expenditure
by the rigidity of the Constitution and the weakness of the tariff, was
seen clearly. The parties that had defined their electoral appeals on the
basis of the tariff looked less relevant and had to adapt their appeals as
new parties entered an increasingly crowded and chaotic electoral field.
At a time when political differences were becoming more confusing
and people were demanding greater clarity in political terminology, the
Report of the Royal Commission on Dominion-Provincial Relations suggested that income taxation might also have held promise as an instrument for increasing the legibility of competing political programs,
provided that it was powerful and unitary.

4

A Modern Measure? The Income Tax Sublime and the Left–Right Spectrum, 1940–45

Ministers of finance are not generally celebrated for their linguistic self-consciousness, though speaking is clearly part of their job. Rudolf Goldscheid's oft-cited line that "the budget is the skeleton of the state stripped of all misleading ideologies" is true, but in practice budgets are never presented without carefully tailored rhetorical clothing.[1] Finance ministers have to be careful with words; their public pronouncements are crafted to convey authority, caution, responsibility, and, at appropriate times, worry. Successful expression of these qualities depends on the convincing use of language to which politicians rarely draw attention. So when J.L. Ilsley rose in the House of Commons to begin his budget speech on June 23, 1942, his preliminary declaration was remarkable. "Last year," he said, "I referred to the financial requirements of 1941–42, which were difficult to define clearly, as 'staggering.' Confronted now with much larger requirements, set out as the simplest sums in arithmetic, I must perforce drop all adjectives and try to state, as clearly as one who isn't a prophet may state, what they mean in terms of the future."[2] Ilsley's remarks reflect his sense of being at the centre of a daunting political project. The scale of public finance in the early 1940s was overwhelming. The categories and language through which the minister of finance had made sense of previous budget provisions no longer accommodated the numbers necessary to cover the dominion's anticipated expenses. By drawing attention to the poverty of the available vocabulary, the minister was marking the stunning situation of public finance at the time – what we might call the income tax sublime.

The unprecedented scale of public finance in the early 1940s, when an unprecedented burden of public spending was shared among an unprecedented number of individual taxpayers, created a situation that overwhelmed people's ability to make sense of it. The income tax sublime produced a conceptual void that, having been marked by Ilsley in his budget speech, had to be filled with a new imaginary. That new imaginary, which tied the universality of income taxation to the universality of social programs that provided economic security, is what Shirley Tillotson has called "the citizenship of contribution."[3] The income war tax, since its introduction in 1917, had only taxed high incomes. Income taxation had only affected most people as an idea, not as an experience. It had been very powerful in the rhetoric that it had produced by suggesting a set of political possibilities. Critics decried it as a weak creature and found it wanting. Over its first two decades, its weakness made it an object of controversy and concern and arguably made it more important and powerful rhetorically than a more fiscally powerful and ubiquitous income tax would have been. Ilsley's budget speech marked the moment when the powerful possibility of income taxation became a powerful social fact, what Bob Russell has called a "fiscal revolution," in which Ilsley, appointed as the minister of finance in 1940 with a mandate to enact the fiscal recommendations of the Rowell-Sirois Commission, set out to make dominion taxation powerful and universal.[4] Faced with resistance from some provinces, the dominion government had to act alone, acting as if the provinces had acquiesced and forcing a retreat formalized into a surrender with a series of tax rental agreements between the various provinces and the dominion.

The forceful resolution to the fiscal crises of the 1930s was accompanied by an increasingly sophisticated use of left and right to illustrate differences among political parties. Speakers in the previous decade more often than not framed their placement of parties on a left–right axis as a question, but by the early 1940s the positioning of parties was becoming more uniform, and people were speaking more confidently about it. Coming out of the Depression, with a broad consensus on the need to address inequality, differences were most often framed as a choice between minor reform and radical reform. The Cooperative Commonwealth Federation, as the parliamentary party most identified with the latter option, was confident in the knowledge that the world was headed in its direction in the early 1940s. The ruling Liberals tended to define themselves as moderate reformers, but in fact the governing party was generally resistant to the implementation of social programs that would entail permanent heavy spending and therefore heavy taxation.[5] The Liberal-CCF dyad created an identity crisis for the Conservatives, who could either campaign to the right of the Liberals as opponents of reform or stake out an uncertain and unprecedented middle ground. What this meant for the party's political fortunes has been explored at length in J.L. Granatstein's *The Politics of Survival*.[6] But the party's identity crisis also had a rhetorical dimension: it mobilized immense intellectual and political energy, in a few short years producing conferences, declarations, a name change, and a complex leadership arrangement. The extensive rhetorical parsing in *Saturday Night*, the leading Conservative magazine of the period, is a unique documentary record of an early, anxious encounter between vividly self-aware right-wing intellectuals and the modern political imaginary.

The income war tax, which had begun as a purely political tax on high incomes in 1917, and whose possibilities had been the object of imaginative fantasies in the previous two decades, became in 1941 and 1942 a tax paid by almost everyone and therefore powerful. Inspired by the logic of Keynesianism and pressured by the exigencies of the war, the dominion spent more and borrowed more than it ever had; inspired by the visions of the Rowell-Sirois Commission and the exigencies of the war, the dominion taxed more people more steeply than it ever had. People who had been immune to the effects of income tax, who had called for a progressive income tax as a way to punish the rich, now discovered that there was a bottom end to the curve of progressivity and that they were at it. People struggled to make sense of numbers that were without precedent and rates of taxation that, as Donald Creighton said, "would have been terrifying even if imaginable only a few years before."[7] The experience of the citizenship of contribution was novel for taxpayers still reeling from the uncertainties of the interwar period and still fluent in nineteenth-century partisan appeals. It affected politics in new ways, and it forced the government and opposition parties to define their identities in its shadow. By the end of the Second World War, a new imaginary of universal citizenship materialized by the taxpayer-funded social state was securely in place and, with it, the language of left and right.

"A POWERFUL INSTRUMENT": INCOME TAXATION IN THE BUDGETS OF 1941 AND 1942

After the release of the Rowell-Sirois Report and in the opening months of the Second World War, the dominion government used its taxing powers to become the indisputably dominant player in the country's internal economy, eclipsing the expanded role that the provinces had taken since the 1890s. The strengthening of the federal income tax was a predictable outcome of a number of simultaneous political factors that had developed over the course of the previous three decades. The demand of western farmers for some form of tariff relief necessitated a shift of the tax base from indirect to direct taxation, which the farmers had explicitly acknowledged in their declaration in Ottawa in 1910. Starting in the 1920s, Maritimers began pushing for a more formalized system of federal-provincial aid, to be financed by a more aggressive federal program of taxation. When the dominion relied exclusively on the tariff for its revenue, the Maritimes' demand for increased federal taxation would have been incommensurable with the western one for tariff relief; the advent of federal income taxation in 1917 opened a new avenue to the resolution of both demands. This solution really became clear, however, only when the Depression of the 1930s exposed the fiscal weakness of provinces and municipalities, responsible for poor relief, and necessitated federal aid for western as well as Maritime provinces.

The Rowell-Sirois Report had clarified what had been on many people's minds for a long time, providing a blueprint for the solution to all of Confederation's fiscal crises that hinged on the expansion of the federal government's taxing power. The resistance of three provinces to the implementation of the report, however, meant that the rational solution worked out by the commission was scuttled. Instead, a less ambitious and less final resolution was hammered out through the sheer force of the federal government's political will, emboldened by the requirements of war finance – a resolution that laid the groundwork for a postwar era in which the implementation of schemes of social reform existed as a possibility. Specific policies regularly encountered resistance in the names of provincial rights and private property rights, so the possibility never materialized as proponents of social reform intended or expected. But the transformation in the federal power of taxation in the period was staggering, even if the lack of a political will to use that power disappointed many.

Although the memory of the 1930s undoubtedly lay behind the growth of federal taxation, the war was the greater immediate factor in pushing and justifying the agenda. Expenditures for war mobilization expanded rapidly in the first three years of the war, requiring the full use of all possible sources of financing, including taxation. The federal government was keen to frame its imposition of unprecedented burdens on taxpayers as a war requirement, as in a 1943 Department of National Revenue advertisement claiming that "income tax dollars are not ordinary dollars ... they are Victory dollars ... necessary dollars to help win the war."[8] The tax burdens were justified by the state as the necessary corollary to necessary spending for war. But the financial requirements of the war were also seen through new economic eyes conditioned by new ideas. Along with the memory of the 1930s, the ideas of public finance that arose from the 1930s allowed the particular strategy and precluded other strategies for paying for the war. A new economic orthodoxy, identified in particular with the ideas of John Maynard Keynes, gave greater legitimacy to massive spending as a stimulant to an underperforming economy, downplaying the risks of inflation that treasurers had traditionally cited as a reason for keeping budgets tightly balanced. These new ideas of how to finance state expenditures gave the intellectual underpinnings for how the federal government paid for the war, as Ken Norrie and Doug Owram point out. "Whereas in World War I the government had hoped to run 'business as usual,'" they say, "no such illusions existed in World War II."[9] Rather than restraining spending, the government opted to finance its spending on a pay-as-you-go basis. The vastly expanded taxation that this approach required had salutary effects not only on limiting the federal government's reliance on credit (though the government did borrow unprecedented amounts of money in the war) but also on curtailing spending and thereby controlling inflation. Although the war provided the immediate rationale and the political justification for massive increases in public spending, that is, the memory of the 1930s and the new economic perspectives that arose from that preceding period determined the federal government's decision to increase tax levels so dramatically.

The proposals in the Rowell-Sirois Report calling for a massive expansion of the taxing role of the federal government therefore found fertile soil in the political context of the first years of the war. With so much spending required solely by the federal government for defence purposes clearly assigned to Ottawa under the British North America Act, it was much more difficult for the provinces to complain that the federal government was invading a sphere of taxation that rightfully belonged to the provinces than it was when the expanded federal tax revenues were intended to pay for social programs that the JCPC had interpreted as belonging exclusively to the provinces. As in the First World War, increased taxation was linked to loyalty and commitment to the war, the difference being that the federal government in this case was moving toward increased taxation for reasons other than its political resonance during wartime and therefore was less half-hearted in its imposition of tax burden and its invasion of provincial tax territory. Resistance to the imposition of the increased federal taxation, though it was literally effective in scuttling an amendment to the BNA Act as envisioned by the Rowell-Sirois Report, was weak when it came to resisting the direct invasion of federal taxing power in part because of wide popular acceptance of the need for war finance as well as the fairness of a tax based upon income.

Another important factor in explaining the political climate in which the recommendations of the Rowell-Sirois Report were acted on was the fear of socialism. Political elites were concerned that widespread dissatisfaction with capitalism arising from the memory of the 1930s would sweep the CCF to power. It was widely recognized that a more powerful federal income tax would be used to finance transfer payments to help poor provinces fund equalizing social programs as well as federal programs to insulate people from income insecurity. These measures had been rejected earlier as dangerously socialist in that they undermined both the incentive for individual citizens to work hard and the pressure on legislators to restrain public spending. Realistically, however, most defenders of free enterprise in the 1940s believed that some reforms were necessary for capitalism to survive another economic slump or even another election. They were willing to accept what they regarded as a little socialism to prevent a lot of socialism, and a strengthened federal power of taxation was therefore somewhat grudgingly accepted as the price of maintaining a stable system of free enterprise.

The financial and administrative requirements of the war, the fear of socialism if capitalism was not reformed, and the memory of the 1930s therefore combined to create a context in which the expansion of federal power as envisioned in the report of the Rowell-Sirois Commission was difficult to resist. Some provincial governments did resist the implementation of the report, however, and successfully scuttled the amendment to the BNA Act that would have codified a new dominion-provincial relationship and nullified the JCPC's interpretive stranglehold on the development of tax-and-spend regimes under the BNA Act. As with the scuttling of the commission in its hearing stages, the charge was led by Ontario, with support from Alberta and British Columbia. At the dominion-provincial conference on the Rowell-Sirois recommendations in January 1941, where Ilsley offered the provincial representatives the chance to discuss the terms under which the dominion would begin taxing incomes, Ontario Premier Mitchell Hepburn and his western allies Duff Pattullo of British Columbia and William Aberhart of Alberta walked out after a few minutes of discussion to signify their refusal of the terms of debate. Although dominion-provincial unanimity was required to amend the BNA Act, Ontario's intransigence was especially problematic because of its lucrative tax base and was central to the entire question of whether tax revenues would be federal or provincial.

Ontario's intransigence denied the dominion and the champions of dominion power the concrete and unassailable victory that they had envisioned: a revised and modernized BNA Act. However, it did not mark the end of the dominion's ambition to dominate income taxation. Instead of working with the provinces to come to an agreement about a changed relationship, federal authorities decided to move unilaterally, effectively invading territory that they had asked the provinces to surrender willingly. Shortly after Hepburn nixed the operationalization of the Rowell-Sirois scheme, Ilsley, in his budget speech of April 29, 1941, declared the dominion's intention to act alone, in defiance of the provinces' opposition, to become the sole taxing power. Unconsciously echoing Creighton's historical contribution to the Rowell-Sirois Report, which claimed that the architects of Confederation spoke of taxation "as if speaking of an undivided power," Ilsley constructed the 1941 budget around the premise that the dominion would impose income taxation on persons and corporations as "if the provinces were not in those fields."[10]

Rather than extracting a constitutional amendment that would recognize a superior right to tax on behalf of the dominion, Ilsley and his officials simply made the latent but considerable powers in the original BNA Act manifest, presenting the provinces with a unilateral *fait accompli.* Having failed to secure an invitation to take over income taxation for the country as a whole, the dominion invited itself to take up much the same role envisioned by the Rowell-Sirois Report, using its superior capacity, its constitutional supremacy, the requirements of the war economy, and the memory of the 1930s to overcome all conceivable opposition. Although a generation of reform-minded intellectuals bitterly regretted the provinces' role in scuttling the revision of the BNA Act to reflect a division of powers more amenable to the development of tax-and-spend policies, in fact the dominion's unilateral invasion of unceded provincial tax territory had much the same practical effect in terms of reversing the decentralization of fiscal power that the JCPC had effected in the 1890s.

Resigned to the dominion's dominance of the income tax field, one by one the provinces signed agreements officially ceding their right to tax incomes to the dominion for the duration of the war – some more willingly than others. These tax-sharing agreements traded other forms of revenue or spending for the surrendered fiscal capacity and, in many cases, were much like what the provinces had desired, openly, since the 1920s or before. Pushed to new and unprecedented levels of spending by the exigencies of the war, the dominion took on the central fiscal role imagined for it, acting for the first time in the central role in which the generation of the 1930s had envisioned it. Although this role was formally only a wartime exception to the constitutional sparring that characterized Confederation, like the introduction of the income war tax in the previous war, it was an exception that would become a rule – a rule from which other possibilities dangled.

Through the sheer force of its blunt constitutional fiscal supremacy, the dominion government in the early 1940s unilaterally imposed much the same scheme as had been proposed by the Rowell-Sirois Commission. The report, as the culmination of the intellectual and political work arising from the fiscal and constitutional crises of the 1920s and 1930s, had called on the dominion to become the single taxing authority through mutual agreement on a revised Constitution, the widely shared goal of reformers interested in a dominion-provincial scheme that admitted more redistributive potential than the tariff-fed pre-1914 dominion did. The right of the dominion to levy any tax that it wanted, enshrined in the British North America Act but traditionally declined, and embodied apologetically and disappointingly in the income war tax, was the key to the resolution of the post-Rowell-Sirois impasse. Ironically, after the BNA Act and the income war tax had been repeatedly declared in the past decade poor instruments in desperate need of modernization, these weak, ungainly, outworn instruments were what the dominion used unilaterally to overcome and nullify the provinces' resistance to federal intrusion.

"Terrifying Even if Imaginable": The Income Tax Sublime and the Citizenship of Contribution

The political, economic, and social requirements of military mobilization necessitated a break with the past in the early 1940s, as they had in 1917, accelerating an already existing modernization of politics by tying it to the unquestioned necessity of the war. Both wars followed immediately after a period of economic depression and political quagmire, and both led to political and fiscal innovations that were welcomed as long-term solutions to structural problems. The difference was that, while in the former the government was half-hearted in its fiscal reforms and more dedicated to political modernization, in the latter the government was resistant to any reforms other than fiscal ones. Both wars led to major changes in dominion taxation, but in the 1939–45 war the sense of novelty was concentrated more in taxation. This was in part because, whereas the pre-1914 critique of tariff politics was tied to certain sections of the public, the pre-1939 critique of the Constitution was widespread and had been absorbed and articulated by the federal government in the Rowell-Sirois Report. The sense that something had to be done was widely shared; how much of a change was needed, and whether the change was ultimately to overturn capitalism or prevent its overturning, was up for debate. The need for a break with the past was all but unanimously accepted.

The sudden expansion of the dominion's taxing power in the early 1940s resolved many of the constitutional and fiscal crises of the previous decades, but it created new conceptual problems. The vast increases in the rates and base of the income war tax created a sense of radical novelty in Canadian politics. The scale of taxation was the principal focus of the sense of novelty in the early 1940s. By the time the Second World War began, federal income taxation had existed for more than twenty years and was no longer novel. What was novel was making the tax universal, adjusting its curve of progressivity so that middle-income earners also paid taxes. The budgets of the early 1940s, by universalizing the income tax, necessitated a new understanding of what the tax was intended to do. Having entered into political life on the wings of the slogan "conscription of wealth," the income war tax had to be reimagined when it became something to which everyone was subject in relation to the ability to pay. The enormous scale of taxation, and the lack of a rhetoric through which to make sense of that scale, created an income tax sublime, a sense of radical novelty that overwhelmed the language with which people understood the federal state and its taxing power.

This sense of being on new and uncertain political terrain is reflected clearly in Ilsley's budget speech of June 23, 1942. "It is a most difficult task," he told the House of Commons, "to deal with sums of the magnitude involved here."[11] In that budget, as in the preceding two budgets, the dominion was taxing more people at higher rates than ever before and spending and borrowing more than in any previous year. Ilsley called it a "sobering experience" to design a tax policy "affecting such large fractions of the incomes of our people."[12] In an article on tax increases a year earlier, *Saturday Night* had opined that "business men and private citizens read the figures and blinked."[13] The sense of shock at the levels of taxation involved in the dominion budgets of the early 1940s clearly reflects the lack of a conceptual apparatus for making sense of an income tax to which almost everyone gave a substantial portion of income. It was new and unfamiliar and had to be actively understood.

A large part of the shock of the budgets of the early 1940s was the contrast to the 1930s, when the economic depression combined with the more moderate levels of taxation had kept dominion revenues low. The recovery (much of it, as in 1915–16, fuelled by war production) combined with the sharper rates and broader base to create what Ilsley called a "greatly increased" revenue. As he said in the 1942 budget speech, "our present estimate is that they will total $1,481 million, an increase over the previous year of $609 million, or approximately 70 per cent. This is some $34 million higher than I forecast in presenting the budget last year, and is nearly three times the Dominion's pre-war revenue."[14] The other key transformation was the shift from the tariff as the primary source of revenue to direct taxes – a contributing factor in the massive increases that the dominion easily effected. As Ilsley said,

> total tax revenues are now estimated at $1,360,915,000 as compared with $778 million in the preceding fiscal year. In contrast with previous years, direct taxes on income and profits made the largest contribution to the total. The graduated tax on personal incomes, the 18 per cent corporation tax and the special tax on dividends and interest produced $404 million, more than 80 per cent in excess of last year's yield.[15]

A sudden increase in tax rates, and therefore in revenue, was possible only because it was accomplished with an income tax, rather than the inflexible and ungainly tariff.

The key factor in the changes to the income war tax in the early 1940s was the extension of the tax burden into moderate incomes. Previously, the income tax had been, and had been understood as, a tax on high-income earners. Following the logic of the Rowell-Sirois Report, which underlined the importance of filling in "the trough in the curve of progressivity" (the low rate of taxation payable by middle-income earners), the revisions of 1941 and 1942 made a different class of income earners subject to the income tax.[16] That this task was a political challenge was certainly the position of *Saturday Night*, which pointed out in early 1941 that "to popularize direct taxation with one million people who have never before consciously paid a direct tax to the government ... is the stupendous task before the Dominion Department of National Revenue."[17]

New and strange about income taxation were that almost everyone paid it. This not only added to the administrative burden of collecting the tax but also meant the enshrinement of the citizenship of contribution. It was Ilsley's job to make sense of it and, in the meantime, to register empathy with taxpayers by flagging his own vertiginous sense of its modernity.

Beyond his budget speeches, Ilsley addressed the practical challenge of how to make sense of income taxation directly, speaking to groups of taxpayers in the aftermath of the tax changes to explain and defend the reforms. Speaking in 1942 to a meeting of the Trades and Labour Congress of Canada, for example, Ilsley reminded his audience that "we all agree it is the fairest tax and the best tax. It is the best way of taxing on the basis of ability to pay." He specifically addressed the resentment that he imagined unionized workers would feel at being made to pay taxes on low incomes. He reminded them carefully that an income tax "is preeminently the type of tax that labour has supported in the past, and which all those devoted to democratic ideals have upheld." Celebrating its modernity, Ilsley called income taxation the "foundation stone of social progress." Echoing critiques of the tariff and celebrations of the income war tax when it was introduced, he said that "we know too well that we are paying it – it is not hidden in the price of something we buy." This meant, though, that it was "not a painless tax." Specifically addressing possible resentment at having to pay taxes on low incomes, he said that "the result is that as we have increased it, and extended it down into the lower brackets, which we had to do in order to get any large revenue out of it, we have all discovered that this very good medicine tastes pretty bad when we have to take it ourselves."[18] Although his speech was a response to antitax sentiment, its core message was that the income tax was, and should be, powerful. The fairest tax, the one that is the most visible and therefore the most democratic, Ilsley asserted, should be powerful. Having emphasized the fairness and importance of the tax, he claimed to take great pride in the fact that his government had "gradually built up the income tax in Canada to be a powerful instrument."[19] The eagerness of the minister to underline the strength of the tax, and explicitly to align his government with increasing the strength of it, underscored the popularity of income taxation in the period.

In his budget speech, meanwhile, Ilsley had specifically demurred from any class-based conscription of wealth associations with the tax. The income war tax was originally a tax on high incomes, not on the incomes of all earners; his reforms extended the tax downward so that it was an odd opportunity to invoke the distribution of wealth. Nevertheless, Ilsley claimed that he was asked to consider the possibility of imposing a ceiling on incomes, a point beyond which earnings would be taxed at a rate of 100 percent. In response to this idea – which only he raised in the debate – Ilsley replied that

> there may be some political allurement in the principle of establishing by legislation an absolute limit on personal incomes, instead of adhering to the principles of progressive taxation even though at very high rates. I can only say that there have been too many difficult and far-reaching decisions to be made in framing this budget for me to give any consideration to its political adornment.[20]

The insistence that the budget was simply about trying to make sense of vast sums of money needed for vast and unavoidable endeavours, not to perform a kind of radical gesture as in 1917, was clear.

Ilsley's remarks reflect a desire to present a new understanding of the income war tax, to make sense of its new gargantuan form in the light of current politics, and to remove it from its previous associations. In contrast to the original passage of the income war tax, when opposition members tore into the government for the pallor of its approximation of the principle of the conscription of wealth, the Ilsley reforms were not an occasion for fiery statements about punishing the rich. Neither was the revised income tax, strong enough on its own to fund the pre-1914 dominion budget many times over, greeted as a sure avenue to the abolishment of the tariff. The dominion income tax was no longer a *possibility*, no longer a repository of possible versions of itself. It was simply a tax. Now its modernity lay in the fact that it was so large and powerful and so universal. In his attempts to make that experience and idea normal, Ilsley was helping his audience to understand the radical novelty in which they were living. As the tax increases became normal and the postwar world came into view, the question of what to do with the immense fiscal power that the provinces and the people had entrusted in the dominion became central. The answer invariably referenced the cataclysmic memory of the 1930s, but it took a range of forms – a range that speakers made sense of by mapping it onto a spectrum from left to right.

AN "INTELLIGIBLE LINE OF CLEAVAGE": PARTY DIFFERENCES AND THE CITIZENSHIP OF CONTRIBUTION

The dizzying prospect of universal income taxation that Ilsley had to meet as finance minister also confronted the political parties as they sought to

define their appeals and their differences from one another. The immensity
of the budget, the debt, the tax base, and the national revenue signalled a
new era with new possibilities, one that the parties had to evaluate as the
first station on the road to their own versions of modern politics. There
was a general consensus that the new tax regime had saved Confederation
from the nightmare of the Depression in the 1930s, but the dream of the
future, appropriately, was an object of division. The CCF emphasized in
its pamphlets and speeches the need for greater equality of income and
social status. It underscored that a truly equal society would operate on
generally cooperative principles rather than competition; ultimately, that
is, the CCF wanted to replace capitalism with an entirely different economic system. In the short term, though, the party consistently called for
greater and more progressive taxation to equalize income, even if the call
was half-hearted in relation to its calls for a complete social and economic
transformation. The popularity of the CCF was tied to its willingness to
use radical methods to establish social security, in contrast to the Liberals
and Conservatives, who had done little to alleviate the economic catastrophe of the 1930s while it was occurring. Even though it was not in power
or even the official opposition, the CCF was the party that seemed most
clearly to be aligned with the enthusiasm to transform capitalism through
economic planning and therefore the most connected to the popularity
of the new tax regimes.

For the Conservatives, the new tax arrangements created something of
an identity crisis. The increasing currency of the language of left and right
made political analysis easier but more awkward for the Conservatives,
acutely aware in the 1940s that being positioned on the right was a recipe
for political oblivion. The possibility of using the state to effect some
equalization of incomes was very popular, so the left side of the spectrum was the implicitly favoured and sought-after position. The troubling prospect of becoming a superfluous fringe party to the right of the
Liberals or a superfluous replica of the Liberals in the centre haunted the
Conservatives in the early 1940s. The problem and attempted solutions
produced a lot of linguistic self-consciousness among conservative intellectuals, especially in *Saturday Night*. Out of this work came a new set of
policies and ideals that reflected an attempt to bridge the divide between
safeguarding capitalism and transforming it. The Progressive Conservative Party, which emerged alongside the new tax possibilities, embodied
this attempt by reform-minded party intellectuals who sensed that it was
time to adapt. Because of pressure from donors primarily interested in
opposing the establishment of a permanent tax-and-spend regime after

the war, the party was less eager to define itself in terms of its position on equality and taxation, and it turned instead to a purely modernist party identity, obfuscating as much as possible its distance from the other parties on the political spectrum.

The need for clarity in political language was noted repeatedly in *Saturday Night* during the early 1940s. A letter in late 1943, which the editors titled "Words and Meanings," pointed out that "democracy, to function at all as a form of government, requires a citizenry capable of carrying on at least intelligible discussion." This meant that there had to be generally agreed upon meanings and understandings of the terms involved. "When two people mean different things by the same word and are each determined to stick to their own definition of it," the writer asked, "what hope is there for intelligent discussion?"[21] At the same time, the editors were keen not to become too attached to static identities or labels, positive or negative. In an editorial in 1940 entitled "Names Are Not Important," B.K. Sandwell, the editor of *Saturday Night,* argued that the fear of socialism should not serve as the basis for resisting important or necessary reforms.[22] This meant that one had to be both clear and subtle in one's use of political terms. Intelligent stewardship of political language was a key responsibility of politicians, according to Sandwell. In another editorial the same year, he wrote that "one of the most important functions of Parliament in relation to the people [is] ... formulating and clarifying the issues upon which the people are to choose between different groups of politicians who are asking for their support."[23] This was crucial to the meaningful function of democracy in a parliamentary system. As Sandwell argued in 1942,

> for the successful functioning of a parliamentary democracy it is essential that there should be an alternative political group ready to take over the government when the occupying political group ceases to command the support of the electorate. It is also important that the electors should know who that alternative political group is and what it stands for; since otherwise they are merely voting to throw the old group out and without any knowledge of what they are going to put in.[24]

For democracy to be meaningful, voters had to be able to choose between party banners that clearly differed from one another on the issues that mattered most to them.

The conservative *Saturday Night* was particularly concerned about the Conservative Party's lack of political clarity. The party was disadvantaged in the early 1940s by being identified most clearly with the problems of the 1930s and with the laissez-faire ideology that prevented government action to aid the unemployed. But it was also beset by an identity crisis, an uncertainty about where it fit in the political spectrum. To be an effective party in a modern party system, the Conservatives would have to distinguish themselves clearly from both the Liberal Party and the CCF, both much better defined. "The make-up and tendencies of the C.C.F.," the 1942 editorial claimed, "are fairly clear to the electors today: it is a socialist party with certain reservations in respect to the 'family farm.' The make-up and tendencies of the Conservative party are both thoroughly obscure, and it is highly desirable that they should cease to be obscure as soon as possible."[25] The desirability of finding a role and a position that reflected the modern political situation was reflected in a number of calls for new political cleavages in the early 1940s. With the release of the Rowell-Sirois Report, for instance, and its calls for reforming the Constitution to centralize taxing power in the dominion, Sandwell noted that the recommendations might serve as a useful new measure for differences between the Conservatives and the Liberals:

> It would probably do no harm if the two major parties should be definitely differentiated from one another by their concept of the proper direction in which the constitution should trend. This would provide a much more permanent, vital and intelligible line of cleavage than the outworn differences about high and low tariffs, which has been becoming less significant with each succeeding year.[26]

This comment was made in passing and contradicted somewhat the warm praise that the conservative magazine had for the report's recommendations. However, it reflected a consistent desire to see the Conservative Party define itself in modern ways and, more generally, to see a more modern and meaningful system of party differences adhered to in politics.

Positioning the party and reviving its fortunes were high ideals made more difficult by the emerging political imaginary. As discussions on how to make the party relevant continued through the early 1940s, commentators increasingly underscored the problem of the language of political differences. As one article in 1942 noted, "neither the 'Liberal' nor the 'Conservative' party, as we have it today, fits the classical definition of Liberalism and Conservatism." The parties did not represent what they once meant or were believed to mean. It was not just that the Conservatives were unclear but also that the system of differences was unclear. "It is impossible to imagine anything more essentially 'Tory' than Canada's present Liberal party," the writer argued, claiming that "the waning of the Conservative party was due not so much to predominating left-wing sentiment in the Dominion as to the usurpation of Toryism's historic place by the Liberals."[27] If, as the writer noted, the differences between the parties was no longer meaningful – if the Liberals were in fact Tory – on what basis did people vote? According to some authors, the force of memory, of what the party had once stood for rather than its current position, dictated party allegiance. "Emotional appeals divide us by resurrecting the past," argued Armour Mackay in 1943.[28] Party sentiment was not about disagreement on issues but about a sense of shared belonging that no longer had any real social fact behind it. The time when "Canadians could be divided into two political groups, Liberals and Conservatives," was also a time "when you knew, or if you didn't know you could soon find out the political creed of all your neighbours," and "when every substantial citizen of the village, town or city was known to be either a Liberal or Conservative. And you could drive up and down the rural concessions and point to this farmer and that and tell to what party he owed his allegiance."[29] That the issues at stake had changed, and that these labels were no longer meaningful to people in the immediate way that they had been a generation before, were often repeated. The meanings attached to the established political parties were becoming obscure, and differences that seemed to be crucial were losing force. Many commentators and correspondents would have agreed that the "freedom to choose between a Liberal or a Conservative has become a joke."[30] For proponents of the Conservative Party, the challenge was to make their party meaningful in the modern political imaginary, to invest it with a new purpose by giving it a specific role and purpose.

In trying to define exactly the purpose of the Conservative Party, *Saturday Night* contributors showed a growing comfort and familiarity with the left–right spectrum as a way of arraying political positions. The popularity of the CCF, and its effect on the party system as a whole, was a common theme in comments on the future of Canadian politics and on how parties would compete for popular support and power. Contributors to the magazine generally believed that "Canada seems to be dividing itself into two main groups, both of whom want abundant living, wider enjoyment of the fruits of democracy for all its citizens," but "one group hopes to bring about the better order through regulated capitalism, the other plumps for socialism."[31] Given this reality, "the proper task of the Conservative party," as J.L. Granatstein argued, "was to concentrate on scuppering the C.C.F."[32] Whether this task was better accomplished by being strong or being weak – or disappearing altogether – was the question. All options were apparently on the table. A *Saturday Night* editorial from 1942 asked "those ... who wish to maintain the private enterprise system" to consider "whether they can do this best by sinking their party identity in that of an anti-Socialist party combining elements from all the existing non-Socialist parties, or by continuing an independent existence as a middle-of-the-road party prepared to support moderate measures and to veto extreme measures whether they come from the Left or from the Right." The editorial expressed concern that the first option, an antisocialist coalition of Liberal and Conservative, would be read as reactionary – like the Union government in 1917 – and potentially play into the hands of the CCF. "On the other hand," it concluded, "if Socialism is the real issue there seems little use in a division of parties which takes no cognizance of it."[33] Sandwell and the majority of *Saturday Night* contributors favoured another solution, however. As early as 1940, the editor was arguing that "the proper position for the Conservative party to take is one well to the left of Liberalism."[34] A few weeks later another contributor claimed that "there is no room for the Conservative party to the right of the King government." The Liberals' investment in social security and their commitment to preventing a return of the economic catastrophe of the 1930s were so minimal, he argued, that positioning the party between the Liberals and the CCF was the more viable solution. "Where can the Conservative party go, then," he asked, "but to the left of the Liberal party?"[35]

The fear of a two-party system in which one party favoured socialism and the other capitalism was a major motivating force in trying to come up with a purpose for the Conservative Party in the new political situation. Again, this concern was expressed in left–right terms and reflected a growing familiarity with that way of describing political differences. J.M. Macdonnell, a Conservative strategist keen on reforming the party, was particularly vocal in his concern about "a two-party cleavage in Canada in which the two parties would be strongly Right and strongly Left respectively," in which case "the party system would be unable to function" in its normal parliamentary fashion.[36] In 1942, Macdonnell asked *Saturday Night* readers this question: "Is it conceivable that every few years we do something equivalent to changing our whole economic system?" He criticized

those who suggest a union of the two old parties, leaving two parties, a party of the Right, the result of a fusion between Liberals and Conservatives, and a party of the left, the C.C.F. This would create a situation where the wide gulf between the philosophies of the two parties thus formed would ... make the party system unworkable and, worse still, would produce an economic civil war.[37]

In a private letter on March 24, 1942, to another Conservative, Macdonnell elaborated on this theme:

If we disappear ... we then open the way to a lamentable situation. The C.C.F. will become the Opposition. They will attract the Leftist elements. All others, and particularly all reactionaries, will congregate in the other Party and we shall have a class war ... If one is an out and out socialist, the other an out and out individualist, a general election means in effect a revolution.[38]

Using the language of left and right, Macdonnell was arguing for the continuation of the Conservative Party as a bulwark against an overly stratified party system that would mean the end of parliamentary democracy. Editorials in *Saturday Night* essentially endorsed this view, lending support to the importance of maintaining two strong national parties opposed to the CCF. However, if the Conservative Party was to play a role in reversing the trend toward socialism, it had to offer something that suggested change to voters, or its continued existence would perilously draw support from the Liberals and bring the CCF to power.

Concerns like those expressed in *Saturday Night* about the prospects of a two-party system dominated by the CCF were the primary motivating factor in the modernization of the Conservative Party in 1942. In the course of a few months, after veering sharply to the right under the de facto leadership of Arthur Meighen, the party adopted an unofficial platform that reflected the desires of Conservatives to position themselves left of the Liberals, changed the name of the party, and absorbed a new leader from outside the party. All of these efforts were evaluated and discussed in *Saturday Night* in the language of left and right, with implicit or explicit reference to an agenda of social programs designed to moderate income inequality. The party's modernization was demonstrably a response to a new political imaginary that defined political differences along a left–right axis – an imaginary that arose in response to the threat and promise of income taxation.

The modernization began with a policy conference held at Port Hope in September 1942. A self-selected group of Conservative Party members who favoured moving the party toward a policy of support for the welfare state met and drafted a set of policy statements. Since none of the attendees was a party leader, the Port Hope policies were unofficial and quickly became a subject of debate in the party. *Saturday Night* greeted the Port Hope development as an important and promising step in repositioning the party. Showing a fluent familiarity with the left–right spectrum, the editor exulted in the knowledge that "it will not, after Port Hope, be possible for the Conservative party to attempt to insinuate itself to the Right of the Liberals." The clear purpose of the party after Port Hope, he argued, "is to seek public approval as a party somewhat further Left than the Liberals but not so disturbingly Left as the C.C.F."[39]

The next stage in the transformation of the Conservative Party was a convention held in Winnipeg in November, at which the general direction of the party implicit in the Port Hope declaration was given official force. At the centre of activity in Winnipeg was John Bracken, a long-time premier of Manitoba who had ruled the province throughout the 1930s despite the economic and constitutional crises that occasioned the defeat of every other provincial premier. A long-time member of the Progressive Party, Bracken owed his political survival to his fondness for and deftness at parliamentary coalitions, and he was widely respected as an intelligent and nonpartisan political reformer. Bracken was pursued by the Conservative Party leadership leading up to Winnipeg and ultimately agreed to stand as a leadership candidate provided that the party change its name to Progressive Conservative, a label that he could more comfortably and convincingly champion. In one day, therefore, the party was renamed and absorbed a new leader previously identified with a very different political outlook.

There was a lot of excitement about Bracken himself. He was described by one contributor as "a national solvent" who would clean up dominion politics and get it working again.[40] The name change brought mixed responses, often from a single commentator. Stephen Leacock claimed in advertising copy that he wrote and signed endorsing Ontario Conservative leader George Drew that adopting the new name amounted to "recognizing a thing in name after it has long existed as a fact."[41] A few months before, though, Leacock had spoofed the name with a humorous tale of a party meeting in which the members were trying to find a name that "would mean progressive and yet mean conservative" but "couldn't get it." The group had tried "both the name Forward Party and the name Backward Party, and ... the name Backwards-and-Forwards Party." Eventually, someone suggested "the title *The Non-Party Party*," and everyone jubilantly agreed.[42] Given Bracken's background in the Progressive Party, a group that defined itself to a large extent by its refusal to behave like a political party, and whose meaning was generally applied to mean non-partisan, this was an apt punchline.

Installed as the new leader of the renamed party, Bracken began the difficult process of defining what it meant. This was a delicate matter since it involved reconciling nearly antithetical strains and traditions yet being intelligible to voters. The party had been defined in recent years in part by the fierceness of its commitment to free enterprise; although the Bracken leadership, building upon the Port Hope conference and Bennett's New Deal, hoped to get beyond this association, it could not sever these bonds entirely. This was partly because the personnel and structure of the party had not changed and partly because there had been considerable popular support for the Conservative Party in previous elections that might shift to the Liberals if the new party became too adventurous in embracing alternatives to traditional liberal capitalism. In reframing the party's position in the aftermath of the name change, Bracken had to be progressive without being too unconservative: he had to steer the party away from the right shore without landing on the left.

Bracken finessed his party's position on the left–right spectrum, in large part, by invoking modernism, casting his party as the one that would renew free enterprise by clearing away the past. Rejecting both the traditionalist position and the reactionary position of the established right, that is, he hoped to replace the CCF as the party of the future by associating free enterprise with modernity. In a speech in 1944, he said that "we are out to make the Progressive Conservative Party the party that will sever the bonds which tied us to scarcity in the past and release the forces that will give us abundance in the future."[43] Implicitly addressing the contention, arising out of the 1930s, that capitalism was exploitative and dehumanizing, Bracken said that "we must save the driving force of our system, but the system must be made to yield full results in human welfare."[44] Echoing Ilsley's 1942 budget speech, he claimed for his new party the role of modernists, freeing the economy from the constraints of the past, opening the way to the unimaginable future. The party, Bracken said,

> is the answer of those who would set our present economic system free from the ignorance and limitations of the past, change it from the restrictive economy we have known, and turn it into an expanding economy which will make possible the production and distribution of material, goods and services on a scale never before considered possible by man.[45]

In invoking his vision of the party as the embodiment of modernity, he seldom if ever pointed to any specific policies that would express this position. Indeed, his position was precarious from the start because his party would never support any substantial deviation from its traditional positions; his role was almost immediately reduced to that of a palatable figurehead for what was, in the context of the public values of the 1940s, an unpalatable party.[46] His public statements are interesting and relevant not as reflections of actual policies but as windows into the political rhetoric of the 1940s. For example, when, in the same speech in 1944, Bracken asked rhetorically whether voters would be convinced of the party's legitimate shift away from a previous reactionary stance, he answered that

> we will convince people of this truth when we convince them that we believe in the right of the people to the full use of the greater production of goods and services that we can now produce from our natural resources; and when we can convince them that we believe in the right of the people to a more equitable distribution of that production on the basis of more fair rewards for work done and service given.[47]

Bracken was trying to convince people to vote against a party campaigning on transforming the Canadian economy substantially to make it operate on principles of public service rather than greed. In responding, he offered a vision of a more equitable society in which everyone had the right to share in the fruits of a modernized economy. This, as vague and apologetic as it was, passed for a right-wing electoral position in the Canadian politics of the 1940s.

In contrast to the focus on modernity and the attempt to downplay right-wingism in the Progressive Conservative position, the Cooperative Commonwealth Federation was more blunt in the 1940s about its place on the left–right spectrum. Like the PC Party, the CCF was struggling with identity issues, having entered the decade with a confusing division in the leadership over the question of Canada's participation in the war. But the CCF enjoyed the comparative advantage that its program of a planned economy under democratic rule was broadly thought to be the blueprint for the future, even by people unsympathetic to it. This consensus gave the party confidence in stating its position openly. The memory of the 1930s again played a part in that the CCF was seen as the party most likely to effect a clean break with the past of unregulated and insecure capitalism, a promise that the Liberals and PCs could offer only half-convincingly. At the same time, a residual fear of socialism required that the party be careful with its rhetoric and package its socialism as reasonable rather than extreme. Although the party ultimately proposed nationalizing the "commanding heights" of industry and instituting a planned economy, income taxation, with its easy promise of equalization of wealth without revolution, was key to how the CCF defined its immediate agenda.

This crucial role for income taxation in the party's immediate, but not ultimate, policy goals was expressed in a number of ways. Most directly, in the CCF's 1943 policy handbook *Make This Your Canada*, David Lewis and Frank Scott proposed that "all incomes above three thousand should continue to be taxed at the present rate and to this should be added the recommendation of a ceiling on income" – the 100 percent tax rate declined by Ilsley as too political.[48] Slightly less directly, the 1944 pamphlet *What Is Democratic Socialism?* said that, under a CCF government, social services "designed to provide equality of opportunity for all citizens" would be paid for, in the immediate future, by "heavy taxation on high incomes and inheritances." However, this would only be during "the period of transition from a capitalist society," following which "the revenue for social security will come from socialized industry."[49] Clearly, the CCF was not interested in being merely a taxing-and-spending government, though that would be the acknowledged first step. Party leader M.J. Coldwell, echoing these sentiments in *Left Turn, Canada* (1945), called on the citizenship of contribution. The dominion was already taxing heavily to pay for the war, he said. "Since the war began and up to and including 1944, we have appropriated seventeen and one-half billion dollars in our various wartime budgets. This is nearly two-thirds of the value of everything we included in all the wealth of all the people of Canada in the year 1927."[50] The awesome fiscal capacity that this demonstrated was important, Coldwell pointed out, for avoiding a return to 1930s social conditions through public spending on social programs. However, he cautioned, invoking the memory of the 1930s, no substantial change had been made to the Canadian economy other than the massive increase in tax revenue. Unless public spending was applied thoughtfully to remedying social problems likely to undermine the economy after the war, there was no certainty that the bad old days would not recur. As Coldwell said, "if the present system continues, with the present lack of planning for the future welfare of the country and its people, Canada will again face unemployment, deflation, and financial and economic depression."[51] High dominion taxation was only a preliminary step, one that opened up the possibility of funding comprehensive social services but not in itself a solution to the social crisis of capitalism.

Underlying the CCF endorsement of the high taxation introduced at the dominion level to pay for the war was the "billions for peace" argument that, in the words of Coldwell, "a nation which can spend billions for war must spend millions for peace, to improve the spiritual, cultural, as well as the economic condition of the people."[52] Invoking the memory of the 1930s, commentators from various political positions drew attention to the double standard that applied to spending for military necessity versus spending for social necessity and inferred that popular opinion would not stand for a return to prewar parsimony from the federal government. In his speech defending universal taxation to the Trades and Labour Congress, for example, Ilsley proclaimed the importance of devoting the equivalent investment to social security after the war as was being devoted to the war:

> We must conceive and carry out social insurance with the same boldness and thoroughness with which we have raised the income tax for war purposes. We must have the same courage and faith in financing useful peacetime development as we have had to apply in financing the war. We must retain the confidence that we have gained in the war, and shake off forever the frustration which fell upon us in the 1930s.[53]

There was nothing in Ilsley's speech to suggest what precisely the government would do with its peacetime billions, or even any particular priority for social spending, but the general concept that wartime taxation levels would be applied long term to prevent another economic catastrophe like that in the 1930s is clear. Similarly, Sandwell noted in *Saturday Night* at the start of the upward slope of wartime taxation that

> the most widespread source of bewilderment among ordinary Canadians today is, I am confident, the fact that a nation which could not, five years ago, raise the necessary money to put a few thousand unemployed citizens to work on producing things which would add to the health, comfort and happiness of the whole population, is now able without difficulty to raise vastly greater sums to put a few thousand citizens to work fighting Germany and provide them with very expensive implements of destruction with which to diminish the health, comfort and presumably also happiness of Germany.[54]

The Conservatives of *Saturday Night* shared with the Liberal finance minister and the socialists of the CCF the belief that something was wrong with a society that refused to tax in order to spend on social welfare.

Sandwell was more doubtful that people would have accepted the 1940s level of taxation in the 1930s, but he was equally insistent that times had irrevocably changed. When Leonard Marsh, a social scientist and civil servant with ties to the CCF's brain trust League for Social Reconstruction and the Liberal mandarinate, released a report calling for major federal investments in social security in 1943, another *Saturday Night* contributor wrote that taxpayers already exposed to high levels of taxation would have no difficulty with the cost of the programs:

> With the country acclimated to budgetary expenditures of around four billions [sic] for war purposes, little popular objection is anticipated for an expenditure of a quarter of that amount for peacetime protection of the people from economic insecurity as proposed by Dr. Marsh in his rough outline of a social security program. With Parliament appropriating around fifty per cent of the national income to defence from external enemies, resistance to the outlay of a quarter of the sum for provision against internal want is not likely to be very strong.[55]

Clearly, a wide consensus existed, and extended across political differences, that income taxation was about financing social spending. This link between taxing and spending was the basis for new left–right political differences that people were using with increasing sophistication and confidence.

That the CCF's policies best reflected the overall public mood was expressed most often, by party sympathizers and critics, with reference to the left–right spectrum. Although there were references to socialism, and to a drift toward socialism, in general what was noted was a more amorphous predilection for which the notion of a spectrum was a more useful instrument. The title of Coldwell's 1945 book, for instance, *Left Turn, Canada,* implied a general swing of the public mind, as a descriptive but more importantly a prescriptive utterance. An article in *Saturday Night* in 1944 similarly was titled "Is the Commonwealth Swinging to the Left?"[56] Another author a year earlier linked the CCF's popularity to "political agnosticism," arguing that the apparent radicalism of the public imagination was more accurately an invitation by an open-minded electorate to be wooed by a party's promises. "Politically," he said, "Canadians may be divided into radicals, reactionaries and political agnostics, and the party or political leader who can catch the imagination and win the support of that last group should be able to determine Canada's future political policy." Although he rejected the thesis of a leftward drift, the author still saw modern political difference as more fluid and more based upon

specific appeals than previous party differences, which were fixed and
social. And even this dissent was phrased ultimately as the emergence of
a spectrum: "Today a more exact division would be: those on the right,
the reactionaries; those on the left, the radicals; and those in between, the
fence-sitters. And how the fence-sitters have multiplied!"[57] Political difference was increasingly understood as being arrayed on a left–right spectrum, and people were aware of the novelty of such an understanding.

The sense that high levels of taxation were to be permanent and that
the governing Liberals had to take steps to undermine the CCF's strong
position as the party that would decisively woo the electorate with its ambitious visions of planned economies led to intense anticipation of government action in the mid-1940s. The release of the Marsh Report calling for
federal investment in social programs in March 1943 increased this anticipation, though no action immediately followed.[58] More than a year later G.C.
Whitaker wrote in *Saturday Night* that "Canadians at large are decreasingly
trustful of the old parties, if not of the old order itself, [and] large numbers
of them all over the country are looking towards the end of the war for pie
in the sky." Whitaker cited a poll in which four of five respondents said that
they wanted a different kind of society after the war. Prime Minister King,
he said, can "read the writing on the wall and must even now be drafting an
answer to it."[59] Finally, in the summer of 1944, the government introduced
legislation to create a federal Family Allowance, to be paid on a per-child
basis directly from the dominion treasury to mothers; although there was
some grumbling from Bracken and other Progressive Conservatives, the
legislation quickly passed unanimously in the House of Commons. The most
expensive thing ever undertaken by the dominion other than the Second
World War itself, the Family Allowances Act was the first universal social
program and the first to be funded by universal income taxation.[60]

The Family Allowance, for better or worse, answered the question of
what unprecedented levels of taxation were intended for and what they
could do. Although Marsh and other proponents of social reform were
lukewarm on the Family Allowance, they clearly reflected the general
spirit of the age in providing "a 'floor' of minimum provision, ... providing a firm foundation on which to build an equitable structure."[61] They
also represented the Liberal Party's bid to displace the CCF as the party
of postwar social development and, in the words of a *Saturday Night*
editorial, took the party "far to the moderate left, not too far from the
moderate right."[62] Coupled with the income tax expansion earlier in the
1940s, the Family Allowance for the first time created a permanent, peacetime justification for high taxation and allowed people to make sense of

the modernity of universal taxation by tying it to an equally vertiginous spending project – the essence of the citizenship of contribution.

The Family Allowance, then, provided an example of the spending of dominion revenue from universal taxation. Beyond their political reson-ance, the federal taxing and spending innovations were also discussed by *Saturday Night* in terms of their costs to individual taxpayers and, more abstractly, capitalism itself. The cartoons on the financial page, in par-ticular, often demonstrated a more worried and less enthusiastic attitude toward extravagances of taxing and spending. One cartoon in March 1943 (the same issue in which Marsh's recommendations were announced) showed a beaming John Q. Public embracing an apparent gift of social security from a government dressed as Santa Claus, who omin-ously holds a bill, to be presented next, in his other hand (Figure 4.1).

A BILL TO BE PAID !

FIGURE 4.1   The cost of social programs 1: "A Bill to Be Paid" shows a man joyously receiving what appears to be a wonderful gift, when in fact he is about to be presented with a sobering bill. The images suggested that John Q. Public was easily impressed by government generosity and paid little attention to what was behind it: taxes. The financial page of *Saturday Night* regularly ran articles, editorials, and cartoons that were critical or dismissive of public support for tax-funded welfare state proposals. | James Allen, *Saturday Night*, March 27, 1943, 37.

The message of the cartoon was that social security was tied inextricably to increased taxation. This message was repeated later when the Family Allowance was introduced. When it was first discussed in *Saturday Night* in 1941, the author stated flatly that "the first question that will be asked about family allowances is what they would cost."[63] When they were introduced three years later, of course, the high levels of taxation necessary for the war had transformed people's expectations of which costs could be borne. Still, a cartoon depicting a nervous and rattled taxpayer watching as a stork drops yet another burden in his baby carriage (Figure 4.2) made the point that social programs were

NEW ARRIVAL: "I WANT IN, TOO!"

FIGURE 4.2   The cost of social programs 2: "New Arrival" shows an anxious man watching Family Allowances being added to his burden. The taxpayer is dressed in a three-piece suit, indicating wealth, but his clothing has become worn out, suggesting that he has hit hard times. He is also represented as clearly old and male, perhaps to underscore the ridiculousness of his having to care for babies. In contrast to John Q. Public in Figure 4.1, this taxpayer does not appear to have any sympathy for social spending, which he feels only as a burden. The financial section, in which Allen's cartoons appeared, expressed a much more cautious and nervous position on the emergence of a tax-funded welfare state than the political pages edited by B.K. Sandwell. | James Allen, *Saturday Night*, October 16, 1943, 45.

expensive and meant hardship for the taxpayer. Even in presenting a cautious view of taxing and spending innovations, these representations drove home the message that taxation was for social spending, separating it from the cost of the war.

At the end of 1945, the government introduced a *White Paper on Employment and Income.* Released by Minister of Reconstruction C.D. Howe, it signalled the government's intention to amend but not reverse the political economy of war when hostilities ended. Tax rates would be lowered from their punishing wartime levels to encourage investment, but the government would continue to use its taxing power to direct economic activity and, crucially, prevent catastrophic 1930s-style levels of unemployment. The *White Paper,* coming after Ilsley's marking of the novelty of high taxes, gave universal income taxation a legible and permanent purpose. The role of income taxation, for a government committed to a rhetoric of cautious reform, was to moderate unhealthy and dangerous extremes in the economy.

As J. Harvey Perry and others have noted, the *White Paper* signalled a fundamental shift from finance to economics in treasury questions: a tax measure was used as much to influence economic behaviour and effect a social policy outcome as to raise money. This shift, rather than being simply a wartime tendency, continued into the postwar period. After the war, when the need for government spending was less acute and more open to debate, and when popular support for high levels of taxation was less immediately forthcoming, budgets became smaller. But they never returned to their pre-1930s sizes or to any size that could be funded by anything other than a graduated income tax.[64] Just as important was the shift to the taxation of personal income as the core of the tax system. Personal income taxation became the form of taxation most felt by Canadians, other than those with very low incomes, exempt even from universal income tax. It remains the form of taxation on which our implicit understanding of the political spectrum rests. Paying income tax is at the centre of our practice of modern citizenship and was put there in the early 1940s.

Over the decades that followed, Perry's judgment has become a historiographical truism. The *White Paper* is widely seen as the announcement of a changed perspective on the role of the federal government, and of the effects of its taxation, in the wider economy and society. Rather than simply paying for costs necessary for the bare functioning of the state apparatus, taxation becomes a central instrument in a new social practice of interventionist government policy. Where taxation was previously thought of as a financial necessity, with the *White Paper* it became an instrument of economic management. The government adjusts its levels of taxation to effect changes in the economy and, in particular, to manage levels of unemployment. Although scholars are divided on the extent to which the *White Paper* committed the government to a policy of full employment or even reflected a truly Keynesian commitment to using the state to manage the economy, the more general argument that the government had announced a permanent change in how it understood the effects of its tax measures is widely accepted.[65] As Perry says, this changed role arose from the experiments in war finance and planning for postwar reconstruction but was undeniably a legitimization of the more active role envisioned for the federal government in managing the economy through a centralized income tax envisioned in the report of the Rowell-Sirois Commission.[66] It reflected a new vision of the role of the state's fiscal capacity: interventionist, not apologetic; economic, not just financial.

What Perry did not say is that characterizing the dominion income tax as a rudder for the national economy amounted to a demotion from how it had been seen previously. In the three decades leading up to the *White Paper*, a dominion income tax had been understood in various ways as a fundamentally political instrument, not a narrowly fiscal one. Critics of the rhetorical effects of the tariff understood bitterly the centrality of taxation to electoral politics and longed for a clearer tax as the basis of a clearer system of differences. The Rowell-Sirois Report, as we saw in Chapter 3, proposed a dominion income tax of the kind that the income war tax became in the early 1940s. One advantage, the report pointed out, was that it could serve as a more transparent expression of the policy intentions of the governing party. Rather than being an important instrument with which the federal government could rationalize investment and stimulate growth, for most of its history the income war tax was seen as an instrument that could rationalize our political thought and stimulate our sense of the politically possible – a political instrument rather than simply an economic one. Throughout the early decades of the twentieth century, income taxation was cast as the solution to the inequities of the tariff system and as the engine of a new, modern, political imaginary. If in the postwar era Perry and others could remark, awed and impressed, on the role to which the *White Paper* had assigned the taxing authority, it was because income taxation had become so central, and the political modernization that it was expected to effect so clearly under way, that the greater and more abstract role was no longer worthy of comment.

***

In the first few years of the 1940s, the dominion fiscal capacity expanded dramatically. Inspired by the report of the Rowell-Sirois Commission, which had envisioned a single, legible, and coherent taxing authority as the solution to the constitutional and fiscal crises of the 1930s, and made necessary by the intransigence of some provinces in opposing a plan that would see the dominion tax its citizens to pay for social services in other provinces, the dominion's unilateral occupation of the entire income tax field was a revolution in public finance. By massively expanding the number of those taxed and the amount of revenue coming into the dominion treasury, it opened new vistas of political possibility that had to be made sense of, in the short term by the cost of the war, in the long term by a range of partisan visions of the role of a newly vigorous federal taxing power in crafting a postwar society.

The modernist break with the past of universal income taxation and previously unimagined federal spending power had to be made intelligible by the various parties vying to be given control of the immense power represented by the dominion fiscal state. For the democratic socialists of the CCF, the most direct inheritors of the tradition of political modernism that had been pushing for a powerful direct tax since 1910, the immediate plan was simple: use the taxing power to effect an equalization of incomes by spending on social programs. The governing Liberals demonstrated how this approach worked with the introduction of the Family Allowance in 1944, but otherwise they cautiously controlled the extent to which heavy taxation burdened free enterprise. The Progressive Conservatives struggled with their position on the spectrum of possibilities and sought as much to obfuscate as to clarify what they would do post-1945 if elected. All parties, and all political actors, increasingly used the left–right terminology as a shorthand for their relationship with the citizenship of contribution.

By the mid-1940s, when the *White Paper on Employment and Income* was released, no one invested income taxation with much imaginative heft. In a sense, the tax became irrelevant intellectually, as an object of political fantasies, once it was established as a blunt and overpowering fact of life. Once it was powerful as a tax, that is, it quickly lost its power as a possibility. Income taxation took on its contemporary status as a dull and shadowy burden, and the expectations that it had been invested with either became redundant or were absorbed by the partisan melee – the left–right spectrum of modern political differences. The first half of the 1940s, when income taxation became a universal obligation and the parties struggled to make sense of it and their intentions regarding its possibilities, was the end of the period of active modernization of politics and the beginning of what we recognize as the modern political imaginary.

Conclusion: Income Taxation, Democracy, and the Modern Political Imaginary

A modern political imaginary, a new way of representing political difference, emerged in the first decades of the twentieth century. Where previously politically engaged people had identified themselves as Liberals or Conservatives, largely on the basis of their attitude toward British nationalism, after 1945 they were more likely to position themselves and their political attitudes along a spectrum, left to right, on the basis of the extent to which they wanted the state to intervene in the distribution of income. The dominion two-party system, tied to the nationalist appeals of the protective tariff, had been replaced by a multiparty system in which various possibilities for using the treasury to alter the distribution of income were presented to the electorate. Income taxation did not exactly replace the tariff – in fact it was a small part of the dominion's total revenue when it was introduced in 1917 – but the possibilities that it suggested slowly displaced the tariff as the primary basis of political differences in dominion politics. By the time income taxation became a universal and defining fact of political life, and the potential basis for large-scale social programs, the left–right spectrum was the most common instrument for imagining the field of political differences.

This new imaginary arose to some extent from conscious rhetorical invention that sought to expose the limitations of the tariff-defined two-party system inherited from the nineteenth century. At first, the critique took the form of people's enlightenment that set out to energize or else eliminate the party system. Organized farmers and industrial workers entered into electoral politics forcefully in the 1910s, first as critics of the parties hoping to influence the Liberals in particular to take up a position against the tariff, later as founders of third parties. These groups forcefully undermined the nationalist imagery of the tariff by characterizing it as exploitative and regressive, changing the politics of taxation, and reframing politics as being between the old political parties on the one hand and the people broadly on the other. By 1921, when farmer- and labour-identified third parties held seats in the House of Commons and power in some provinces, the old party labels had been significantly displaced as meaningful poles of political differences – a victory for those who saw them as corrupt, misleading, and hopelessly anachronistic.

In place of the old party labels, people began to use other language by the 1920s and 1930s, at first cautiously and uncertainly and with explicit reference to the novelty of third parties but with growing confidence. Reformers, faced with unprecedented problems of economic dislocation and fiscal collapse, had inequality on the brain when thinking of what a new, more transparent system of difference could be anchored to: a new citizenship of contribution that provided an abstract and universal burden of fiscal responsibility that could be used to fund redistributive social programs. By the 1940s, when the Rowell-Sirois Report served as the inspiration for a radical increase in the income war tax, the words *left* and *right* were being used fluently by speakers to make sense of a crowded field of possibilities.

The development of income taxation at the dominion level in Canada, then, far from simply being a technical tale of forms and figures, is in some sense a story about democracy. It is a social, cultural, and intellectual history of how people set out to transform political rhetoric by shifting the burden of public finance onto what they believed was a more supple, more intelligible, and fairer form of tax. Accounts of the transformation of dominion politics in the 1930s and 1940s, such as that by Doug Owram, underscore the role of intellectuals in changing how the government worked in the period leading up to 1945. An account of fiscal politics as democratization, conversely, underscores the role of less elite actors in shaping modern politics. University-trained experts in political science certainly played key roles in parties and in the government, particularly in the period of the Rowell-Sirois Commission and after. However, by looking beyond these actors, by tracing the emergence of a new way of doing politics back to the destruction of the old tariff-defined party system, we find more and different voices, and we gain a new perspective on how the conditions of possibility for the postwar welfare state were established.

This points to what Martin, Mehrotra, and Prasad mean when they suggest that fiscal history can "rewrite conventional accounts of modernity" by drawing attention to the conditions under which the possibility of political struggle over the welfare state emerged.[1] The historiography of the postwar welfare state generally "ignores the revenue side of the budget."[2] Scholars fall prey to the popular perception that, because taxes are technical, their history will be lifeless and dull. For people who paid harshly exploitative taxes that provided minimal fiscal capacities, taxes were not a dull but an important and immediate part of their political lives. Their resistance to the tariff, the rhetoric that they used in discussing it, was the necessary condition for the later development of a powerful dominion state that could contemplate projects such as the Family Allowance. To turn back further to taxes as the condition of possibility of a given political difference is to gain a new perspective on politics itself. To examine what Shirley Tillotson calls the "moral and symbolic meaning of taxation" changes the very notion of what political history is, whom it is about, and why we write it.[3]

This book makes clear that the increased use of left–right differentiation was a significant liberation. It was the product of an explicit and implicit project to clarify the language of political differences, and it entailed significant rhetorical, political, and intellectual work. It was, to use Ian McKay's term, "people's enlightenment," a democratic semantic revolution, even if some of its champions were patrician or even reactionary. It was one of the great modern projects and, by making possible the development of a welfare state, created the possibility of other great modern projects. It was a liberation from the stultifying and limiting representations of political discourses that had kept effective decision making in the hands of a narrow elite in the nineteenth century despite a formally generous white male suffrage. The emergence of a political imaginary in which parties vie over how to use income taxation as an instrument to equalize wealth is an important element in the democratization of the fiscal power of the state and therefore of modern democracy.

This shift in perspective is related historiographically to new political history. This history is more than a return to political topics once deemed unfashionable; it is the incorporation of the intellectual projects of social and cultural history into the history of the political. Social history and cultural history emerged as the dominant areas of inquiry after the 1960s because it was important to interrogate how society and culture were structured and how power worked through them. Social and cultural historians trace the development of common practices and assumed norms to show the struggles that produced them. Social and cultural history asks how "this" – the world of meanings and equivalences that surrounds us – became normal and, by being normal, invisible. Political history, during the ascendancy of social and cultural history, largely cut itself off from these kinds of inquiries; rather than interrogating norms, more often it reproduced them, taking current political logic as natural, speaking its language, and accepting its representations of difference. New political history, inspired by social and cultural history, asks the following questions. How did we get here? How did the political categories through which we order our world, of which we are rarely consciously aware, come to surround us? How did this political world become normal?

Studying the history of a time when income taxation was widely discussed is vital to such a project. An expanded dominion income tax was broadly supported in the early twentieth century not only because it was necessary for the war but also because it was a better tax, a more efficient and democratic tax, than what Canadians had known before. Many people actively chose to be taxpayers; they were highly engaged in debates about taxation and informed through these debates about what made a tax good or bad. The expansion of the taxing capacity of the dominion, on which the later development of the welfare state was contingent, was itself contingent on their engagement and the intelligent and often bitter attention that people gave to discussions of fiscal politics. Their consent to be taxed, that is, their willingness to be contributing citizens, arose from their intellectual engagement, their enlightenment.

It is difficult for us to think of income taxation as a democratic project because we are accustomed to a neoliberal perspective that sees the social obligation of taxation as a burden. Hailed by the government and the market as savvy self-promoters, we struggle to see the relationships made possible by taxing and spending as a liberation. In part, this is because the democracy of the midcentury fiscal state was never fully realized and because new identities other than those of income stratification have taken on greater significance since the 1960s. But more than anything else, it is the outcome of a powerful alternative rhetoric that seeks to alienate people from discussions of fiscal questions in a reverse people's enlightenment and a conceptualization of political differences that undoes much of the clarity introduced by the left–right spectrum.

To see income taxation as worthy of intelligent reflection, and to take an interest in the rhetoric through which people understood its power, is to resist a powerful imperative in our society to see taxation as a difficult and dull topic and to see our experience of taxation as a meaningless, technical burden that weighs pointlessly on individuals. Our uninterest in taxation surrenders the consideration of the relative burdens and benefits of our fiscal system to those who can devote all of their time to the endeavour or afford to pay others to do so for them. Our tax system, which weighs lightly on high-income earners and heavily on low- to middle-income earners, is a reflection of our collective boredom with fiscal politics: we have the tax system of people who don't want to talk about taxes.

This book shows that tax doesn't make itself interesting; rather, people make tax interesting. It is up to us to make fiscal questions interesting to one another, to engage with the possibilities of taxation, and to make public finance into an intelligible terrain on which we can struggle for the world that we want. It is up to us to make it interesting to each other by using rhetoric to open up new possibilities and, like the farmers and workers in 1911 and 1917, expose the absurdities and injustices written into the tax system and the wider system that supports and legitimizes it. This book will have done some justice to the material if it makes a contribution to the renewal of people's enlightenment by sketching a renewed citizenship of contribution.

Notes

INTRODUCTION

1 Adrian Humphreys, "NDP Making Huge Gains as Canada Tilts Leftward: Poll," *National Post*, May 28, 2012, http://nationalpost.com/2012/05/28/ndp-making-huge-gains-as-canada-tilts-leftward-poll/.

2 Stephen Leacock, *The Unsolved Riddle of Social Justice* (Toronto: S.B. Gundy, 1920), 141. Leacock's anguished perspective on Canadian politics in the post–First World War period, and his attraction to income taxation as a corrective, are discussed in Chapter 2.

3 J. Harvey Perry, *Taxes, Tariffs, and Subsidies: A History of Canadian Fiscal Development*, 2 vols. (Toronto: University of Toronto Press, 1955).

4 Bob Russell, "The Politics of Labour-Force Reproduction: Funding Canada's Social Wage," *Studies in Political Economy* 18 (1984): 67. This article was the first scholarship that I read on income taxation in Canada, and its historical narrative, culminating in the Ilsley reforms and the introduction of Family Allowances, undoubtedly affected the research and writing of this book. I'm indebted to Russell even if our claims are unrelated and somewhat at odds and to James Struthers for urging me to look up Russell's article.

5 See Elsbeth Heaman, *Tax, Order, and Good Government* (Montreal and Kingston: McGill-Queen's University Press, 2017), and Shirley Tillotson, *Give and Take: The Citizen-Taxpayer and the Rise of Canadian Democracy* (Vancouver: UBC Press, 2017), which, with *The Terrific Engine*, constitute the only monographs ever written by Canadian historians on taxation. That all three end up being published within less than a year is remarkable, though not entirely surprising to the authors, who have been in professional communication for years and are very familiar with each other's projects.

6 Donald Wright, *The Professionalization of History in English Canada* (Toronto: University of Toronto Press, 2005), 53.

7 Underhill cited in Carl Berger, *The Writing of Canadian History* (Toronto: University of Toronto Press, 1976), 66.

8 Donald Creighton, *The Commercial Empire of the St Lawrence, 1760–1850* (Toronto: Ryerson Press, 1936); Donald Creighton, *British North America at Confederation* (Ottawa: Queen's Printer, 1937). The idea that the book echoes Creighton's contribution to the commission is from Berger, *The Writing of Canadian History,* 215–16. See also Donald Wright, *Donald Creighton: A Life in History* (Toronto: University of Toronto Press, 2015), 136–41, which supports the claim generally but notes that the report's "Creightonian overtones were necessarily muted" (140).

9 Doug Owram, *The Government Generation: Canadian Intellectuals and the State 1900–1945* (Toronto: University of Toronto Press, 1986); Barry Ferguson, *Remaking Liberalism: The Intellectual Legacy of Adam Shortt, O.D. Skelton, W.C. Clark, and W.A. Mackintosh, 1890–1925* (Montreal and Kingston: McGill-Queen's University Press, 1993). Two books that cover ground similar to that in my book, David Laycock's *Populism and Democratic Thought in the Canadian Prairies* (Toronto: University of Toronto Press, 1990) and Walter D. Young's *Democracy and Discontent: Progressivism, Socialism, and Social Credit in the Canadian West* (Toronto: McGraw-Hill Ryerson, 1978), are less focused than Owram and Ferguson on university-trained intellectuals but nonetheless primarily concerned with identifying strains of recognizable political ideas rather than studying how people used language.

10 New political history as such has not been defined or outlined by scholars. See Larry Glassford, "The Evolution of 'New Political History' in English-Canadian Historiography: From Cliometrics to Cliodiversity," *American Review of Canadian Studies* 32, 3 (2002): 347–67, for an overview that does not reflect the current rebirth and is too eager for a return to, rather than a rethinking of, political history of the Creighton-Underhill type. Glassford cites Ian Radforth and Allan Greer, eds., *Colonial Leviathan: State-Formation in Mid-Nineteenth-Century Canada* (Toronto: University of Toronto Press, 1992), and Nancy Christie, *Engendering the State: Family, Work, and Welfare in Canada* (Toronto: University of Toronto Press, 2000), as examples of publications that point in that direction.

11 The founding of the Political History Group in the Canadian Historical Association in 2009 was a key marker of this rebirth. Also notable were the lecture series Re-Imagining the Political, held at Carleton University in 2008, and the conference Transformation: State, Nation, and Citizenship in a New Environment, held at York University in 2011.

12 Ian McKay, "The Liberal Order Framework: A Concept of Reconnaissance," *Canadian Historical Review* 81, 4 (2000): 616–78. See also Michel Ducharme and Jean-François Constant, eds., *Liberalism and Hegemony: Debating the Canadian Liberal Revolution* (Toronto: University of Toronto Press, 2009), which includes McKay's essay and critical commentaries by other historians.

13 Two examples are Jarrett Rudy, *The Freedom to Smoke: Tobacco Consumption and Identity* (Montreal and Kingston: McGill-Queen's University Press, 2005), and Darren Ferry, *Uniting in Measures of Common Good: The Construction of Liberal Identities in Central Canada* (Montreal and Kingston: McGill-Queen's University Press, 2008).

14 Perry, *Taxes, Tariffs, and Subsidies;* W. Irwin Gillespie, *Tax, Borrow, and Spend: Financing Federal Spending in Canada, 1867–1990* (Ottawa: Carleton University Press, 1991); Robert B. Bryce, *Maturing in Hard Times: Canada's Department of Finance through the Great Depression* (Montreal and Kingston: McGill-Queen's University Press, 1986).

15 Besides the new monographs by Tillotson and Heaman cited above, see, in particular, Shirley Tillotson, "The Family as Tax Dodge: Partnership, Individuality, and Gender in

the Personal Income Tax Act, 1942 to 1970," *Canadian Historical Review* 90, 3 (2009): 391–425; Elsbeth Heaman, "'The Whites Are Wild about It': Taxation and Racialization in Mid-Victorian British Columbia," *Journal of Policy History* 25, 3 (2013): 354–84; and Andrew Smith, "Toryism, Classical Liberalism, and Capitalism: The Politics of Taxation and the Struggle for Canadian Confederation," *Canadian Historical Review* 89, 1 (2008): 1–25.

16 Isaac William Martin, Ajay Mehrotra, and Monica Prasad, eds., *The New Fiscal Sociology: Taxation in Comparative Historical Perspective* (Cambridge, UK: Cambridge University Press, 2009). The term "fiscal sociology" was coined by Joseph Schumpeter, "The Crisis of the Tax State," in *The Economics and Sociology of Capitalism,* ed. Richard Swedberg (Princeton, NJ: Princeton University Press, 1991), 101.

17 Martin et al., *The New Fiscal Sociology,* 2.

18 J.A. Laponce notes in *Left and Right: The Topography of Political Perceptions* (Toronto: University of Toronto Press, 1981) that the opposition has ancient origins, with the right generally linked to authority, stability, and virtue and the left linked to disorder, chaos, and evil. Christian morality underlined subjugation to legitimate authority and saw the left as being the side of the devil seeking to undermine the rule of God and his designates, represented as the right. The word *right* has other meanings that link it to authority: it also means "true" and "legally sacrosanct privilege." In politics, however, the left is more dominant in the sense that it comes first in the set (we say "left and right," not "right and left") and in the sense that it is used more often as a self-description. Laponce explains this shift by noting that, "compared to religious and social systems, politics – democratic politics especially – is a system of challenge and opposition; it seeks 'reequilibrium' through disequilibrium" (44).

19 Laponce points out in *Left and Right* that the English-speaking democracies "had lesser need than France for an overarching duality" because they "already possessed a two-party system and had experienced very few changes in the names of their two parties" (52) – an observation that fits with the chronology of this book. McKay's "The Liberal Order Framework" underlines the ideological similarity of Canada's long-standing parliamentary government and opposition, Liberal and Conservative.

20 Thomas Carlyle, *The French Revolution* (New York: Modern Library, 2002), 185–86.

21 Carlyle, *The French Revolution,* 186.

22 For the geographical diffusion of the terminology of "left" and "right" across Europe in the late nineteenth century, see Laponce, *Left and Right,* 52–54.

23 Carlyle, *The French Revolution,* 179.

24 David Harvey, *Paris, Capital of Modernity* (London: Routledge, 2003), 1.

25 Tim Armstrong, *Modernism: A Cultural History* (London: Polity Press, 2005), 82. "Creative destruction" is a term coined by Joseph Schumpeter, used by Harvey to characterize the redesign of Paris by Georges-Eugène Haussman in the period following the 1848 uprising. See Harvey, *Paris,* 2. Schumpeter was an economist of the Austrian school who argued, echoing Marx, that economic growth under capitalism constantly had to revolutionize itself, destroying the old in order to make way for the new. See Joseph Schumpeter, *Capitalism, Socialism, and Democracy* (London: Routledge, 2003), 83. Schumpeter was also an advocate of historical studies of taxation, claiming in an influential essay that "fiscal history" is "the thunder of world history." Schumpeter, "The Crisis of the Tax State," 101.

26 Carlyle, *The French Revolution,* 179.

27 Quoted in Ian McKay, *Reasoning Otherwise: Leftists and the People's Enlightenment in Canada, 1890–1920* (Toronto: Between the Lines, 2008), 16.

28 McKay, *Reasoning Otherwise*, 62.

29 McKay, *Reasoning Otherwise*, 62.

30 Shirley Tillotson, "A New Taxpayer for a New State: Charitable Fundraising and the Origins of the Welfare State," in *Social Fabric or Patchwork Quilt: The Development of Social Policy in Canada*, ed. Raymond B. Blake and Jeff Keshen (Peterborough, ON: Broadview Press, 2006), 162. Although the term "citizenship of contribution" appears in Tillotson's later *Contributing Citizens: Modern Charitable Fundraising and the Making of the Welfare State, 1920–1966* (Vancouver: UBC Press, 2008), I use the earlier article here because its discussion is more definitional.

31 Tillotson, "A New Taxpayer for a New State," 164. In some sense, it echoes T.H. Marshall's concept of social citizenship, though with more emphasis on the responsibility to pay than on "rights" conferred by the state and more emphasis on the novelty of the shift rather than its consistency with a whiggish unfolding of liberal rights. See T.H. Marshall and Tom Bottomore, *Citizenship and Social Class* (London: Pluto Press, 1992), 3–49. Marshall proposed in a series of lectures in 1949 that liberal citizenship was comprised of civil rights, political rights, and social rights, conferred in succession and at different times.

32 "Political modernism" draws on other people's understanding of what modernism is and how it expresses itself politically, but no one uses the term as such. See my article "'The Rich ... Should Give to Such an Extent that It Will Hurt': 'Conscription of Wealth' and Political Modernism in the Parliamentary Debate on the 1917 Income War Tax," *Canadian Historical Review* 93, 3 (2012): 382–407.

33 Quentin Skinner, *Visions of Politics,* vol. 1, *Regarding Method* (Cambridge, UK: Cambridge University Press, 2002). David Banoub presented a paper on rhetorical analysis at the Underhill Graduate Colloquium at Carleton University in 2009. His paper introduced me to Skinner's work, and subsequent discussions with him have guided my understanding and use of it.

34 Skinner, *Visions of Politics,* 1:176.

35 Quoted in Skinner, *Visions of Politics,* 1:4.

36 Skinner, *Visions of Politics,* 1:1. The phrase is widely used in reference to Skinner's method.

37 Skinner, *Visions of Politics,* 1:3.

38 One of Skinner's favourite examples is C.B. Macpherson, who argued that parliamentarians in the English Civil War were fighting for something that he called "possessive individualism," which appears nowhere in any document of the time and, Skinner argues, would have meant nothing to the people to whom Macpherson ascribes it as an ideal. See C.B. Macpherson, *The Political Theory of Possessive Individualism: Hobbes to Locke* (Oxford: Oxford University Press, 1962).

39 I use the term "modernism" here in preference to "modernity" because it defines an urge rather than a condition. David Harvey defines modernism as a "movement" and modernity as a "condition" in *The Condition of Postmodernity: An Enquiry into the Origins of Cultural Change* (London: Basil Blackwell, 1989), 10. His distinction informs the terminological preference for "political modernism" in my book.

40 Curiously, though scholars from various disciplines have claimed new theoretical ground on the basis of the term "imaginary," often it is left undefined and used without terminological or etymological attribution, as if it were being coined anew each time. One attraction of the term, as well as a reason for its recent proliferation, seems to be that it has no

immediately recognizable meaning and purpose, in contrast to terms such as "discourse" and "hegemony," which have well-established theoretical lineages and potentially constraining methodological and political resonances. The imaginary is particularly appealing to authors who want to claim new conceptual ground and reach nonspecialists and don't want to overburden their prose with a towering, prefabricated theoretical edifice.

41 Ernesto Laclau and Chantal Mouffe, *Hegemony and Socialist Strategy: Towards a Radical Democratic Politics* (London: Verso Books, 1985), 155.

42 Charles Taylor, *Modern Social Imaginaries* (Durham, NC: Duke University Press, 2005), 25.

43 Taylor, *Modern Social Imaginaries,* 25.

44 In the Westminster system, a white paper announces a general direction in policy and is often exploratory rather than definitive. (Pierre Trudeau's government's politically explosive 1969 white paper on Indian policy is often referred to simply as "the White Paper," leading to confusion regarding other white papers.) The 1945 white paper was called simply "Employment and Income"; however, the title *White Paper on Employment and Income* is more familiar and therefore used here.

CHAPTER 1: A CLEAR LINE?

1 The 1911 election, called "the most important election in Canadian political history," was once the object of significant scholarly interest. Paul Stevens, ed., *The General Election 1911: A Study in Canadian Politics* (Toronto: Copp Clark, 1970), 1. Because of the issues at stake and the outcome, it attracted historians writing on different aspects of politics. Reciprocity and its threat to manufacturing, railway, and finance interests in eastern Canada have been examined by scholars of Canadian business as well as (more critically) some scholars of political culture. The role of Henri Bourassa's nationalist movement in defeating Laurier in Quebec has also been examined extensively. There is considerable scholarship on party organization, seen for a period in the 1960s as the determining factor in the outcome of the Liberal defeat. Both W.L. Morton and John English have seen the 1911 election as the first act of a larger drama of political party formation: in English's *The Decline of Politics* (Toronto: University of Toronto Press, 1977), of the formation of the union government in the First World War, and in Morton's *The Progressive Party in Canada* (Toronto: University of Toronto Press, 1950), of the western development of a Progressive Party after the war. Only in surveys such as Robert Craig Brown and Ramsay Cook's *Canada 1896–1921: A Nation Transformed* (Toronto: McClelland and Stewart, 1974) was the election examined from the perspective of reciprocity and defence. Patrice Dutil and David MacKenzie's recent *Canada 1911* (Toronto: Dundurn, 2011) is the first monograph to attempt to integrate the story of English and French Canada. Dutil and MacKenzie, like I do in this chapter, see the election as "a moment marking out a transition from an older political culture to a more modern one" (303), but their focus is more on the words and actions of Laurier and Borden than on the reciprocity issue and the organized farmers' role in framing it. On the whole, the argument and emphasis in this chapter are most similar to Morton's, though with more particular attention paid to the role of the *Grain Growers' Guide* and to the language of political contestation generally.

2 "The Election Results," editorial, *Grain Growers' Guide* 4, 9 (1911): 5. Editorials in the *Grain Growers' Guide* were not signed, but Roderick McKenzie was the editor throughout the period examined in this chapter.

3 Stephen Leacock, "The Great Election in Missinauba County," *Montreal Daily Star*, May 25, 1912, 22. The story was later collected in *Sunshine Sketches of a Little Town* (London: John Lane, 1912), 124. In the book, "stupendous" is changed to "tremendous." For other changes between the newspaper version and the book, see Gerald Lynch, "From Serialization to Book: Leacock's Revisions to *Sunshine Sketches of a Little Town*," *Studies in Canadian Literature* 36, 2 (2011): 96–111. Albert Moritz and Theresa Moritz point out in *Stephen Leacock: His Remarkable Life* (Markham, ON: Fitzhenry and Whiteside, 2002) that Leacock often spoke during 1910–11 in support of the Conservative Party's defence of the tariff and note that "his addresses were packed with factual material, convincing arguments and even, it appears, emotional rhetoric" (148). They suggest that "Leacock's satirical view of the election may have emerged in the hindsight of 1912, as he worked on *Sunshine Sketches*" (147). The idea that Leacock write a humorous story with a Canadian setting for the *Star* came from B.K. Sandwell, a journalist who later became editor of *Saturday Night* (149).

4 Leacock, *Sunshine Sketches*, 124.

5 See Gerald Lynch on Leacock as a Tory humanist in *Stephen Leacock: Humour and Humanity* (Montreal and Kingston: McGill-Queen's University Press, 1988), 3–23.

6 J. Harvey Perry, *Taxes, Tariffs, and Subsidies: A History of Canadian Fiscal Development*, vol. 1 (Toronto: University of Toronto Press, 1955), 52.

7 O.D. Skelton, *General Economic History of the Dominion 1867–1912* (Toronto: Publishers' Association of Canada, 1912), 146.

8 Ben Forster, *A Conjunction of Interests: Business, Politics, and Tariffs, 1825–1879* (Toronto: University of Toronto Press, 1986), 180.

9 Forster, *A Conjunction of Interests*, 199.

10 For contemporary accounts, see the remarks by Macphail and the *Grain Growers' Guide* in this chapter. For historians, see Michael Bliss, who wrote in *Northern Enterprise: Five Centuries of Canadian Business* (Toronto: McClelland and Stewart, 1987) that "the Liberals finally came to power under Wilfrid Laurier in 1896 only after they let manufacturers know well in advance that they were 'safe' on the National Policy" (300), and Robert Craig Brown and Ramsay Cook, who remarked in *Canada 1896–1921: A Nation Transformed* (Toronto: McClelland and Stewart, 1974) that the 1893 convention was the start of the party's attempt "to redeem itself from its free trade past" (10).

11 *Tariff Reforms, Freer Trade, Reduced Taxation* (Toronto: Ontario Liberal Association, 1896), CIHM microfiche series no. 11463, 2.

12 Quoted in *Tariff Reforms, Freer Trade, Reduced Taxation*, 14.

13 Quoted in *Tariff Reforms, Freer Trade, Reduced Taxation*, 14.

14 Quoted in *Tariff Policy of the Government* (Toronto: Ontario Liberal Association, 1904), CIHM microfiche series no. 76123, 14.

15 Quoted in *Tariff Policy of the Government*, 15.

16 *Tariff Policy of the Government*, 15.

17 *The Tariff Issue in Canada: The Attitude of the Two Parties Regarding It* (Toronto: Ontario Liberal Association, 1902), CIHM microfiche series no. 77291, 16.

18 *Tariff Issue in Canada*, 16.

19 André Siegfried, *The Race Question in Canada* (New York: Appleton, 1907), 141–42.

20 Siegfried, *The Race Question in Canada*, 142.

21 Siegfried, *The Race Question in Canada*, 143.

22 Siegfried, *The Race Question in Canada*, 143.

23 Siegfried, *The Race Question in Canada*, 143.

24 Siegfried, *The Race Question in Canada*, 144.

25 Andrew Macphail, *Essays in Politics* (London: Longmans, Green 1909), 179.

26 Macphail, *Essays in Politics*, 183.

27 Macphail, *Essays in Politics*, 189.

28 Macphail, *Essays in Politics*, 158.

29 Macphail, *Essays in Politics*, 182.

30 Morton, *The Progressive Party in Canada*, 26.

31 See Ian McKay, *Reasoning Otherwise: Leftists and the People's Enlightenment in Canada, 1890–1920* (Toronto: Between the Lines, 2008), passim. His work, and the concept of people's enlightenment specifically, are discussed in detail in the introduction.

32 James Speakman, "The Tariff," *Grain Growers' Guide* 3, 4 (1910): 7. The article was a letter from Speakman, director of United Farmers of Alberta, to Laurier – one of many letters from farmer leaders printed that day.

33 W.D. Lamb, "Sifton and the Tariff," letter, *Grain Growers' Guide* 3, 5 (1910): 12.

34 "Protection and Revenue," editorial, *Grain Growers' Guide* 3, 15 (1910): 6.

35 "Different Ways of Looking at It," editorial, *Grain Growers' Guide* 2, 51 (1910): 6.

36 James Finlay, "For the Farmers," letter, *Grain Growers' Guide* 3, 21 (1910): 16.

37 "Protection and Revenue," editorial, *Grain Growers' Guide* 3, 15 (1910): 6.

38 "Canadian Farmers: The Facts about Preference," editorial, *Grain Growers' Guide* 2, 50 (1910): 9.

39 "Trade and Loyalty," editorial, *Grain Growers' Guide* 3, 33 (1911): 6.

40 "The Last Word," editorial, *Grain Growers' Guide* 4, 7 (1911): 5.

41 Zummerzet, "Bumkum and Flap-Doodle," letter, *Grain Growers' Guide* 3, 4 (1910): 12. Zummerzet was one of several correspondents whose letters were published under pseudonyms such as Jack O'Lantern and Unitas, a tradition in English journalism dating back to the eighteenth century.

42 "The Politics of Business," editorial, *Grain Growers' Guide* 3, 4 (1910): 6.

43 "Ontario Will Help the West," editorial, *Grain Growers' Guide* 3, 1 (1910): 5.

44 W.D. Lamb, "Sifton and the Tariff," letter, *Grain Growers' Guide* 3, 5 (1910): 12.

45 J.L. Williamson, "On Party Rule," letter, *Grain Growers' Guide* 3, 17 (1910): 17.

46 G.E. Wainwright, "The Future Outlook," letter, *Grain Growers' Guide* 4, 11 (1911): 14.

47 Frederic Kirkham, "Mr. Kirkham Returns Again," letter, *Grain Growers' Guide* 2, 52 (1910): 14.

48 "On to Ottawa," editorial, *Grain Growers' Guide* 3, 14 (1910): 6.

49 "Let There Be Light," editorial, *Grain Growers' Guide* 3, 17 (1910): 6. The title phrase and variations of it appeared regularly.

50 "What Protection Means," editorial, *Grain Growers' Guide* 2, 50 (1910): 6 (this editorial cited Laurier's speech at a Liberal Party convention in Ottawa in 1893); "What about the Tariff?," editorial, *Grain Growers' Guide* 2, 50 (1910): 6.

51 "Protection and Morals," editorial, *Grain Growers' Guide* 4, 11 (1911): 5.

52 "Sir Wilfrid's Reply," unsigned article, *Grain Growers' Guide* 3, 4 (1910): 11. The article paraphrased a speech by Laurier in Red Deer, Alberta, on August 11, 1910.

53 Untitled editorial, *Grain Growers' Guide* 4, 18 (1911): 6.

54 "Direct Taxation," editorial, *Grain Growers' Guide* 3, 50 (1911): 6.

55 David Ross, "On the Tariff," letter, *Grain Growers' Guide* 3, 13 (1910): 20.

56 "Who Pays the Tariff?," editorial, *Grain Growers' Guide* 3, 12 (1910): 6.

57 See Henry George, *Progress and Poverty: An Inquiry into the Causes of Industrial Depressions, and of the Increase of Want with Increase of Wealth* (New York: Appleton and Company, 1881). The single tax was a widely influential idea applied in some form in a few cities in western Canada for a short time. As Elsbeth Heaman notes in the unpublished manuscript chapter "The Single Tax vs the Supply-Side State: Revisiting a Western Canadian Experiment," the single tax was powerful and important at the turn of the century because it served as "a kind of middle ground between the two metatheories" – socialism and liberalism (33). (See my similar claim for the "conscription of wealth" in Chapter 2.) However, this malleability, a political strength of the idea at the time, has consigned the single tax to "a no-man's-land between two great conflicting interpretations of history: material and liberal" (4). This claim is countered by Ramsay Cook, who devotes a chapter of *The Regenerators: Social Criticism in Late Victorian English Canada* (Toronto: University of Toronto Press, 1985) to George's ideas and his influence on social reformers (107–22), and by Ian McKay, who discusses the single tax briefly in *Reasoning Otherwise*, noting George's reforms as being an important bridge between liberal and socialist thinking and pointing out that many later leftists migrated left through the single tax idea (85–86). On the practical side, J. Harvey Perry has paid significant attention to the single tax in *Taxes, Tariffs, and Subsidies*, devoting an entire chapter to analyzing the taxation of undeveloped land in new cities in western Canada and concluding that taxing unearned increments worked only because of the "exceptional and non-recurring condition of the times": that is, a "land boom of extravagance never witnessed before or since in Canada [which] reached its peak during these years" (1:131). These treatments, though, ignore the greater political significance of the single tax idea itself as a case of what Heaman calls "popular state-formation" (25).

58 "Direct Taxation," editorial, *Grain Growers' Guide* 3, 50 (1911): 6.

59 Joseph Schickl, "Re: Land Taxation," letter, *Grain Growers' Guide* 2, 50 (1910): 14.

60 "Western Leaders' Ideals," unsigned article, *Grain Growers' Guide* 3, 22 (1910): 20. The article was paraphrasing the remarks of E.A. Partridge, head of the United Farmers of Alberta, to the Canadian Club in Toronto on December 19, 1910.

61 John R. Symons, "Taxation on Land Values," letter, *Grain Growers' Guide* 3, 45 (1911): 18.

62 Fred W. Green, "Some Henry George Nuts," letter, *Grain Growers' Guide* 3, 47 (1911): 18.

63 Unitas, "What Is Taxation," letter, *Grain Growers' Guide* 4, 5 (1911): 10.

64 C.S. Watkins, "Direct Taxation Welcome," letter, *Grain Growers' Guide* 4, 4 (1911): 10.

65 "We Must Pull Together," editorial, *Grain Growers' Guide* 3, 2 (1910): 6.

66 "We Must Pull Together."

67 "Cleansing Political Life," editorial, *Grain Growers' Guide* 3, 12 (1910): 18. Mariana Valverde argues in *The Age of Light, Soap, and Water* (Toronto: McClelland and Stewart, 1991) that images of cleanliness and light were crucial to how moral reformers conceived of their work and its importance (38–43). Farmers who defined protection as corruption and saw their work as bringing cleanliness and light to politics were undoubtedly counting on the same "inspiring imagery" that Valverde outlines (41).

68 Jack O'Lantern, "Let There Be Light," letter, *Grain Growers' Guide* 3, 17 (1910): 18. Saint George slew a dragon and was the patron saint of England; invoking such a symbol of Britishness might have been an attempt to play to ethnic fears and desires in the multicultural Prairies.

69 J.A. Stevenson, "The Battle for Democracy in Canada," *Grain Growers' Guide* 3, 14 (1910): 11. This article was also cited by Morton in *The Progressive Party in Canada*.

70 G. Swanton, "Light in the Darkness," letter, *Grain Growers' Guide* 2, 50 (1910): 14.
71 Stevenson, "The Battle for Democracy in Canada," 11.
72 Stevenson, "The Battle for Democracy in Canada," 11.
73 "Condemn Extreme Partyism," editorial, *Grain Growers' Guide* 3, 33 (1911): 4. The phrase was attributed to Manitoba organizer J.W. Scallion, who used it in a speech in Virden, Manitoba, on March 8, and it was used repeatedly by the editors in the weeks that followed.
74 See McKay, *Reasoning Otherwise*, passim.
75 J.E. Paynter, "The Forward Movement," letter, *Grain Growers' Guide* 3, 16 (1910): 18. Paynter was identified as the secretary of the Comrades of Equity, a farmers' organization.
76 "Organize and Get Your Rights," editorial, *Grain Growers' Guide* 3, 13 (1910): 6.
77 *The Siege of Ottawa* (Ottawa: Canadian Council of Agriculture, 1911), 11.
78 *The Siege of Ottawa*, 12.
79 *The Siege of Ottawa*, 18.
80 *The Siege of Ottawa*, 22.
81 *The Siege of Ottawa*, 22.
82 *The Siege of Ottawa*, 49.
83 *The Siege of Ottawa*, 50.
84 "We Asked for Bread and You Gave Us a Stone," *Ottawa Evening Journal*, December 17, 1910, 1.
85 Canada, *Debates of the House of Commons*, December 16, 1910, 1454 (Robert Borden).
86 T.A. Russell, "The Grain Growers and the Manufacturers," in *Proceedings of the Canadian Club, Toronto, for the Year 1910–1911* (Toronto: Warwick Brothers and Rutter, 1911), 127, 117.
87 Ramsay Cook, *The Politics of John W. Dafoe and the* Free Press (Toronto: University of Toronto Press, 1963), 43.
88 "Mr. Russell's Reply to the Farmers," editorial, *Manitoba Free Press*, January 4, 1911, 4.
89 "Mr. Foster's Broadside," editorial, *Manitoba Free Press*, January 10, 1911, 4.
90 "Tariff Reduction Theme of Debate," editorial, *Manitoba Free Press*, January 19, 1911, 1.
91 "Tariff Reduction Theme of Debate," editorial, *Manitoba Free Press*, January 19, 1911, 1.
92 "Free Trade in All Farm Products: Lower Duties on Manufactured Goods," *Manitoba Free Press*, January 27, 1911, 1.
93 Dutil and MacKenzie, *Canada 1911*, 182.
94 Quoted in Dutil and MacKenzie, *Canada 1911*, 184.
95 Cook, *The Politics of John W. Dafoe*, 46.
96 "Reciprocity the Issue," editorial, *Grain Growers' Guide* 4, 2 (1911): 5.
97 G.E. Wainwright, "The Future Outlook," letter, *Grain Growers' Guide* 4, 11 (1911): 14.
98 Quoted in "Porritt's Election Views," *Grain Growers' Guide* 4, 13 (1911): 9.
99 O.D. Skelton, "Canada's Rejection of Reciprocity," *Journal of Political Economy* 19, 1 (1911): 731.
100 Skelton, "Canada's Rejection of Reciprocity," 726. A similar claim was made by Fielding in the House of Commons: "This is the reciprocity we begged the United States for thirty years to give us ... The leading gentleman on the opposite side of the House [the Conservatives] went down to Washington ... to ask for the very reciprocity that is now before the house." Quoted in Dutil and MacKenzie, *Canada 1911*, 158.
101 Skelton, "Canada's Rejection of Reciprocity," 728.
102 Skelton, "Canada's Rejection of Reciprocity," 727.

103 Charles W. Humphries, "Mackenzie King Looks at Two 1911 Elections," *Ontario History* 56, 3 (1964): 205.
104 Terence A. Crowley, "Mackenzie King and the 1911 Election," *Ontario History* 61, 4 (1969): 194.
105 Macphail, *Essays in Politics,* 167.
106 Quoted in Norman Hillmer, "Citizen Entrepreneur, 1908–1914" (unpublished chapter of a biography ofSkelton, 2009), 23.
107 Edward Porritt, *The Revolt in Canada against the New Feudalism: Tariff History from the Revision of 1907 to the Uprising of the West in 1910* (London: Cassell, 1911), 27.

CHAPTER 2: THE BRINK OF THE ABYSS

1 *Royal Commission on the Parliament Buildings Fire* (Ottawa: King's Printer, 1916). Chaired by Duncan McTavish, it was better known as the McTavish Commission.
2 This phrase is borrowed from Anthony Read, *The World on Fire: 1919 and the Battle with Bolshevism* (London: Jonathan Cape, 2008).
3 Stephen Leacock, *The Unsolved Riddle of Social Justice* (Toronto: S.B. Gundy, 1920), 12. This was his first serious book on a contemporary issue, his previous publications having been humourous novels, textbooks, and history books. Leacock was sympathetic to the Conservative Party and became an ardent opponent of leftism late in his career, but students of his political thinking have consistently underlined its subtlety. Gerald Lynch identifies Leacock in his book *Stephen Leacock: Humour and Humanity* (Montreal and Kingston: McGill-Queen's University Press, 1988) as a Tory humanist somewhat akin to what Gad Horowitz would later describe as Red Tory but with less explicit sympathy for the left; see his "Conservatism, Liberalism, and Socialism in Canada: An Interpretation," *Canadian Journal of Economics and Political Science* 32, 2 (1966): 143–71. Myron J. Frankman, in his essay "Stephen Leacock, Economist," in *Stephen Leacock: A Reappraisal,* ed. David Staines (Ottawa: University of Ottawa Press, 1986), 52, connects Leacock to Thorsten Veblen, the American sociologist and social critic. Ian McKay, in *Reasoning Otherwise: Leftists and the People's Enlightenment in Canada, 1890–1920* (Toronto: Between the Lines, 2008), 87, points out that Leacock at a young age was a follower of utopian socialist Edward Bellamy.
4 Leacock, *The Unsolved Riddle of Social Justice,* 13.
5 Canada, *Debates of the House of Commons,* August 2, 1917, 4108 (George Graham).
6 Canada, *Debates of the House of Commons,* August 17, 1917, 4652 (Charles Murphy).
7 Canada, *Debates of the House of Commons,* August 17, 1917, 4641 (Michael Clark).
8 Canada, *Debates of the House of Commons,* August 17, 1917, 4639 (Federick Forsyth Pardee).
9 John English, *The Decline of Politics: The Conservatives and the Party System 1901–20* (Toronto: University of Toronto Press, 1979), 53–69.
10 Library and Archives Canada (LAC), Sir William Thomas White Papers, boxes 1–4, consist of correspondence between White and various banking executives and Canadian officials in London, sharing intelligence about Canada's standing as a credit risk.
11 R.T. Naylor, "The Canadian State, the Accumulation of Capital, and the Great War," *Journal of Canadian Studies* 16, 3–4 (1981): 29.
12 W. Irwin Gillespie in *Tax, Borrow, and Spend: Financing Federal Spending in Canada, 1867–1990* (Ottawa: Carleton University Press, 1991), 56–60, devotes considerable space

to the many objections of dominion finance ministers, from Richard Cartwright in the 1870s to White in the 1910s, to direct taxation. A representative quotation is George Foster's remark: "I would like to see the man who could be elected in any constituency on a policy of direct taxation" (56). H.V. Nelles in *The Politics of Development: Forestry, Mines, and Hydro-Electric Power in Ontario, 1849–1941* (Montreal and Kingston: McGill-Queen's University Press, 1974), 46, has also noted that the peculiarities of Ontario's resource policies can be largely explained by the province's fear of "the 'bugbear' of direct taxation."

13 "On account ... of the serious interruption of ocean commerce which is bound to ensue by reason of the hostilities I apprehend that our imports, and consequently our revenues, may be more seriously curtailed and reduced and it would appear to me that we may face a situation in which the [previous] estimate of revenue will not be reached." Thomas White to Robert Borden, August 3, 1914, LAC, Sir William Thomas White Papers, box 3.

14 During the debate on the income war tax, F.B. Carvell cited his own suggestion in August 1914 that income tax should be introduced to pay for the war. See *Debates of the House of Commons*, July 25, 1917, 3769–70. Frederick William-Taylor, chairman of the Bank of Montreal, then Canada's largest bank and a key ally of the federal treasury, and B. Edmund Walker, chairman of the Canadian Bank of Commerce, wrote to White on August 10, 1914, to say that income taxation was an option that, however unpopular, would be accepted. LAC, Sir William Thomas White Papers, box 3. White's description of income tax as a "minor" tax is highlighted in J. Harvey Perry, *Taxes, Tariffs, and Subsidies: A History of Canadian Fiscal Development*, vol. 1 (Toronto: University of Toronto Press, 1955), 151.

15 W.A. Mackintosh noted shortly after the war that "issue after issue of tax exempt bonds put a premium on large incomes to be paid out of the taxes of the ordinary consumer." Quoted in Hugh Grant, "Revolution in Winnipeg, 1919," *Labour/Le travail* 60 (2007): 174. Richard Krever, "The Origin of Federal Income Taxation in Canada," *Canadian Taxation* 3, 2 (1981): 184, also notes that some Liberal members "pointed out that, without an income tax, raising revenue through bonds would mean that the poorer pay to the richer citizens of the country."

16 O.D. Skelton, *Canadian Federal Finance* (Kingston: Jackson Press, 1915), 86.

17 "The Burden of Government," editorial, *Industrial Banner*, November 3, 1916, 6.

18 "The Burden of Government."

19 "The High Cost of Living," editorial, *Industrial Banner*, September 1, 1916, 6.

20 "Now Is the Time," editorial, *Industrial Banner*, September 15, 1916, 2.

21 "Immoral Profits," editorial, *Industrial Banner*, March 9, 1917, 4.

22 Myer Siemiatycki, "Munitions and Labour Militancy: The 1916 Hamilton Machinists' Strike," *Labour/Le travail* 3 (1978): 132.

23 Siemiatycki, "Munitions and Labour Militancy," 131–32.

24 Siemiatycki, "Munitions and Labour Militancy," 133.

25 "It Is Up to the Government," editorial, *Industrial Banner*, June 16, 1916, 2.

26 "The Spirit of Revolt Is Everywhere Apparent," editorial, *Industrial Banner*, August 25, 1916, 1.

27 "Workmen and Recruiting," editorial, *Industrial Banner*, June 30, 1916, 2.

28 Under the Military Service Act, Class 1 recruits, who were the first priority and, as it turned out, the only ones to be actually conscripted, had to be unmarried, without children, and between the ages of twenty and thirty-five. Canada, *The Military Service Act: Its Meaning and Effects* (Ottawa: King's Printer, 1917), 1.

29 "Labour Will Demand Better Conditions after the War," editorial, *Industrial Banner*, September 15, 1916, 1.
30 "The Government Has Promised There Shall Be No Conscription," *Industrial Banner*, October 20, 1916, 1.
31 "Will the Government Allow Wealth to Go Free Now Labor Is to Be Conscripted?," *Industrial Banner*, May 25, 1917, 1.
32 "Labor Is on Guard!," editorial, *Industrial Banner*, June 1, 1917, 4.
33 McKay, *Reasoning Otherwise*, 434.
34 "A Battle for Place and Power," editorial, *Industrial Banner*, June 22, 1917, 4.
35 Stephen Leacock, *National Organization for War* (Ottawa: King's Printer, 1917), 3.
36 Leacock, *National Organization*, 3.
37 Leacock, *National Organization*, 4.
38 Leacock, *National Organization*, 9, 3.
39 Newton Rowell, *Conscription of Wealth* (n.p.: n.p., [1917?]), 4.
40 Rowell, *Conscription of Wealth*, 9.
41 Rowell, *Conscription of Wealth*, 9.
42 "Political Action," editorial, *Industrial Banner*, July 7, 1916, 2. The phrase was common in the *Banner* in this period.
43 "Political Action."
44 "Political Action."
45 "The Awakening," editorial, *Industrial Banner*, December 15, 1916, 4.
46 "Thus the war-induced epidemic of general strikes, which one prominent unionist dubbed 'Winnipegitis,' found its earliest germination in Toronto." Siemiatycki, "Munitions and Labour Militancy," 141.
47 Canada, *Labour Gazette* (Ottawa: King's Printer, 1917), 847–49.
48 Quoted in "Asks that Canada 'Conscript' Wealth," unsigned article, *New York Times*, July 4, 1917, 4.
49 "The Awakening," editorial, *Industrial Banner*, December 15, 1916, 4.
50 Krever, "Origin of Federal Income Taxation in Canada."
51 English, *The Decline of Politics*, 106.
52 Krever, "Origin of Federal Income Taxation in Canada," 185.
53 Quoted in Krever, "Origin of Federal Income Taxation in Canada," 187.
54 As J. Harvey Perry notes in *Taxation in Canada* (Toronto: University of Toronto Press, 1951), 308, "generally the members of the Opposition conduct almost the entire debate and to an observer unfamiliar with this fact it would appear from its tenor that the budget had been pretty much a dismal failure."
55 Canada, *Debates of the House of Commons*, June 22, 1917, 2576.
56 Canada, *Debates of the House of Commons*, June 22, 1917, 2576.
57 Canada, *Debates of the House of Commons*, June 22, 1917, 2576.
58 Canada, *Debates of the House of Commons*, July 10, 1917, 3187.
59 Canada, *Debates of the House of Commons*, July 10, 1917, 3187.
60 Canada, *Debates of the House of Commons*, July 10, 1917, 3187.
61 Canada, *Debates of the House of Commons*, August 17, 1917, 4561; Leacock, *National Organization for War*, 9.
62 Canada, *Debates of the House of Commons*, September 15, 1917, 5885.
63 Canada, *Debates of the House of Commons*, August 17, 1917, 4640.
64 Canada, *Debates of the House of Commons*, August 27, 1917, 5005–6.

65   Canada, *Debates of the House of Commons*, September 8, 1917, 5553.
66   "Public Sentiment Demanding Conscription of Wealth," editorial, *Industrial Banner,*
     October 5, 1917, 1.
67   Quoted in English, *The Decline of Politics*, 222.
68   Quoted in English, *The Decline of Politics*, 222.
69   Gregory S. Kealey, *Workers and Canadian History* (Montreal and Kingston: McGill-
     Queen's University Press, 1995), 289–319.
70   Craig Heron and Myer Siemiatycki, "The Great War," in *The Worker's Revolt in Canada
     1917–1925*, ed. Craig Heron (Toronto: University of Toronto Press, 1998), 35.
71   O.D. Skelton, *Canadian Federal Finance II* (Kingston: Jackson Press, 1918), 2.
72   Perry, *Taxes, Tariffs, and Subsidies*, 1:163–64.
73   *Debates of the House of Commons*, February 26, 1919, 49.
74   C.W. Peterson, *Wake Up, Canada! Reflections on Vital National Issues* (Toronto: Macmil-
     lan, 1919), 280.
75   Peterson, *Wake Up, Canada!*, 281.
76   Peterson, *Wake Up, Canada!*, 282.
77   Peterson, *Wake Up, Canada!*, 283.
78   Leacock, *The Unsolved Riddle of Social Justice*, 30.
79   Leacock, *The Unsolved Riddle*, 10–11.
80   Skelton, *Canadian Federal Finance II*, 1.
81   Leacock, *The Unsolved Riddle of Social Justice*, 140–41.

CHAPTER 3: THE CURVE OF PROGRESSIVITY

 1   When Rogers died in an airplane crash in June 1940, political economist and civil ser-
     vant W.A. Mackintosh wrote warmly of his colleague, saying that "people instinctively
     trusted" him and "believed unhesitatingly in the soundness of his standards and the right-
     ness of his motives." See "Obituary: Norman McLeod Rogers, 1894–1940," *Canadian
     Journal of Economics and Political Science* 6, 3 (1940): 476. A few weeks before his death,
     however, Rogers was described by Conservative Party leader R.J. Manion to the *Windsor
     Star* as an "irresponsible little falsifier" and an "unscrupulous man." See J.L. Granatstein,
     The Politics of Survival: The Conservative Party of Canada, 1939–1945 (Toronto: University
     of Toronto Press, 1967), 45.
 2   Canada, *Debates of the House of Commons*, January 23, 1939, 217–18.
 3   Lara Campbell, *Respectable Citizens: Gender, Family, and Unemployment in Ontario's Great
     Depression* (Toronto: University of Toronto Press, 2009), 3. She notes that the historiog-
     raphy on the Depression is "fragmented and incomplete" (7).
 4   Following the convention of identifying royal commissions by their chairs, the Royal
     Commission on Dominion-Provincial Relations takes its name from Newton Rowell,
     who chaired it until 1938, and Joseph Sirois, who replaced him. The scholarly literature
     on the Rowell-Sirois Commission is extensive, reflecting its importance in the develop-
     ment of the postwar federal state and its attraction to political scientists and histori-
     ans as a subject. Of the older studies, the two most important for this chapter have
     been J. Harvey Perry's account of the tax questions addressed by the commission and
     Doug Owram's book on intellectual engagement with constitutional questions as part
     of a wider culture of reform. See J. Harvey Perry, *Taxes, Tariffs, and Subsidies: A History
     of Canadian Fiscal Development*, 2 vols. (Toronto: University of Toronto Press, 1955),

307–24; and Doug Owram, *The Government Generation: Canadian Intellectuals and the State 1900–1945* (Toronto: University of Toronto Press, 1986), 221–53. Of the more recent studies, T. Stephen Henderson's emphasis on the role of Nova Scotia's commission (the Jones Commission) in laying the groundwork for the Rowell-Sirois Commission is most similar to this chapter's and is cited throughout. See T. Stephen Henderson, "A New Federal Vision: Nova Scotia and the Rowell-Sirois Report, 1938–48," in *Framing Canadian Federalism: Essays in Honour of John T. Saywell*, ed. Dimitry Anastakis and P.E. Bryden (Toronto: University of Toronto Press, 2009), 51–74. Matt James's argument that advocates of left materialist agendas had to focus strategically on improving conditions of possibility resonates with this chapter's, but ultimately the focus is different. See Matt James, *Misrecognized Materialists: Social Movements in Canadian Politics* (Vancouver: UBC Press, 2006), 13–26.

5 Canada, *Report of the Royal Commission on Dominion-Provincial Relations*, 3 vols. (Ottawa: J.O. Patenaud, King's Printer, 1939), 2: 111.

6 Canada, *Report on Dominion-Provincial Relations*, 2: 112.

7 See J.L. Granatstein, *The Ottawa Men: The Civil Service Mandarins, 1935–1957* (Toronto: Oxford University Press, 1982); Owram, *The Government Generation;* and Barry Ferguson, *Remaking Liberalism: The Intellectual Legacy of Adam Shortt, O.D. Skelton, W.C. Clark, and W.A. Mackintosh, 1890–1925* (Montreal and Kingston: McGill-Queen's University Press, 1993). Granatstein's account is the most narrowly biographical, portraying a small group of like-minded men rising to power. Owram's cast of characters is larger, the narrative arc is longer, and the wider social forces that gave rise to a governmental culture hungry for expertise are exhaustively painted in. Ferguson's version is a hybrid of the two approaches, focusing on a small number of linked scholar-bureaucrats but providing a wider context for them. Granatstein's work reflects the insistent ossification of interpretive approaches in political history during the ascendancy of social and cultural history. The intellectual history of politics that Owram and Ferguson represent tends to reify ideas and intellectuals but is more easily brought into conversation with other approaches and is therefore more valuable.

8 See the introduction for a discussion of this term as it is used here.

9 James, *Misrecognized Materialists*, 22.

10 James, *Misrecognized Materialists*, 23.

11 Quoted in James Struthers, *No Fault of Their Own: Unemployment and the Canadian Welfare State, 1914–1941* (Toronto: University of Toronto Press, 1983), 128. The first quotation is from a debate in the House of Commons in early 1935, and the second is from a letter in the Bennett papers.

12 Michiel Horn, *The League for Social Reconstruction: The Intellectual Origins of the Democratic Left in Canada, 1930–1942* (Toronto: University of Toronto Press, 1980), 131–32.

13 League for Social Reconstruction, *Social Planning for Canada* (Toronto: Nelson, 1935), 501.

14 F.R. Scott, "The Privy Council and Mr. Bennett's 'New Deal' Legislation," 1937, in *Essays on the Constitution: Aspects of Canadian Law and Politics* (Toronto: University of Toronto Press, 1977), 92.

15 Untitled editorial, *Canadian Forum* 16, 187 (1936): 5; untitled editorial, *Canadian Forum* 16, 194 (1937): 6.

16 Untitled editorial, *Canadian Forum* 16, 194 (1937): 6.

17 J. Alex Aikin, "Rewriting the National Constitution," *Canadian Forum* 15, 174 (1935): 207.

18 The discussion of Maritime Rights in this chapter draws heavily from E.R. Forbes, *The Maritime Rights Movement, 1919–1927* (Montreal and Kingston: McGill-Queen's University Press, 1979), which linked the movement to wider movements of progressive reform in the early twentieth century, and to a lesser extent from Don Nerbas, "Revisiting the Politics of Maritime Rights," *Acadiensis* 37, 1 (2008): 110–30, which portrayed it as "a self-legitimizing movement of the local elite" (112). The research and analysis of Nerbas are more rigorous and precise, but his argument is ultimately unconvincing in what, for this book, are key places. Nerbas makes no mention, for example, of the phrase "fiscal need." The claim that regional agitators could "make demands upon the Dominion government while simultaneously rejecting the principle of the redistributive role of state intervention" ignores the centrality of social programs to the goals of the region, as well as the resistance of the dominion, which clearly reflected a fear of fiscal commitments that would ultimately be redistributive. Nerbas also cites labour leaders' support for Maritime Rights demands as evidence of the hegemony of business leadership, even though labour would have had its own reasons for supporting measures that would slow outmigration and deindustrialization. This chapter draws on his research but sticks closer to Forbes in its overall interpretation of the movement's character and purpose.

19 Ernest R. Forbes, *Challenging the Regional Stereotype: Essays on the 20th Century Maritimes* (Fredericton: Acadiensis Press, 1989), 112.

20 Forbes, *Challenging the Regional Stereotype*, 112.

21 Other than Thomas Wakem Caldwell, elected as a Progressive in the riding of Victoria-Carleton in New Brunswick in 1921, all of the members elected in New Brunswick, Nova Scotia, and Prince Edward Island in the 1921, 1925, and 1926 federal elections were either Conservatives or Liberals. Compared with Manitoba, which in 1921 elected eleven Progressives, three Liberals, and one Labour member, it's easy to see why the Maritimes were perceived as being more politically traditional than the west. This is, however, a mistaken impression.

22 Forbes, *The Maritime Rights Movement*, 86.

23 Diary of William Lyon Mackenzie King, quoted in John Herd Thompson and Allen Seager, *Canada 1922–1939: Decades of Discord* (Toronto: McClelland and Stewart, 1985), 109.

24 Forbes, *The Maritime Rights Movement*, 127.

25 *Journal of the Canadian Bankers' Association*, 1925, quoted in Thompson and Seager, *Canada 1922–1939*, 111.

26 Norman McLeod Rogers, *A Submission on Dominion-Provincial Relations and the Fiscal Liabilities of Nova Scotia with the Canadian Federation* (Halifax: King's Printer, 1934), 160–61.

27 Stephen Henderson, "A New Federal Vision: Nova Scotia and the Rowell-Sirois Report, 1938–1948," in *Framing Canadian Federalism: Essays in Honour of John T. Saywell*, ed. Dimitry Anastakis and P.E. Bryden (Toronto: University of Toronto Press, 2009), 51, 54.

28 Rogers, *A Submission on Dominion-Provincial Relations*, 88.

29 Norman McLeod Rogers, "A Crisis in Federal Finance," *Canadian Forum* 15, 170 (1934): 54.

30 Rogers, "Crisis in Federal Finance," 54.

31 Norman McLeod Rogers, "One Path to Reform," *Canadian Forum* 15, 171 (1934): 98.

32 Rogers, *A Submission on Dominion-Provincial Relations*, 193.

33 Canada, *Report of the Royal Commission on Financial Arrangements between the Dominion and the Maritime Provinces* (Ottawa: King's Printer, 1935), 9.

34 Canada, *Report on Financial Arrangements*, 9.
35 Canada, *Report on Financial Arrangements*, 9.
36 Canada, *Report on Financial Arrangements*, 6.
37 Canada, *Brief of the Dominion of Canada* (Ottawa: King's Printer, 1935), 81.
38 Canada, *Brief of the Dominion of Canada*, 82.
39 Canada, *Brief of the Dominion of Canada*, 83.
40 Canada, *Report on Financial Arrangements*, 23.
41 Quoted in Henderson, "A New Federal Vision," 56.
42 There were other internal sources of pressure for a commission, such as the Bank of Canada, a newly established institution of the dominion government, and its staff of university-trained political economists. J.J. Deutsch and Alex Skelton were hired by the bank in 1936 and immediately set to work investigating the finances of Manitoba and then Saskatchewan and Alberta. Their reports were released internally one by one through the winter and spring of 1937 and then published in book form. Granatstein says in *The Ottawa Men* that these reports allowed Graham Towers, president of the bank, to pressure King successfully to call the commission (60–61). Undoubtedly, though, the agitation for a renewed fiscal federation began outside the civil service and was effectively expressed inside it later.
43 Quoted in Larry Glassford, *Reaction and Reform: The Politics of the Conservative Party under R.B. Bennett 1927–1938* (Toronto: University of Toronto Press, 1992), 137.
44 Untitled editorial, *Canadian Forum* 16, 192 (1937): 6. This phrase and variations of it were used regularly in the *Forum* in this period.
45 W.L. Morton, *The Progressive Party in Canada* (Toronto: University of Toronto Press, 1950), 151.
46 "Falsifying Election Issues," editorial, *Canadian Forum* 19, 223 (1939): 140.
47 Graham Spry, "Politics," *Canadian Forum* 15, 177 (1935): 324.
48 Untitled editorial, *Canadian Forum* 16, 183 (1936): 4.
49 David Lewis, "The C.C.F. Convention," *Canadian Forum* 16, 188 (1936): 7.
50 "Red Herridge or Red Herring?," editorial, *Canadian Forum* 19, 223 (1939): 139.
51 "Red Herridge or Red Herring?," 139.
52 G. McLure, "The C.C.F. and Mr. Herridge," *Canadian Forum* 19, 224 (1939): 192.
53 Spry, "Politics," 324.
54 Frank Underhill, "A Socialist Analysis [of the New Deal]," *Canadian Forum* 15, 173 (1935): 168.
55 Eugene Forsey, "The Taxpayers' Money," *Canadian Forum* 19, 222 (1939): 107.
56 Canada, *Dominion-Provincial Conference, Tuesday, January 14, 1941 and Wednesday, January 15, 1941* (Ottawa: King's Printer, 1941), 73.
57 "The C.C.F.'s Opportunity," editorial, *Canadian Forum* 17, 199 (1937): 155. The editorial continues that "historians are only snobs who attach themselves to the successful and call them the bearers of destiny."
58 Dorothy Steeves, "A British Columbia View," *Canadian Forum* 20, 238 (1940): 239.
59 Canada, *Report of the Royal Commission on Dominion-Provincial Relations* 1: 42–43.
60 *British North America Act and Amendments 1867–1927* (Ottawa: J.O. Patenaude, 1935). The pencil mark appears on page 19 in Skelton's copy, D.A. (Alex) Skelton Fonds, Queen's University Archives, box 1.
61 League for Social Reconstruction, *Social Planning for Canada*, 327, 338–44.
62 Canada, *Report of the Royal Commission on Dominion-Provincial Relations*, 1: 214.

63 Canada, *Report on Dominion-Provincial Relations*, 1: 214.
64 Canada, *Report on Dominion-Provincial Relations*, 1: 214.
65 Canada, *Report on Dominion-Provincial Relations*, 1: 214.

CHAPTER 4: A MODERN MEASURE?

1 Quoted in Joseph Schumpeter, "The Crisis of the Tax State," in *The Economics and Sociology of Capitalism*, ed. Richard Swedberg (Princeton, NJ: Princeton University Press, 1991), 100. The line, which first appeared in Goldscheid's 1917 book *Staatssozialismus oder Staatskapitalismus* (State Socialism or State Capitalism), referred to the budget itself, the numerical revenues and expenditures, not the written or spoken document. Schumpeter and Goldscheid were Austrian social scientists in the early twentieth century who sought to move public finance to the centre of the analysis of modern society. Schumpeter wrote that "the spirit of a people, its cultural level, its social structure, the deeds its policy may prepare – all this and more is written in its fiscal history, stripped of all phrases" (101). Interest in Schumpeter in particular has been rising, as evidenced by the return of the term "fiscal sociology" in the title of a recent collection of essays on taxation, *The New Fiscal Sociology: Taxation in Comparative and Historical Perspective*, ed. Isaac William Martin, Ajay K. Mehrotra, and Monica Prassad (Cambridge, UK: Cambridge University Press, 2009).
2 Canada, *Debates of the House of Commons*, June 23, 1942, 3577. The work of parliamentary rhetoric in establishing authority, and the scholarly study of that work, are discussed in Chapter 3. Here my focus is on Ilsley's role in marking – and making sense of – the radical novelty of universal income taxation.
3 The term refers to change in the "moral and symbolic meaning of taxation" whereby all citizens contribute through taxation to fund programs that benefit everyone. See Shirley Tillotson, "A New Taxpayer for a New State: Charitable Fundraising and the Origins of the Welfare State," in *Social Fabric or Patchwork Quilt: The Development of Social Policy in Canada*, ed. Raymond B. Blake and Jeff Keshen (Peterborough, ON: Broadview Press, 2006), 162–64. See Chapter 1 for a discussion of this term and its use in this thesis.
4 Bob Russell, "The Politics of Labour-Force Production: Funding Canada's Social Wage, 1917–1946," *Studies in Political Economy* 13 (1984): 67. Russell places the revisions to the dominion income tax in the early 1940s in the context of a discussion on the Marxist idea of reproduction of the labour force, arguing that "the partial socialization of wage income" effected by the Ilsley revisions to the income war tax and the "vastly extended general revenues of the [dominion] state" that they produced "made possible social-wage entitlements such as the family allowance scheme" (66). Although Russell's theoretical concerns are different from mine, the outline of events is roughly the model for this chapter in particular and to some extent for the book as a whole. I am indebted to James Struthers for directing me to the Russell article years ago when I first expressed interest in the origins of dominion income taxation.
5 For the federal Liberals' wartime social policy positions, see James Struthers, "Unequal Citizenship: The Residualist Legacy in the Canadian Welfare State," in *Mackenzie King: Citizenship and Community*, ed. John English, Kenneth McLaughlin, and P. Whitney Lackenbauer (Toronto: Robin Bass Studio, 2002), 169–85. Struthers argues that Ottawa's development of welfare state measures under King's leadership was limited and cautious and that concerns about excessive tax burdens were key in these considerations (175, 174).

6 J.L. Granatstein, *The Politics of Survival: The Conservative Party of Canada, 1939–1945* (Toronto: University of Toronto Press, 1967), offers a straightforward narrative of the party's difficulties, underlining the awkward policy shifts during the Manion-Meighen-Bracken era, but ties these difficulties to the popularity of the CCF and social welfare policies rather than to the novelty of universal income taxation and the left–right spectrum. In this chapter, my focus is on the increasing ubiquity of left–right language as a medium for representing political possibilities and differences rather than the difficulties of the Conservative Party per se.

7 Donald Creighton, *The Forked Road: Canada 1939–1957* (Toronto: McClelland and Stewart, 1976), 52. The fact that J. Harvey Perry also underlines the challenge that universal taxation posed to the political imagination – noting that "increasing federal revenues ninefold in the short period of five years" was "an accomplishment that would not have been deemed possible in 1939" – suggests that Ilsley's reforms were an important generational experience that was quickly forgotten and has not interested scholars since. J. Harvey Perry, *Taxes, Tariffs, and Subsidies: A History of Canadian Fiscal Development*, 2 vols. (Toronto: University of Toronto Press, 1955), 1:329. For the purposes of my study, Creighton's and Perry's accounts offer an interesting case of ambiguity between primary documents and historiography, given that they were written sometime after the fact by people deeply invested in the events described. Neither Creighton nor Perry links the awe-inspiring effect of the universalization of income taxation to the increasing ubiquity of the left–right spectrum, the key argument of this chapter.

8 Advertisement, *Saturday Night*, June 12, 1943, 15; ellipses in the original.

9 Ken Norrie and Doug Owram, *A History of the Canadian Economy* (Toronto: Harcourt Brace Jovanovich, 1991), 519. Owram also notes in *The Government Generation: Canadian Intellectuals and the State 1900–1945* (Toronto: University of Toronto Press, 1986), 296, that "in the First [World] War the government had attempted to run the war without disrupting the traditional approach to finance," and he cites mandarin John J. Deutsch's judgment that in the earlier war "the government thought that heavy direct taxation would be a deterrent to expansion and private enterprise which it had done so much to promote," whereas the Second World War could only be won by "detailed planning, a high degree of centralized direction of economic forces, and effective coordination." Owram's overall argument in *The Government Generation* is that the war years marked a significant change in the federal government's approach to governing.

10 Quoted in Perry, *Taxes, Tariffs, and Subsidies*, 2: 537.

11 Canada, *Debates of the House of Commons*, June 23, 1942, 3578.

12 Canada, *Debates of the House of Commons*, June 23, 1942, 3578.

13 P.M. Richards, "The Taxes Make Us Blink," *Saturday Night*, May 3, 1941, 27.

14 Canada, *Debates of the House of Commons*, June 23, 1942, 3574.

15 Canada, *Debates of the House of Commons*, June 23, 1942, 3574.

16 Bob Russell, "The Politics of Labour-Force Reproduction: Funding Canada's Social Wage, 1917–1946," *Studies in Political Economy* 13 (1984): 59, 65. The quoted phrase is from *Report of the Royal Commission on Dominion-Provincial Relations*, 3 vols. (Ottawa: J.O. Patenaud, King's Printer, 1939), 1: 214, which is discussed in the previous chapter.

17 W.A. McKague, "Muddling through Our New Tax Structure," *Saturday Night*, February 15, 1941, 30.

18 J.L. Ilsley, *Sharing the Cost of War: An Address before the Trades and Labour Congress of Canada, Quebec City* (Ottawa: National Liberal Federation, 1942), 9–10.

19 Ilsley, *Sharing the Cost of War,* 9.
20 Canada, *Debates of the House of Commons,* June 23, 1942, 3584.
21 Dudley A. Bristow, "Words and Meanings," *Saturday Night,* December 25, 1943, 3.
22 B.K. Sandwell, "Names Are Not Important," editorial, *Saturday Night,* December 7, 1940, 25.
23 B.K. Sandwell, "Parliament's Function," editorial, *Saturday Night,* February 10, 1940, 3.
24 B.K. Sandwell, "The Conservative Problem," *Saturday Night,* May 30, 1942, 1.
25 Sandwell, "The Conservative Problem," 1.
26 Untitled editorial, *Saturday Night,* March 30, 1940, 3.
27 Henry Bayne Macdonald, "The Conservative Revival," *Saturday Night,* February 14, 1942, 20.
28 Armour Mackay, "Winnipeg Result Gives Us Time to Think," *Saturday Night,* January 9, 1943, 14.
29 A.C. Forrest, "Political Agnosticism Big Factor in C.C.F. Rise," *Saturday Night,* October 2, 1943, 8.
30 J.E. DeWolf, "Too Narrow Freedom," *Saturday Night,* August 8, 1942, 2.
31 Corolyn Cox, "Bialystok-McGill-Oxford-Ottawa," *Saturday Night,* April 3, 1943, 2.
32 Granatstein, *The Politics of Survival,* 150.
33 "Winnipeg and Socialism," editorial, *Saturday Night,* November 21, 1942, 8.
34 B.K. Sandwell, "The Conservative Party," editorial, *Saturday Night,* April 6, 1940, 3.
35 L.L.L. Golden, "Conservative Party – Which Way?," *Saturday Night,* April 20, 1940, 10.
36 "Party or Rebellion," editorial, *Saturday Night,* July 11, 1942, 3.
37 J.W. Macdonnell, "Can We Return to Freedom?," *Saturday Night,* July 11, 1942, 7.
38 Quoted in Granatstein, *The Politics of Survival,* 126.
39 Granatstein, *The Politics of Survival,* 134.
40 Armour Mackay, "Winnipeg Result Gives Us Time to Think," *Saturday Night,* January 9, 1943, 14.
41 Stephen Leacock, "George Drew and Conservatism," *Saturday Night,* July 24, 1943, 11.
42 Stephen Leacock, "Optimism for Wartime: Good News! A New Party!," *Saturday Night,* March 20, 1943, 16.
43 John Bracken, *The Party – Its Future* (Ottawa: Progressive Conservative Association of Canada, 1944), 4.
44 Bracken, *The Party,* 1.
45 Bracken, *The Party,* 5–6.
46 Granatstein, *The Politics of Survival,* 63.
47 Bracken, *The Party,* 3.
48 David Lewis and Frank Scott, *Make This Your Canada: A Review of CCF Policy and History* (Toronto: Cooperative Commonwealth Federation, 1943), 181.
49 Carlyle King, *What Is Democratic Socialism?* (Ottawa: CCF National Office, 1943), 21.
50 M.J. Coldwell, *Left Turn, Canada* (Toronto: Duell, Sloan, and Pearce, 1945), 144.
51 Coldwell, *Left Turn, Canada,* 145–46.
52 Coldwell, *Left Turn, Canada,* 188.
53 Ilsley, *Sharing the Cost of War,* 2.
54 B.K. Sandwell, "War Gets Things Done," editorial, *Saturday Night,* March 22, 1941, 14.
55 G.C. Whitaker, "No Security Legislation This Winter," *Saturday Night,* March 27, 1943, 9.
56 Stanley McConnell, "Is the Commonwealth Swinging to the Left?," *Saturday Night,* August 5, 1944, 26.

57 A.C. Forrest, "Political Agnosticism Big Factor in C.C.F. Rise," *Saturday Night*, October 2, 1943, 8.

58 Owram, *The Government Generation*, 291.

59 G.C. Whitaker, "What New Strategy Will King Adopt to Meet the CCF?," *Saturday Night*, June 24, 1944, 8.

60 Raymond B. Blake, *From Right to Needs: A History of Family Allowances, 1929–92* (Vancouver: UBC Press, 2009), 98, 104. The Family Allowance, Blake argues, "exceeded any previous peacetime administrative organization in both size and scope" (125).

61 Owram, *The Government Generation*, 311. Owram argues that the introduction of family allowances reflected the victory of macroeconomic planning over social welfare priorities in reconstruction (310–15). Anne Fromer, "Social Security for Canada," *Saturday Night*, March 20, 1943, 6.

62 Quoted in Granatstein, *The Politics of Survival*, 165.

63 Henry Somerville, "The World Movement for Family Allowances," *Saturday Night*, June 14, 1941, 15.

64 Perry, *Taxes, Tariffs, and Subsidies*, 2:384–85.

65 Owram, *The Government Generation*, 317, argues that the *White Paper* showed the extent to which "the expert had triumphed in Ottawa" and demonstrated that "the state was committed to a set of policies and expenditures unprecedented in Canadian history."

66 Perry, *Taxes, Tariffs, and Subsidies*, 2:382.

CONCLUSION

1 Isaac William Martin, Ajay Mehrotra, and Monica Prasad, "The Thunder of History: The Origins and Development of the New Fiscal Sociology," in *The New Fiscal Sociology: Taxation in Comparative and Historical Perspective*, ed. Isaac William Martin, Ajay Mehrotra, and Monica Prasad (Cambridge, UK: Cambridge University Press, 2009), 2.

2 Martin et al., "The Thunder of History," 26.

3 Shirley Tillotson, "A New Taxpayer for a New State: Charitable Fundraising and the Origins of the Welfare State," in *Social Fabric or Patchwork Quilt: The Development of Social Policy in Canada,* ed. Raymond B. Blake and Jeff Keshen (Peterborough, ON: Broadview Press, 2006), 162.

Bibliography

Government Documents

Canada Year Book, 1916–1917. Ottawa: King's Printer, 1917.

Debates of the House of Commons, 1910, 1916–17, 1919, 1939, 1941–42.

Debates of the Senate, 1917.

Dominion-Provincial Conference, Tuesday, January 14, 1941 and Wednesday, January 15, 1941. Ottawa: King's Printer, 1941.

Labour Gazette. Ottawa: King's Printer, 1917.

Report of the Royal Commission on Dominion-Provincial Relations. 3 vols. Ottawa: J.O. Patenaud, King's Printer, 1939.

Report of the Royal Commission on Financial Arrangements between the Dominion and Maritime Provinces. Ottawa: King's Printer, 1935.

Royal Commission on the Parliament Buildings Fire. Ottawa: King's Printer, 1916.

Archival Materials

Proceedings of the Canadian Club, Toronto, for the Year 1910–1911. Toronto: Warwick Brothers and Rutter, 1911.

Rogers, Norman McLeod. *A Submission on Dominion-Provincial Relations and the Fiscal Liabilities of Nova Scotia with the Canadian Federation*. Halifax: King's Printer, 1934.

The Siege of Canada. Ottawa: Canadian Council of Agriculture, 1911.

The Tariff Issue in Canada: The Attitude of the Two Parties Regarding It. Toronto: Ontario Liberal Association, 1902.

Tariff Policy of the Government. Toronto: Ontario Liberal Association, 1904.

Tariff Reforms, Freer Trade, Reduced Taxation. Toronto: Ontario Liberal Association, 1896.

Library and Archives Canada

Bracken, John. *The Party – Its Future* (pamphlet). Ottawa: Progressive Conservative Party, 1944.

Ilsley, J.L. *Sharing the Cost of War* (pamphlet). Ottawa: National Liberal Federation, 1942.

–. *Sharing the Cost of War: An Address before the Trades and Labour Congress of Canada, Quebec City.* Ottawa: National Liberal Federation, 1942.

King, Carlyle. *What Is Democratic Socialism?* (pamphlet). Ottawa: CCF National Office, 1943.

The Military Service Act – Its Meaning and Effects (pamphlet). Ottawa: King's Printer, 1917.

Rowell, Newton. *Conscription of Wealth* (pamphlet). N.p.: n.p. [1917].

Sir William Thomas White Papers. R4279-0-1-E.

McGill University Rare Book Room

Leacock, Stephen. *National Organization for War* (pamphlet). Ottawa: King's Printer, 1917.

Queen's University Archives

D.A. (Alex) Skelton Fonds.
J.J. Deutsch Fonds.
Norman McLeod Rogers Fonds.

Newspapers and Magazines

Canadian Forum, 1934–40.
Grain Growers' Guide, 1910–11.
Industrial Banner, 1916–17.
Manitoba Free Press, 1911.
New York Times, 1917.
Ottawa Citizen, 1917.
Saturday Night, 1939–45.

Secondary Sources

Armstrong, Tim. *Modernism: A Cultural History.* London: Polity Press, 2005.

Berger, Carl. *The Writing of Canadian History: Aspects of English-Canadian Historical Writing, 1900–1970.* Toronto: University of Toronto Press, 1976.

Blake, Raymond B. *From Rights to Needs: A History of Family Allowances in Canada, 1929–92.* Vancouver: UBC Press, 2009.

Bliss, Michael. *Northern Enterprise: Five Centuries of Canadian Business.* Toronto: McClelland and Stewart, 1987.

Brown, Robert Craig, and Ramsay Cook. *Canada 1896–1921: A Nation Transformed.* Toronto: McClelland and Stewart, 1974.

Bryce, Robert B. *Maturing in Hard Times: Canada's Department of Finance through the Great Depression.* Montreal and Kingston: McGill-Queen's University Press, 1986.

Campbell, Lara. *Respectable Citizens: Gender, Family, and Unemployment in Ontario's Great Depression.* Toronto: University of Toronto Press, 2009.

Carlyle, Thomas. *The French Revolution.* New York: Modern Library, 2002.

Christie, Nancy. *Engendering the State: Family, Work, and Welfare in Canada.* Toronto: University of Toronto Press, 2000. https://doi.org/10.3138/9781442674479.

Coldwell, M.J. *Left Turn, Canada.* Toronto: Duell, Sloan, and Pearce, 1945.

Cook, Ramsay. *The Politics of John W. Dafoe and the* Free Press. Toronto: University of Toronto Press, 1963. https://doi.org/10.3138/9781442653092.

–. *The Regenerators: Social Criticism in Late Victorian Canada.* Toronto: University of Toronto Press, 1985.

Creighton, Donald. *British North America at Confederation.* Ottawa: King's Printer, 1937.

–. *The Commercial Empire of the St Lawrence, 1760–1850.* Toronto: Ryerson Press, 1936.

–. *The Forked Road: Canada 1939–1957.* Toronto: McClelland and Stewart, 1976.

Crowley, Terence A. "Mackenzie King and the 1911 Election." *Ontario History* 61, 4 (1969): 181–96.

Ducharme, Michel, and Jean-François Constant, eds. *Liberalism and Hegemony: Debating the Canadian Liberal Revolution.* Toronto: University of Toronto Press, 2009.

Dutil, Patrice, and David MacKenzie. *Canada 1911.* Toronto: Dundurn, 2011.

English, John. *The Decline of Politics: The Conservatives and the Party System, 1901–1920.* Toronto: University of Toronto Press, 1977.

Ferguson, Barry. *Remaking Liberalism: The Intellectual Legacy of Adam Shortt, O.D. Skelton, W.C. Clark, and W.A. Mackintosh, 1890–1925.* Montreal and Kingston: McGill-Queen's University Press, 1993.

Ferry, Darren. *Uniting in Measures of Common Good: The Construction of Liberal Identities in Central Canada.* Montreal and Kingston: McGill-Queen's University Press, 2008.

Forbes, Ernest R. *The Maritime Rights Movement, 1919–1927: A Study in Canadian Regionalism.* Montreal and Kingston: McGill-Queen's University Press, 1979.

–. *Challenging the Regional Stereotype: Essays on the 20th Century Maritimes.* Fredericton: Acadiensis Press, 1989.

Forster, Ben. *A Conjunction of Interests: Business, Politics, and Tariffs 1825–1879.* Toronto: University of Toronto Press, 1986. https://doi.org/10.3138/9781442673229.

Frankman, Myron J. "Stephen Leacock, Economist." In *Stephen Leacock: A Reappraisal,* edited by David Staines, 51–58. Ottawa: University of Ottawa Press, 1986.

George, Henry. *Progress and Poverty: An Inquiry into the Causes of Industrial Depressions, and of the Increase of Want with Increase of Wealth.* New York: Appleton and Company, 1881.

Gillespie, W. Irwin. *Tax, Borrow, and Spend: Financing Federal Spending in Canada, 1867–1990.* Ottawa: Carleton University Press, 1991.

Glassford, Larry. "The Evolution of 'New Political History' in English-Canadian Historiography: From Cliometrics to Cliodiversity." *American Review of Canadian Studies* 32, 3 (2002): 347–67. https://doi.org/10.1080/02722010209481666.

–. *Reaction and Reform: The Politics of the Conservative Party under R.B. Bennett 1927–1938.* Toronto: University of Toronto Press, 1992.

Granatstein, J.L. *The Ottawa Men: The Civil Service Mandarins, 1935–1957.* Toronto: Oxford University Press, 1982.

–. *The Politics of Survival: The Conservative Party of Canada, 1939–1945.* Toronto: University of Toronto Press, 1967.

Grant, Hugh. "Revolution in Winnipeg, 1919." *Labour (Halifax)* 60 (2007): 171–79.

Harvey, David. *The Condition of Postmodernity: An Enquiry into the Origins of Cultural Change.* London: Basil Blackwell, 1989.

—. *Paris, Capital of Modernity*. London: Routledge, 2003.

Heaman, Elsbeth. "The Single Tax vs the Supply-Side State: Revisiting a Western Canadian Experiment." Unpublished chapter, 2012.

—. "'The Whites Are Wild about It': Taxation and Racialization in Mid-Victorian British Columbia." *Journal of Policy History* 25, 3 (2013): 354–84. https://doi.org/10.1017/S0898030613000158.

—. *Tax, Order, and Good Government*. Montreal and Kingston: McGill-Queen's University Press, 2017.

Henderson, T. Stephen. "A New Federal Vision: Nova Scotia and the Rowell-Sirois Report, 1938–48." In *Framing Canadian Federalism: Essays in Honour of John T. Saywell*, edited by Dimitry Anastakis and P.E. Bryden, 51–74. Toronto: University of Toronto Press, 2009.

Heron, Craig, and Myer Siemiatycki. "The Great War, the State, and Working-Class Canada." In *The Workers' Revolt in Canada, 1917–1925*, edited by Craig Heron, 11–42. Toronto: University of Toronto Press, 1998. https://doi.org/10.3138/9781442682566-003.

Hillmer, Norman. "Citizen Entrepreneur, 1908–1914." Unpublished chapter of O.D. Skelton biography, 2009.

Horn, Michiel. *The League for Social Reconstruction: The Intellectual Origins of the Democratic Left in Canada, 1930–1942*. Toronto: University of Toronto Press, 1980.

Horowitz, Gad. "Conservatism, Liberalism, and Socialism in Canada: An Interpretation." *Canadian Journal of Economics and Political Science* 32, 2 (1966): 143–71. https://doi.org/10.2307/139794.

Humphreys, Adrian. "NDP Making Huge Gains as Canada Tilts Leftward: Poll." *National Post*, May 28, 2012.

Humphries, Charles W. "Mackenzie King Looks at Two 1911 Elections." *Ontario History* 56, 3 (1964): 203–6.

James, Matt. *Misrecognized Materialists: Social Movements in Canadian Politics*. Vancouver: UBC Press, 2006.

Kealey, Gregory S. *Workers and Canadian History*. Montreal and Kingston: McGill-Queen's University Press, 1995.

Krever, Richard. "The Origin of Federal Income Taxation in Canada." *Canadian Taxation* 3, 2 (1981): 170–88.

Laclau, Ernesto, and Chantal Mouffe. *Hegemony and Socialist Strategy: Towards a Radical Democratic Politics*. London: Verso Books, 1985.

Laponce, J.A. *Left and Right: The Topography of Political Perceptions*. Toronto: University of Toronto Press, 1981.

Laycock, David. *Populism and Democratic Thought in the Canadian Prairies*. Toronto: University of Toronto Press, 1990.

League for Social Reconstruction. *Social Planning for Canada*. Toronto: Thomas Nelson and Sons, 1935.

Leacock, Stephen. *Sunshine Sketches of a Little Town*. London: John Lane, 1912.

—. *The Unsolved Riddle of Social Justice*. Toronto: S.B. Gundy, 1920.

Lewis, David, and Frank Scott. *Make This Your Canada: A Review of CCF Policy and History*. Toronto: Cooperative Commonwealth Federation, 1943.

Lynch, Gerald. "From Serialization to Book: Leacock's Revisions to *Sunshine Sketches of a Little Town*." *Studies in Canadian Literature* 36, 2 (2011): 96–111.

–. *Stephen Leacock: Humour and Humanity.* Montreal and Kingston: McGill-Queen's University Press, 1988.

Mackintosh, W.A. "Obituary: Norman McLeod Rogers, 1894–1940." *Canadian Journal of Economics and Political Science* 6, 3 (1940): 476–78.

Macphail, Andrew. *Essays in Politics.* London: Longmans, Green, and Company, 1909.

Macpherson, C.B. *The Political Theory of Possessive Individualism: Hobbes to Locke.* Oxford: Oxford University Press, 1962.

Marshall, T.H., and Tom Bottomore. *Citizenship and Social Class.* London: Pluto Press, 1992.

Martin, Isaac William, Ajay Mehrotra, and Monica Prasad, eds. *The New Fiscal Sociology: Taxation in Comparative Historical Perspective.* Cambridge, UK: Cambridge University Press, 2009. https://doi.org/10.1017/CBO9780511627071.

–. "The Thunder of History: The Origins and Development of the New Fiscal Sociology." In *The New Fiscal Sociology: Taxation in Comparative and Historical Perspective,* edited by Isaac William Martin, Ajay Mehrotra, and Monica Prasad, 1–27. Cambridge, UK: Cambridge University Press, 2009. https://doi.org/10.1017/CBO9780511627071.002.

McKay, Ian. "The Liberal Order Framework: A Prospectus for a Reconnaissance of Canadian History." *Canadian Historical Review* 81, 4 (2000): 616–78. https://doi.org/10.3138/chr.81.4.616.

–. *Reasoning Otherwise: Leftists and the People's Enlightenment in Canada, 1890–1920.* Toronto: Between the Lines, 2008.

Moritz, Albert, and Theresa Moritz. *Stephen Leacock: His Remarkable Life.* Markham, ON: Fitzhenry and Whiteside, 2002.

Morton, W.L. *The Progressive Party in Canada.* Toronto: University of Toronto Press, 1950.

Naylor, R.T. "The Canadian State, the Accumulation of Capital, and the Great War." *Journal of Canadian Studies* 16, 3–4 (1981): 26–55. https://doi.org/10.3138/jcs.16.3-4.26.

Nelles, H.V. *The Politics of Development: Forestry, Mines, and Hydro-Electric Power in Ontario, 1849–1941.* Montreal and Kingston: McGill-Queen's University Press, 1974.

Nerbas, Don. "Revisiting the Politics of Maritime Rights." *Acadiensis (Fredericton)* 38, 1 (2008): 110–30.

Norrie, Ken, and Doug Owram. *A History of the Canadian Economy.* Toronto: Harcourt Brace Jovanovich, 1991.

Owram, Doug. *The Government Generation: Canadian Intellectuals and the State 1900–1945.* Toronto: University of Toronto Press, 1986.

Perry, J. Harvey. *Taxation in Canada.* Toronto: University of Toronto Press, 1951.

–. *Taxes, Tariffs, and Subsidies: A History of Canadian Fiscal Development.* 2 vols. Toronto: University of Toronto Press, 1955.

Peterson, C.W. *Wake Up, Canada!* Toronto: Macmillan, 1919.

Porritt, Edward. *The Revolt in Canada against the New Feudalism: Tariff History from the Revision of 1907 to the Uprising of the West in 1910.* London: Cassell, 1911.

Radforth, Ian, and Allan Greer, eds. *Colonial Leviathan: State-Formation in Mid-Nineteenth-Century Canada.* Toronto: University of Toronto Press, 1992.

Read, Anthony. *The World on Fire: 1919 and the Battle with Bolshevism.* London: Jonathan Cape, 2008.

Rudy, Jarrett. *The Freedom to Smoke: Tobacco Consumption and Identity.* Montreal and Kingston: McGill-Queen's University Press, 2005.

Russell, Bob. "The Politics of Labour-Force Reproduction: Funding Canada's Social Wage, 1917–1946." *Studies in Political Economy* 14, 1 (1984): 43–73. https://doi.org/10.1080/19187033.1984.11675632.

Schumpeter, Joseph. *Capitalism, Socialism, and Democracy.* London: Routledge, 2003.

–. "The Crisis of the Tax State." In *The Economics and Sociology of Capitalism,* edited by Richard Swedberg, 99–140. Princeton, NJ: Princeton University Press, 1991.

Scott, F.R. *Essays on the Constitution: Aspects of Canadian Law and Politics.* Toronto: University of Toronto Press, 1977.

Siegfried, André. *The Race Question in Canada.* New York: Appleton, 1907.

Siemiatycki, Myer. "Munitions and Labour Militancy: The 1916 Hamilton Machinists' Strike." *Labour (Halifax)* 3 (1978): 131–51. https://doi.org/10.2307/25139910.

Skelton, O.D. "Canada's Rejection of Reciprocity." *Journal of Political Economy* 19, 9 (1911): 726–31. https://doi.org/10.1086/251921.

–. *Canadian Federal Finance.* Kingston: Jackson Press, 1915.

–. *Canadian Federal Finance II.* Kingston: Jackson Press, 1918.

–. *General Economic History of the Dominion 1867–1912.* Toronto: Publishers' Association of Canada, 1912.

Skinner, Quentin. *Visions of Politics.* Vol. 1, *Regarding Method.* Cambridge, UK: Cambridge University Press, 2002.

Smith, Andrew. "Toryism, Classical Liberalism, and Capitalism: The Politics of Taxation and the Struggle for Canadian Confederation." *Canadian Historical Review* 89, 1 (2008): 1–25. https://doi.org/10.3138/chr.89.1.1.

Stevens, Paul, ed. *The General Election 1911: A Study in Canadian Politics.* Toronto: Copp Clark, 1970.

Struthers, James. *No Fault of Their Own: Unemployment and the Canadian Welfare State, 1914–1941.* Toronto: University of Toronto Press, 1983.

–. "Unequal Citizenship: The Residualist Legacy in the Canadian Welfare State." In *Mackenzie King: Citizenship and Community,* edited by John English, Kenneth McLaughlin, and P. Whitney Lackenbauer, 169–85. Toronto: Robin Bass Studio, 2002.

Taylor, Charles. *Modern Social Imaginaries.* Durham, NC: Duke University Press, 2005.

Thompson, E.P. *The Making of the English Working Class.* London: Victor Gollancz, 1963.

Thompson, John Herd, and Allen Seager. *Canada 1922–1939: Decades of Discord.* Toronto: McClelland and Stewart, 1985.

Tillotson, Shirley. *Contributing Citizens: Modern Charitable Fundraising and the Making of the Welfare State, 1920–1966.* Vancouver: UBC Press, 2008.

–. "The Family as Tax Dodge: Partnership, Individuality, and Gender in the Personal Income Tax Act, 1942 to 1970." *Canadian Historical Review* 90, 3 (2009): 391–425. https://doi.org/10.3138/chr.90.3.391.

–. "A New Taxpayer for a New State: Charitable Fundraising and the Origins of the Welfare State." In *Social Fabric or Patchwork Quilt: The Development of Social Policy in Canada,* edited by Raymond B. Blake and Jeff Keshen, 153–69. Peterborough, ON: Broadview Press, 2006.

–. *Give and Take: The Citizen-Taxpayer and the Rise of Canadian Democracy.* Vancouver: UBC Press, 2017.

Tough, David. "'The Rich ... Should Give to Such an Extent that It Will Hurt': 'Conscription of Wealth' and Political Modernism in the Parliamentary Debate on the 1917 Income War Tax." *Canadian Historical Review* 93, 3 (2012): 382–407.

Valverde, Mariana. *The Age of Light, Soap, and Water: Moral Reform in English Canada, 1885–1925*. Toronto: McClelland and Stewart, 1991.

Wright, Donald. *Donald Creighton: A Life in History*. Toronto: University of Toronto Press, 2015.

–. *The Professionalization of History in English Canada*. Toronto: University of Toronto Press, 2005.

Young, Walter D. *Democracy and Discontent: Progressivism, Socialism, and Social Credit in the Canadian West*. Toronto: McGraw-Hill Ryerson, 1978.

Index

Note: "(f)" after a page number indicates a figure.

Printed and bound in Canada by Friesens
Set in Garamond by Apex CoVantage, LLC
Copy editor: Dallas Harrison
Proofreader: Carmen Tiampo
Indexer: Stephen Ullstrom